W9-AVY-301

DADDY'S GIRL:
A TRAGIC VICTIM OF INCEST

In the late 1940s, a little girl grew up in Toronto—
one who liked to wear pretty dresses and roller
skate with her friends. But no one, not even her
own mother, ever guessed that behind her large grey
eyes Charlotte Vale Allen carried a terrible burden—
an unspeakable secret she shared only with her
father . . .

"It's a long season in hell. Charlotte Vale Allen's story
of incest is told with a candor that is Dostoyevskian in
depth."   —*The Globe and Mail*

"The story of a woman emerging from a nightmare has
the ring of truth."   —*Publishers Weekly*

"Charlotte Vale Allen has courageously brought an old
and horrifying skeleton out of her closet."
                                        —*Toronto Sunday Sun*

"The author's willingness to write about this sensitive
. . . subject is admirable; others might have chosen to
keep such a sorry tale shrouded by secrecy."
                                        —*Los Angeles Times*

"Honest, complex and dramatic . . . The art of auto-
biography at a fever pitch. Charlotte Vale Allen, author
of sixteen works of fiction, is to be praised for DADDY'S
GIRL, her first devastating venture into nonfiction."
                                        —*Toronto Star*

Bantam-Seal Books by Charlotte Vale Allen
Ask your bookseller for the books you have missed

Daddy's Girl

Charlotte Vale Allen

SEAL BOOKS
McClelland and Stewart-Bantam Limited
Toronto

DADDY'S GIRL.

A Seal Book / published by arrangement with
McClelland & Stewart Ltd.

PRINTING HISTORY

McClelland & Stewart edition published October 1980
2 printings through December 1980

Seal edition / October 1981
2nd printing ... October 1981
3rd printing ...... June 1982
4th printing ..... August 1984

All rights reserved.
Copyright © 1980 by Charlotte Vale Allen.
Cover art copyright © 1981 by Bantam Books, Inc.
This book may not be reproduced in whole or in part, by
mimeograph or any other means, without permission.
For information address: McClelland and Stewart Ltd.,
25 Hollinger Road, Toronto, ON M4B 3G2, Canada.

ISBN 0-7704-2037-0

Published simultaneously in the United States and Canada

Seal Books are published by McClelland and Stewart-Bantam Limited.
Its trademark, consisting of the words "Seal Books" and the por-
trayal of a seal, is the property of McClelland and Stewart-Bantam
Limited, 60 St. Clair Avenue East, Suite 601, Toronto, Ontario
M4T 1N5, Canada. This trademark has been duly registered in the
Trademarks Office of Canada. The trademark, consisting of the
word "Bantam" and the portrayal of a rooster, is the property of
and is used with the consent of Bantam Books, Inc. 666 Fifth
Avenue, New York, New York 10103. This trademark has been duly
registered in the Trademarks Office of Canada and elsewhere.

PRINTED IN CANADA

U   13 12 11 10 9 8 7 6 5 4

...for Norman and Lola because, without you,
there would be no me,
...and for Barrie because,
with you, there is music.

Acknowledgments

I WOULD like to thank Larry Freundlich for his belief in this book and in me, and for making a dream reality.

I would also like to express my gratitude to Bella Pomer for her efforts on behalf of this book.

One

I AM thirty-eight, almost thirty-nine years old and afraid of the dark. My seven-year-old daughter sleeps with a night-light. So do I. I don't minimize her fears. I don't dare.

When Jossie is away on weekends with her father, and I am on my own, my house contains a variety of menacing figures. Most predominant: The Man with the Knife. If I remain at home on a Friday or Saturday evening, there is little chance of his showing up. The noise of the television set in the living room or upstairs in my bedroom, combined with my continuing presence within the house, is sufficient to keep him at bay. However, if I've been out for the evening, then, upon entering, it is a sign of my courage that I confront every room, stepping into each doorway with shallow breath, heart knocking, prepared, finally, to come face to face with this lifelong, shadowy horror. He's never there. But he might be.

I'm most vulnerable to the possibility of The Man with the Knife during my preparations for bed. Therefore, certain precautions are observed. I have a transparent shower curtain through which I can keep watch. The television set or the radio is playing in order to create distracting noise. And I keep my eyes open at all times. But I rarely take showers on weekend nights. It's too dangerous. Mornings do well enough. With daylight, I'm returned to rationality and am able to see into all the corners and know there's no one there, there never was.

I've made The Man with the Knife a running joke in my life, one my friends share with me. He has a depth of reality for me and therefore my friends don't minimize my fear. Some of them have their own sets of nighttime menaces.

During the War, my mother installed me in a nursery school in Toronto that was housed in a building of which I remember only the steep stairway, the huge main room, and the storage room.

I don't know what I did. I was a jittery, fidgety, can't-sit-still little girl and probably was simply somewhat more can't-sit-still than usual. Whatever the reason, the teacher locked me into the storage room. For an entire afternoon.

The door closed and locked from outside, my hand on the knob, I turned to confront the dimensions of the darkness. Dry-mouthed, terrified, longing to continue protesting my innocence, I inched along the wall—rough plaster over concrete—trying to see something, anything. Only the yellow-string outline of the door was clear.

Positive there were monsters, all sorts of murderous creatures in the dark getting set to pounce and tear me to bits, I turned to the wall and began rhythmically bringing my forehead hard against the rough plaster. Over and over. Making pain to combat the fear. Once started, the rhythm of the act overtook me, kept it going.

My mother came at last. The door opened and in the doorway were the smiles-turning-to-shock faces of my mother and the teacher. Blood and tears, I staggered toward the protection of my mother's arms, her body. My mother was very upset and angry. Not, as I had hoped and expected, with the teacher, but with me. She cleaned my face with a tissue, then marched me out of the school demanding to know what I'd done. Wincing as she gingerly applied a cold cloth to the shredded skin of my forehead—her face flushed and tight—she said, "You *behave* yourself, dammit! I need you at that goddamned school!"

Why? I hated the place. Stifling, crowded with too many children and busy women who never had the time to stop or to listen. Why did I have to be there? I was three years old. But there was a war on. "I've got three kids to look after!" my mother offered, exasperated. It didn't tell me why. I went back.

The church bells started ringing during playtime and I went to swing on the wrought-iron gate—strictly forbidden—and announced to two other illicit gate-swingers, "The War's over. My Daddy's going to be coming home." They looked at me, impressed. What was the War? And how did I know it was over? I'm not sure. Something to do with the bells, and guess-work. I must have been right because we didn't get punished that day for swinging on the gate.

I was born in January of 1941 just before my father, like a great number of other Canadian men, entered the army for the duration. He was someone I couldn't remember ever having seen. There was no image of him in my mind, no memories, nothing at all. He was just another threat my mother used— "Just you wait till your father gets home!"—in an ongoing attempt to get my two older brothers and me, primarily me, to behave to her specifications. These consisted of doing precisely what we were told, being mute, invisible, and having no desire either to move or be seen. Impossible, of course. The only one of the three of us who seemed most able to live up to her stringent standards was Bobby, my middle brother. We were five years apart, the three of us. Four, nine and fourteen. At fourteen, Will seemed to me a grownup. He also didn't pay any particular attention to my mother's demands. He simply kept silent, for the most part, and disappeared. I couldn't, much of the time, understand what she wanted. I tried ceaselessly to please her, failed, but kept on trying. Bobby, though, worked out fairly much according to her plan.

He was a beautiful, morbidly shy little boy with a mass of curly brown hair, round blue eyes and a choirboy face. He practiced the piano as he was supposed to, did his homework, spent hours making meticulous crayon copies of cartoon characters, and rarely spoke. He had, though, a delightful smile and wonderful laughter. I spent a lot of time trying to make him—or my mother—laugh, and was successful perhaps half the time. It was worth the effort to see his eyes glisten, his mouth reluctantly open, to hear the contagious crescendo of his laughter; to see my mother's fair features flushed with amusement and hear her say, "What a card!"

Bobby was stubborn and as obstinately unmovable as wet cement if something displeased him. Then his face would close down with a slam, set itself into rigidly determined lines and nothing on earth—not even our mother's pleas—could move him. I admired him. I thought he was brave to defy her. To my recollection, she never struck Bobby as she so often did me. He was the recipient of her rare, so-valued embraces, smiles and sympathy. Had I been able to figure out how to be a smaller version of Bobby, I'd have done it instantly in order to be on the receiving end of those infrequent, gentle and caring caresses. Part of me resented Bobby for his success with her. And part of me insisted I didn't care. But I did.

I decided early on that, for reasons undetermined, my mother didn't love me. Once established in my brain, the idea wouldn't go. And so when I wasn't overtly displeasing her for some unsuspectedly defiant reason, I did everything I could think of to charm her, to make her laugh. I sang, I danced, I told silly stories. I hung on her arm, or her skirt, and sometimes she gave me the benefit of an unaccustomed hand tousling my hair, accompanied by what seemed a bewildered smile. Other times, she seemed receptive and the two of us jigged and danced around the kitchen table, laughing and breathless. Until the order came to, ". . . get out of here now. I'm busy."

It had to mean she didn't really love me.

The War ended and my father was going to come home. I waited in a state of high excitement, convinced his return would change everything, make our lives different, better, happier.

He came. A stranger with a mustache and a brown uniform. He and my mother arrived at the nursery to collect me. I was scooped up into the arms of this father with the dark skin and bristly mustache and the round gray eyes, and we went home.

He came home and opened his kitbag and pulled out a stack of bills: money from all over Europe and North Africa. He'd been a communications sergeant. It sounded important. He offered me the money. I looked at it and asked, "Is it good for spending?"

"Not here, it isn't." He was smiling under the mustache.

"I don't think I want it then."

His smile thinned out and I knew I should have said I wanted the money. But it was too late. Bobby asked for it. Daddy threw it across the table to Bobby without looking at him. He was angry with me for not wanting the money.

Delving again into his kitbag, he lifted out a gun; a Luger he called it, and let it lie impressively dull and heavy across the palm of his hand.

My mother screamed. "What is it? A gun?"

"*What is it?*" he mimicked her in a voice I could tell none of us liked. "What the hell does it *look* like? Of course it's a gun. It happens to be a very good Luger."

"We're not having that in this house! The kids could hurt themselves." She stared at the gun with a terrified expression.

"It isn't even loaded, for chrissake! Look!" He held the gun out to her. She shoved his hand away.

"Get it out of here right this minute!" she insisted, red in the face, her eyes on his.

"Okay, okay!" he backed down.

"And you better take it apart first," she added. "I don't want to be responsible somebody picks it up out of the garbage, shoots their head off."

Will muttered, "Waste of a good gun," and my mother killed him with her eyes. He didn't say anything else.

The kitbag also contained several small oil paintings Daddy said he'd done—pointing to his bold black initials printed in the corners—and his mess kit, other items that held no real interest for any of us. The bag was left in a corner of the kitchen and my mother put the food on the table.

Daddy came home from the War and my mother went around for a few days blushing, giddy, smiling; bestowing pats on the head, occasional hugs. There was laughter at the supper table, floating above the salt spills on the oilcloth and empty plates. And then, abruptly, things were just the way they'd been before. Only worse. After her brief spell of appealing good humor, Mother settled down into what seemed to be ongoing anger. And Daddy not only seemed the primary reason for her anger, he also indicated she was the primary reason for his.

We three, ever quick to notice our mother's moodswings, and now Daddy's as well, instinctively avoided the kitchen when the two of them were in there, delaying as long as possible coming to supper; we knew we'd never get through the meal without some sort of incident. In the act of reaching for something, I regularly knocked over the milk bottle and flooded the table. Bobby seemed especially adept at spilling the salt. And Will invariably, innocently, said something that sparked Daddy's anger. Mealtimes became agony. My mother chose this time to talk about money. Her mouth a thin line, she talked about money. We all knew to the penny what things cost, because she told us. "Do you know what this *cost?*" she'd demand if food remained on the plate, or an apple was discarded half eaten. It seemed a never-ending recital of dollars and cents. A price tag to everything. Daddy ignored her, noisily ate his food and refolded the newspaper he kept beside his plate so he could read while he ate; his annoyance with her or with us radiated from him like heat. He muttered occasional comments. "Goddamn woman's probably got the first cent I ever gave her." He folded, refolded the newspaper, reading his way through the meal. A bald man with a mustache, in his undershirt at the kitchen table, his huge belly wedged against the rim, eating one-handedly while he read his paper; the focus of all our eyes until it was safe to get up and leave. Something about him was frightening and I always wanted to tell my mother not to talk to him. *Don't say anything at all; we'll just eat and then go away.*

Perhaps Will understood the anger. But Bobby and I certainly didn't. We simply accepted it, grasped the unspoken rules of ongoing warfare and tried to stay out of the way when the voices got louder, sharper, harder. I tried asking Will and Bobby why things were the way they were, but they shrugged made no attempt to answer and at last began to pretend I hadn't asked yet another silly question.

My mother often called me "troublemaker," and sometimes said I was ". . . worse than the two boys put together." I argued and thereby simply justified her accusations. My every impulse was to prove to her that I didn't *make* trouble, I simply seemed to find myself in it without any effort.

My daughter is a high-energy, low-boredom-threshold little girl. And there's trouble three or four times a week. Rarely anything of epic proportions, but a mirror gets broken, or food is spilled, or a nightgown is ripped, and at those times I hear my voice demanding to know if she knows . . . "what that cost" . . . and other echoes of the past. Traditional arguments mothers present to children. I understand that now. But the combined rage of my parents remains awesome to my mind. I understand the why's and how's, but still feel the panicky grip of anxiety as I examine memories of my parents' consuming antipathy toward one another.

More often than not, our mother defended her three children while my father made it clear—from his looks, his comments, his disdain—that she was a fool who'd bred three more fools. She couldn't ever win.

Crowds—in department stores, in supermarkets, in elevators, on dance floors—frighten me. Something inside my chest begins to flutter, my head fills with noise, and an unreasoning, irrational anger and panic make me want to start shoving aside the bodies to get the people away from me.

Making love in the classic man-on-top fashion is a physical, psychological and emotional agony. My breathing goes hay-

wire, hysteria climbs out of my throat and grabs hold of my
eyelids, and I know it's merely a matter of another few seconds
before my hands open and I helplessly, hopelessly relinquish
my grip on the strings of my sanity.

For years, shopping of any kind was something that so
closely approximated torture that I did it as rarely as possible.
And making love was a fantasy wherein there was nothing at
all wrong with any part of me and it got accomplished with
all the passion and appropriately technicolored flare it was supposed to. I tried both—shopping and lovemaking—repeatedly,
much in the same way that on weekends, I confront my empty
house and the possibility of The Man with the Knife; determined to conquer my panic, my incapacity to perform according to what I'd read in novels, heard about from friends, secretly believed to be the *right* way.

I was rude to salesgirls without being aware of it; rude and
abrupt in order to buy whatever it was I'd come into the store
for and get out again *fast*. Lola, soon after we met, was appalled, and made me aware of how badly I was behaving.
Gradually, her awareness became mine and I was at last able
to stop being so unforgivably, though unintentionally, bad
mannered.

Men, however, were another matter. No one seemed able or
willing to tell me what I needed to know. No one seemed able
to substantiate the wrongness or rightness with me and certainly there weren't any books handy that served to clarify
matters. So, I kept on confronting men one after another, convinced someone would come along and help me make sense
of me, help me become real to me; rescue me. Obviously, I
frequently told myself, it was a question of love. Friends sup-
ported that theory. "If you don't learn to care for someone
now, you never will," I was told. I was almost twenty-six
and believed that had to be right. So I went ahead and willed
myself to fall. And what I fell into was the most obsessive, the
most destructive, the most potentially dangerous relationship
possible for me. I selected an available man, convinced myself
I was in love with him, then set about convincing him. But

there was one saving aspect of it all: Rob had no inhibitions about sex. He loved all of it, everything. And it's hard to maintain an unhealthy view of something when the man you think you're in love with is so wholeheartedly enthusiastic.

He was handy. He was having wife troubles, he admitted. And he was interested. So I stepped into the arena of what was to be an involvement of several years, convinced I was not only in perfect control of myself but also of the situation. After all, I was volunteering myself into it, into love, so why shouldn't I retain the control?

He wanted me. And wanting me had to mean he loved me. I cringe, writing that. It's so pathetic, so horribly naive. But I believed it utterly twelve-odd years ago. What I knew of love had to do with books and movies and a handful of surrogate mothers and fathers I'd found, and nothing at all to do with prior experience, because I really hadn't had any. Not with love, that is. Sex was something else. So, I stepped in, laid myself down, suffered his weight and told myself, You *want* this! And that was true. I did. But nothing happened. No bells, no lightning flashes, no symbolically flickering candles, no waves washing over us. Just a quietly sick belief that whatever spontaneous and natural instincts I might once have possessed had been killed off.

With ever-present determination, an aching sense of guilty mortification, and an overriding need to know, I set about learning how to masturbate. Awful. Embarrassing. Only tolerable because, thank heaven, there was no one to see. It took weeks because I hadn't any idea what I was after, how it was supposed to feel, or even if I was going about it in the right way. But I did it. I managed to circumvent the burnt-out circuits, to find my way to other still healthy ones, and lay in a heap on my sofa bed in that roach-infested Nineteenth-Street apartment in Manhattan feeling the first genuine sense of sexual and self-accomplishment of my life. There wasn't anything physically wrong with me after all. I was okay.

The next time Rob and I made love—on a nutty weekend trip to Atlantic City where the majority of people we encountered mistakenly assumed we were father and daughter —I was fully functioning, and capable of being sexually satisfied. To a point. Rob took all the credit. I had the wits to say nothing. I simply smiled and thought, Up yours, buddy! I did it myself, just as I've always done all the truly important things for myself.

I still, however, cannot bear anyone's body weighting mine down.

Two

MY MOTHER was an exceptionally good-looking woman. In her early thirties, she looked a good ten years younger. She had about her a youthful, surprised expression that was very appealing. With frizzy blond hair, round green eyes, and a smooth, flawless complexion, I thought her far more beautiful than the mothers of my friends. Five-one or so, slim yet rounded, she seemed, when in the company of others, always ready for a good time. But she rarely managed to have the fun she hoped for, and then her features would firm up, thin down and become preoccupied. Her good looks drew me endlessly because they misled me into believing that someone so pretty couldn't possibly really be as angry as she often became. Somewhere inside her, I thought, was the pretty person who went with that startled-fawn expression and the sometime giddy laughter. I could find her only rarely, and when I least expected to: arriving home from a downtown shopping expedition with one of her sisters to present Bobby and me with a bag of broken biscuits or broken chocolate—great treats—and then to sit at the kitchen table with a cup of tea, smiling, while Bobby and I gorged on fragments of rich tea biscuits or chocolate marshmallow hearts whose sticks had broken or whose forms were misshapen. Mouth full, I'd study her, her smile, trying to decide what had prompted her to provide us with this unanticipated pleasure.

My daughter, Jossie, hates to hear me refer to myself as ugly. It upsets her. "You're not ugly, Mom," she insists, her small, lovely features creased. I think all children, at least for a time, think their mothers are beautiful. At some moments, Jossie actually manages to convince me I am. I know I'm not. But my mother was.

The September after my father came home, my mother took me along to the nearby public school. And I listened, a little embarrassed, while she smilingly talked the principal into breaking the age rules so that, at four, I might enter the kindergarten class. I can't remember what she said. I do remember the man's responsive smiles and nods. He agreed.

She told me it was ". . . so I can have some peace and quiet around here."

I was just as happy to be out of the nursery. But my mother's implying that I deprived her of her peace and quiet bothered me. Since Bobby and Will were away all day at school, I couldn't understand, firstly, why she wanted to get rid of me and, secondly, what she intended to do with all that so-called "peace and quiet."

Now, of course, I understand absolutely what she wanted. But back then it seemed further evidence of her dislike of me. I wanted to be with her, to savor our private time alone together. She wanted breathing room, moving-around-room after living through the War with three small children and very little money.

Daddy went back to work, to the job his boss had kept open for him through the War. In just weeks, it was as if he'd always been there in the apartment: a bald man with a pregnant belly, perennially in his undershirt and trousers who smoked nonstop, read the *Star* at the kitchen table while waiting for his supper, and handed his pay packet over to my mother every Friday night.

She'd open the small brown envelope, take out five or ten dollars and give him the money. Their worst arguments took place Friday nights.

"Five lousy bucks for a week's work. Generous of you." His over-full lips would curl into a sneer beneath his brushy mustache.

"I let you handle the money, we'd have nothing to eat by Monday. You'd spend every stinking cent. We've got three kids here. I'm not letting you get your lousy hands on my money."

"Willya listen to that? *Her* money. *My* goddamned money. Who the hell worked for it anyway? Wasn't for me, you wouldn't have a thing."

"Wasn't for you, my life might be halfway decent." She spoke more unhappily than angrily.

"Go on! Keep pushing! Plenty of women who'd be glad to have me. Keep it up! Go on! Just keep pushing!"

"Let 'em have you! I wish to Christ I'd never laid eyes on you. I should've listened to my father. He knew all right. He warned me about you."

"Your father was fulla shit! Just like your idiot mother and asshole sisters!"

Stung, my mother leaped to the defense of her family. "My father," she cried, growing red in the face, "was the best man who *ever lived!* Don't you go bringing *my father* into this! My father was a man who looked after his family, took care of us, didn't treat his kids like garbage. And *you* should talk! Your beaut of a family's no prize. What'd your stinking father ever do for any of you?"

"Where's the goddamned food?"

I sat and watched, listening to the rise and fall of their voices; feeling dizzy, made sleepy by the waves of sound. My eyes moved back and forth between their faces, my head far too full of noise. I understood that my mother loved her family, particularly her late father, and that my father didn't care overly much about families at all. I wondered why none of my friends' parents shouted at each other this way, and fought about paychecks; wondered why these two people were together and married when they didn't at all seem to want to be. It was as if they hated each other.

In bed at night, in the dark, the slightest noise has me instantly alert; paralytically frightened. It's him, of course, The Man with the Knife. Every creak of the heating system in winter, the refrigerator going on and off, the slam of a car door outside is a sure sign of his arrival. No amount of self-persuasion, no amount of night-lighting or rationalization can surmount my fear of his pending arrival. He's downstairs in the kitchen, or on the roof of my bedroom, peering in at me through the big skylight. My heartbeat makes footsteps in my ears; heavy, lumbering footsteps that travel across the kitchen floor toward the spiral staircase that leads up to my bedroom. When he fails to materialize in my room and my heartbeat slows, the footsteps fade. I must, every time, tell myself, It's my damned heartbeat and not The Man with the Knife.

Come the morning, I shake my head at my fears of the night before. Look at the sunshine, those trees! Everything's bright, clean and just as it should be. So what, I ask myself, are you so damned afraid of? The answer, irrational and foolish as ever: The Man with the Knife. Of course. He'll never die and leave me to revel quietly in peaceful nights.

My mother walked me to school on the first day. I wanted to prove I was old enough, sufficiently grown up to handle this new situation alone. Outside the kindergarten room, I told her I'd go in by myself, that I didn't want the other children to think I couldn't find my own way to school.

Surprisingly, she looked hurt, disappointed, which at once made me feel guilty and sorry. She shook her head, saying, "So independent," sounding both admiring and defeated. "Okay," she said and left. I wanted to call her back and say it was all right, she could take me in if she really wanted to. I watched her go, unable to make myself summon her back.

Inside, there were several mothers fussing over their kids.

And I was reassured, slightly contemptuous of the two or
three children who were sniveling, clutching at their mothers,
from moment to moment craning away to look around with
expressions fraught with misery. Why would they cry because their mothers were leaving? The whole idea of school,
as I was given to understand it, was for the mothers to be free
of the kids for an entire morning, and for the kids to be away
from home and mothers, to enjoy their own freedom. Didn't
they know that? As I watched those reluctant kindergartners,
I thought for several moments of how nice it would have
been to bury my face against my mother's warm belly while
her arms encircled and her hands protected me and I protested
the advent of our separation. I turned away to examine the
contents and dimensions of the room.

School was okay. A lot of the games didn't make much
sense to me, but I played them anyway with an odd, uncomfortable sense of being unlike the other kids. I wanted to be
the same, but was unable to throw myself into the games, the
rollicking piano music, the way the others did. I couldn't seem
to feel their excitement, or their disappointment when the
games and music had to end. It was as if I'd lost my prior
knowledge of how to jump and yell and be wholeheartedly
happy. I could feel myself trying, copying the appropriate
gestures and motions, but the harder I tried the more strained
I felt. I constantly studied the others, hoping to find some
clue in their actions that might lead me into being one of them.
But always, my thoughts, the streams of words in my head,
held me away.

The best part of school was the walk there and back every
day. Up the street to the corner of Robinson, then over three
blocks to the school. There was something so purely satisfying about the way the mornings smelled and looked. Small,
perfect gardens offered their final flowers of the season; leaves
burned in the gutters; the way the car tires sounded going
down the road; the streetcars rattled along the street at my
back, their bells clanging as they swayed heavily along the
tracks down Queen Street. Crunching my way through drifts

of leaves, taking my time, I thought about school, about my parents, about how they were always so mad at one another; shouting, angry. Their quieter, companionable times were so rare they were like holidays. And because of their rarity, suspect. Did it mean they'd suddenly decided to like one another and would vent their combined anger on the three of us? Would they fly off together and leave us? It felt oddly better when they displayed their typical animosity toward one another because then I was sure of where we all stood. But why were they the way they were? The effort to think it all through made me just as dizzy as the razor-edged words slicing back and forth across the kitchen table. So it was better just to smell the air, to look up into the chestnut trees, the oaks and maples, to listen to the sounds the tires made on the road. I'd watch, with a strange-feeling hollowness inside, as kids from neighboring houses came across the road, calling out to each other and formed little groups as they headed for school; while I stayed well to the rear, taking my time. I wanted them to turn, smiling, and wave for me to hurry up, catch up, join them.

Life was school in the mornings; in the afternoons the street or the roof outside the back window. The apartment was always so foreign, so quiet in the afternoons. The long, long hall of that railroad apartment with the rooms all on the street side, the two bedrooms at the front overlooking the main street. I could go from room to room and watch people walk along Queen, turn the corner and go on up the block and out of sight. Or I'd sit in Will's room, the smallest of the three bedrooms, the corner front room, and watch the dust dance in the sunshine; like magic, in the interior silence, watching, distantly aware of the traffic outside. Out there, the noise; inside, the quiet and those magic spots dancing in the sunlight. I'd sit, losing time, for hours, and then uncoil myself from the dusty old armchair and wander down the hall to the kitchen. I'd stand in the doorway and watch my mother stirring something in a pan on the stove, her apron pocket always bulging with tissues, her hair rolled smoothly away from her face, her

expression thoughtful, even serene. She might smile, set down
her spoon, and say, "Want to play Casino?" and eagerly, I'd
go for the cards while she made herself a cup of tea and
wiped the oilcloth clean in preparation for our game. I'd watch
her hands—slim and pretty—as she dealt the cards, her big
diamond catching the light, and as we played, we'd talk. Her
voice would be softer, quieter, more musical than the voice
that shattered the air when she and my father argued. She'd
smile, she'd laugh, and for that half hour, I'd feel a welling,
almost sad happiness. Maybe she really did love me after all
and it was me—the things I sometimes said and did—it was my
own fault she didn't love me all the time.

I had an India rubber ball. A good one. I played downstairs
for hours, bouncing the ball against the red-brick wall of the
building, loving the way that ball snapped up from the side-
walk, smacked hard and clean against the wall, then returned
to me. I was a city kid, with city games, accustomed to the
crowds, the many different languages spoken on the streets,
the noises, the sometime litter, the constant movement, the pa-
rades that periodically marched down Queen Street. Un-
daunted by stores or the people who worked in them, I did
my mother's grocery shopping, in possession of a little, always
misspelled list and exact change. I knew by name every kind
of pasta in the long narrow boxes on the floor of the Italian
market owned by the family of my mother's best friend, Rose;
knew that the man behind the counter at the kosher delicates-
sen would slip me a slice off the bologna or salami he was
hand-slicing on the machine, and that the best old sour dills
were always at the bottom of the barrel; knew the father and
sons who ran the Polish meat market and the Jewish brothers,
pharmacists, who owned the building we lived in and ran the
drugstore one floor beneath our apartment. I knew the sound
of approaching streetcars at night, knew my way around the
neighborhood, was confident of the sound of my heels on the
sidewalks. I loved Sunnyside Park and annual visits to the "Ex,"
when I'd hold on to my carefully saved money for the first
hour while we went from one exhibit to another, strolled along

the midway, and then, in the second hour, blow every last cent in a sudden frenzy of desire to win something—an enormous black-and-white teddy bear or a Kewpie doll. I liked to walk along Queen Street holding my mother's hand and looking at the faces of strangers as we made our way over to the Italian market so my mother could chat for fifteen minutes or half-an-hour with her friend Rose, who, with a white apron over her dress, would stand and smoke a cigarette while she kept an eye on the banks of fruit and occasional customers, smiling and talking to my mother. Rose was thin and pretty, with jet black hair and pale porcelain skin; gentle ways. She usually gave me a handful of cherries or a plum to eat, or encouraged me to go on in the back and play with her niece, Rosemary. Rosemary had long blond hair and rather reserved ways and invariably made me feel that she had other things to do and would have preferred not to play with me. For my part, I'd have been happier to stay outside and listen to what my mother and Rose had to say to each other. Their conversations—as did all those my mother had with her sisters or her friends—fascinated me, perhaps because they offered more and different views of my mother; views that were soft and engaging and further conflicted with the one I had of her with my father. I wasn't encouraged to stay and listen.

Every so often, I checked the window wells along the side of our building, looking to see if somebody had lost a dime or a quarter. I knew exactly how I'd get it up, what I'd buy with the money. But I only once saw a nickel down there and then I couldn't get it. Two big boys I didn't know came along. One lifted the heavy iron grate, the other climbed down and got the nickel as I stood watching, protesting that it was mine. They told me to get lost, let the grate slam down, and went off. I was furious and told myself that if I'd been bigger and stronger, I'd have gone after them, beaten them up, and taken back the money.

Upon hearing of this episode, my father—in one of his sometime highly jocular moods when he smiled and became laughingly expansive—sat with my two brothers in the kitchen while I was getting ready for bed, and whimsically created a new breakfast cereal called "Lost." All I remember of it is my father's deep, husky voice as I was passing the kitchen doorway. Choked, nearly speechless with laughter, he was saying, ". . . so, men, the next time your wife goes out to do the shopping, just remember to tell her to get 'Lost.' " He and my brothers roared with laughter. I laughed, too, on my way down the hall. I thought, when he wanted to be, my father was a very bright, very clever and witty man.

In recent years, my brother Will and I have examined our mutual past and our father in particular, trying for a comprehension of the man, his why's and wherefore's. Will believes, and I agree, that in my father's eyes he reached his zenith in the army. Nothing before or after ever allowed him as much freedom or that special, limited brand of responsibility he enjoyed then. And the stories of his escapades survive him.

He told us how his mother, our grandmother, sent a salami to him in Italy. Sent by sea, it took six weeks to get there. He was informed by headquarters to come collect his package because no one would bring it to him. He went to get it then returned to his forward position at the front where he opened the package to find the salami in an advanced, reeking green state of decay. He then, he told us, picked the salami up out of its wrapping and hurled it in the direction of the German lines whereupon four Germans at once stood up and surrendered, claiming it was unfair to have had poison gas used upon them.

In England, he was, he further told us, offered a pack of English cigarettes. They tasted foul and he asked someone, "What the hell're these things made of?"

"Half horseshit and half cabbage," was the reply.

"Thank God!" father exclaimed. "I thought they were *all* horseshit!"

Also, in England, he and his men were on a pre-invasion exercise in the south and kept on the go for twenty-four hours. At the end of this exercise, all the men were exhausted and desperate for food. A British army field kitchen pulled up and began dispensing, of all things, peanut butter sandwiches. The peanut butter was made of soya and the bread appeared to have been baked from sawdust. And to make matters worse, there was nothing to drink. Irate, Father berated the officer in charge of the field kitchen, saying it was a hell of a way to treat men who'd been in the field for twenty-four hours without food. The officer coolly responded, "You chaps're always complaining. Napoleon's army would've been jolly glad to have had this food."

To which Father responded, "Of course they would've! It was *fresh* then!"

He was, when he cared to be, a witty man.

The first time I went to bed with Rob, I said something that amused him and he laughed. In the near-darkness his laughter was such a close replica of my father's that my breath stopped. I froze, staring at him, and told myself this was Rob, *Rob*. But his laughter and his husky whisper made the hair on my arms stand on end, dried my mouth, sent my heartbeat berserk. For several very long moments I couldn't rid myself of the echo inside my head of his laughter. Then I forced myself to lie down, to touch his face, reassure myself it really was Rob.

Daddy.

A cigarette in the dark. The thick smell of smoke, sleep.

We were Jews, I discovered, because I didn't have to go to school on Jewish holidays. But how did we get to be Jews? I wondered, when we didn't, like other Jewish families in the neighborhood, get dressed up in our best clothes and go to synagogue, or *do* anything on these holidays but sit around the apartment and listen to the radio, trying not to antagonize or irritate each other.

My mother told me she'd been raised in an Orthodox household, with separate sets of meat and milk dishes, Friday night services, no activities on Saturdays, bar mitzvahs, all of it. "Your stinking father could care less," she said. "I kept it up as long as I could." But Will's storming out of Hebrew school well before his thirteenth birthday and planned bar mitzvah had been the end of it. And we ate pork, we ate ham. We sat around the apartment on Jewish holidays. The only reminder of our supposed Jewishness came in the form of Yahrtzeit candles my mother lovingly lit once a year for her dead father. A white candle filling the bottom of a stubby kitchen glass with a label in Hebrew glued to the front. The candle sat on top of the icebox until it burned itself out. Then the glass was cleaned, delabeled and put into use. I'd never drink from one of them. I eyed that candle every year feeling fully a pagan, wondering what mysterious powers it invoked. I never did get a satisfactory explanation. I hadn't the faintest idea what being Jewish meant.

The fact that my father could speak Yiddish wasn't extraordinary because he also spoke nine or ten other languages he'd managed to "pick up" here and there. He was able to converse fluently, effortlessly in Russian (his native tongue—he'd arrived in Canada at five, or perhaps eight or nine, no one knew precisely how old he was because his mother forgot and the birth certificate got lost somewhere along the line), Polish, German, French, Italian, Lithuanian, Hungarian, Czechoslovakian, English and several others. His virtuosity with languages amazed and impressed all of us. He liked to show off his skill, but essentially he needed the languages in order to communicate with the people who ran the various machines at the factory where he worked. He chatted away with them, going from one machine to the next, switching languages, and left in his wake a row of beaming, satisfied faces. These people to whom, when I was introduced, I could say no more than hello and goodbye, adored my father, revered him. "He's one hell of a guy, eh?" someone was always saying. And the women gazed after him with high color in their cheeks, eyes bright, mouths smiling. Everyone liked him.

He could be so charming. What my mother called "putting on his act." He was a fairly handsome man, with a once-black, rapidly graying circle of hair round an ever-wider bald spot; large gray eyes, a ruddy complexion, black mustache. He looked Italian. And Italians invariably assumed he was a *paisan* from some unfamiliar region which accounted for his oddly accented Italian. His smile could be dazzling. I saw dozens of women who worked for him who stood, after a chat with him, in an attitude of almost religious devotion as my father continued on his way between the machines. The ladies liked him. He liked the ladies, I was given to understand by veiled accusations made by my mother in the course of Friday-night paycheck arguments.

My father's family was comprised of wide-eyed, laughingly eccentric people. He had four brothers and four sisters, good-looking, dark-haired, dark-skinned people. Their occasional reunions were loud with manic laughter, frantic with jokes and movement; breathless, motiveless excitement among hard drinkers, high-living types.

My mother's family was fairer, more intense, serious. She had three brothers and three sisters. There was an oldest uncle I saw only once and of whom I was, in accordance with my mother's years of awed talk of him, properly respectful and subdued. He was a man in his late fifties or early sixties when I was a very small child. And somewhere in this world, I have cousins, his daughters, women now in their sixties, whom I've never met.

My mother was the youngest in her family.

My father was the oldest in his.

My mother was passionately devoted to her three older sisters and spent hours every day on the telephone talking to one or all of them. The four sisters together were light, two golden-haired women, one darker, and Amy with the flaming, silken-red hair. Their voices and laughter, soft and secretive, intensely intimate, close. The contrast between the families captivated me. My mother was quick to put down Daddy's family as "Crazy damned Russians." They were. But they were so wildly, madly alive that to be with them was as dizzying and thrilling as a ride on the roller coaster at Sunnyside Park. And as potentially dangerous. Because beneath that laughter there always seemed to lurk a kind of madness, a coarse, crude tenacity for life that might be lethal. They all had violent, sudden tempers. Yet I was drawn powerfully to their frenzied ebullience. I wanted always to have the guts to be crazy, to drink neat scotch or vodka and then eat the glass.

With my mother's family, her sisters, I was expected to be more docile, better behaved, less visible. I was allowed, gratifyingly, to brush Aunt Amy's spectacular hair; to paint Aunt Brenda's fingernails; to hug Auntie May who seemed to like small children. But too-loud laughter, too much visibility resulted in one or usually all the sisters joining forces in commiseration with my mother over the only one of her kids who had to go and turn out ". . . like *his* side of the family."

Three

I wanted Christmas to be Christmas, like the pictures in magazines: with a tree and all the trimmings. But the issue of our Jewishness and my mother's insistence that Jews didn't celebrate the holiday defeated my arguments. She wouldn't have anything to do with the holiday other than the giving of gifts if we chose—and I felt we ought to choose to—and the preparation of a big turkey dinner.

It didn't make sense. If we were to have presents and a turkey, why couldn't we have a tree as well? Still, the gift aspect remained and, wanting a doll, in lieu of a younger brother or sister which I'd much have preferred, but in which my mother seemed to have no interest whatsoever, I sat down to print a letter to Santa in my best lettering. Just the way Daddy told me to. And I hung a stocking in the bedroom doorway. On my way to and from school, I imagined the doll, what it would look like, her clothes.

In bed at night, in the light of the flashing red then blue then red of the neon sign from the drugstore—situated directly outside one of the two windows of my room—I tried to muddle through this mystery of Christmas. Certainly nothing in the apartment felt or looked like it, and the only decorations were paper chains and cutouts I'd spent an afternoon making and then hung over my bedroom windows because my mother said she didn't want the stuff all over the place. Yet, when I ran out to the store with the typically misspelled shopping list— sauges, spagti, balony—everyone said "Merry Christmas" and "Same to you," and I did, too; while at home it was much the same as always.

Will, who at fifteen was very tall and, to my mind, highly mature, said, with a smile, "A holiday's a celebration and the only thing either of them would celebrate would be the funeral of the other." Bobby and I laughed appreciatively. I felt disloyal, even bad, though, for laughing. Children weren't supposed to talk that way about their parents.

There was an apple, a tangerine, some nuts, a candy cane in cellophane, some cheap plastic toys and a note in my stocking I unfolded with a feeling of dread to discover I couldn't read the writing. But it looked all too familiar. I ran over to have Bobby read it to me.

He was sitting up in bed with a *Superman* comic, his hair a mass of unbrushed, chestnut curls.

" 'I'm sorry,' " Bobby read, " 'but I ran out of dolls before I got here. Next year I'll make sure you get one. Santa.' "

"Daddy wrote it, didn't he?"

"Sure." He handed me back the note. "It's his writing."

"I knew it!" I was angry, deeply disappointed. "There is no Santa Claus, is there?"

"Nope."

"D'*you* get anything good?"

"Coupla comics. Wanna read one?"

I was too mad even to consider glancing at *Little Lulu* or *Plastic Man*. Why had he told me to write when he'd known all the time there wasn't any such person as Santa Claus?

I sat on the floor in the hall and glared at the door to their bedroom, waiting for it to open. When it did and he came out, I announced, "I'm mad at you!"

"Oh, yeah?" He delivered one of his more engaging smiles. "How come, eh?"

"I didn't get any *doll!*"

"Didn't Santa leave you a note?"

"*You* wrote that! And everyone knows there's no Santa Claus anyway!"

"I told you not to promise her," my mother murmured sleepily from the depths of the bed. "You shouldn't promise the kids things."

"Christmas isn't over yet!" he barked at her over his shoulder, then went on down the hall to the bathroom.

I stood and watched him go.

"You better learn to ignore his promises," my mother said from the bed. "He means them when he makes them but that's as far as it ever goes."

"So why does he promise then?"

"Go figure it out," she said. "He likes the sound of his own voice, thinks he'll make people like him."

"Make people like him?" People already liked him. I'd seen for myself how the employees at the factory responded to him.

"A real charm boy." She yawned and stretched, then looked over at me, not unkindly saying, "Listen, you go around believing what people promise you, you'll end up with nothing. Believe you me. What you get in this life, you get for yourself. Go believe in promises and see where it gets you." The way she spoke and what she said seemed to indicate Daddy had promised her all kinds of things, too; things she'd never received. Was that why he made her so mad?

A short time later, Daddy went out. For a long time. The turkey was already in the oven, the kitchen steamy and good-smelling when he got back with an outsized box, saying, "This got left outside by mistake," and set it down in front of me on the table. He stood on the far side of the table grinning rakishly as he lit a cigarette, saying, "Go on, open it up."

"What is it?"

"Open it and find out." He stood smiling, the cigarette smoke drifting in front of his face. Over by the sink, my mother wiped her hands on her apron, watching us. I had the feeling I shouldn't open the box, but I went ahead. Inside was a doll with stiffly curled blond hair, a frilly pink dress and matching bonnet, white plastic shoes, little white ankle socks.

"Where'd you get that?" my mother was asking quietly as I ran away down the hall to show Bobby the doll.

"Never you mind where. I got it, that's all."

I slowed down at the rising sound of their voices and continued on past Bobby in the living room to the bedroom.

"And where'd you get the money, anyway?" she wanted to know. "That's an expensive thing."

"None of your stinking business where I get my money!"

"They come around this time saying you've been stealing and I'll let you go to jail, rot there for all I care. Not like last time. You'll go to jail and I'll bloody well let you. No going around to your boss with the kids like the last time, begging for you."

"Will you shut the hell up! Nobody said I took any goddamned money! Up to my ass with you, you know that?"

"She didn't need a doll."

"Leave the kid alone. I promised her."

On my knees on the floor, I gazed at the doll propped against the pillow on my bed. Their voices swelled like a storm; like one of the bad boomy ones during the War when my mother came in to wake me so I'd come stand with her in the closet under the stairs while she jumped and said, "*Jesus!*" every time the thunder boomed. And then, when it was all over, she'd laughed, like a little girl, and said, "Okay, you go on back to bed now."

Kneeling on the floor I looked at the doll's too-blue eyes and sticky yellow hair. I touched one poised, ungiving little finger. It was my fault they were fighting this time, because I'd asked for the doll. Now I had it and didn't want it anymore.

I like men. I'm more attracted to them in my fantasies, though, than in real life. Fantasy men are always gifted with tremendous understanding and sympathy and sexual sensitivity and don't say silly things like, "Relax. Just relax," and they find me infinitely desirable. The only part of the fantasies that has any bearing on reality is the desirable part. If one more man tells me to, "Relax, take it easy," I'll put him through the wall. I don't relax even with my closest women friends. I'm someone who finds the most comfort in being busy and active. At my most relaxed, I seem, as a friend recently observed, to be almost visibly vibrating. My energy level is high and telling me to relax serves only to send it even higher. And why should I relax anyway? What for? There are times when I'd like more than anything else to be the casual kind of woman who can take 'em or leave 'em, but I can't seem to be that way about anyone—male or female. I go into every situation hoping for the best, for everything impossible. A good percentage of the time I get it, then don't know what the hell to do with it, how to deal with it, how not to be frightened by having managed to get exactly what I wanted. This applies particularly to men. They display some interest and I start to look for the exits; I have to force myself to sit still and not bolt, tensed for the inevitable contact they're bound to make with some part of me. The odd thing is that once the contact's been made, most of my fear evaporates. It's just getting there that's so damned hard, so damned frightening. It takes some kind of courage to be naked with a stranger, to show yourself—not necessarily physically—with all your flaws and imperfections. I'd like to be as self-contained as I often appear, to sit, serene and expectant, anticipating the contact rather than dreading it.

I doubt, though, I'll ever be that way. The precedent was established far too long ago, far too deeply. I can't believe a man's with me because of me, especially when a far prettier woman was talking to him just a few minutes ago and I saw the way he looked at her. I'm probably second best because the prettier woman turned him down. Am I supposed to be grateful? Or is he more comfortable with me because I, perhaps, seem to represent less of a threat since my externals are not so terribly imposing? Or is he with me because there is about me something that states all too clearly my dreadful compunction to please in order to be liked?

Daddy.
Lighted cigarette puncturing the nighttime darkness. The thickness, the scent of the dark.

It snowed and Bobby and I, in our snowsuits, climbed out through the window to make angels on the back roof. We lay with our mouths open, letting snowflakes melt on our tongues. After a while, we sat in the thick snow by the brick wall on the street side and watched people go in and out of the side entrance to the old North Star Hotel across the street. "The beer parlor," my mother called it. Three or four storeys high, of red brick, with rooms to rent upstairs. Mother forever warned us to "Walk on this side. Stay away from the beer parlor."

Bobby didn't know why. He said, "I guess 'cause they drink over there, get drunk and fight. I don't know. Ask her, not me."

It was an answer of sorts as to why we were to stay away. Since our parents didn't drink, except on very rare occasions when Daddy got out the bottle of whiskey and drank some from a shot glass, I didn't know what to make of "drinking," but decided, in view of my mother's warnings, that it must be a very bad thing. So I further decided never to do it.

A few times, when Daddy's family got together, my mother drank a little faint-colored something and then got very laughy, with bright pink spots on her cheeks and Daddy would say, "Half a glass of grenadine and water, for chrissake, and she's drunk as a skunk," and laughed. But he looked as if he enjoyed watching her laugh, seeing how pretty she looked with the color high in her face.

"How come," I asked Bobby, peering over the side of the roof, "they always fight?"

"Oh," he paused in packing a snowball, "she says he runs

around with women and he's got no sense of responsibility. And he calls her money-mad, says she drives him nuts."

"Was it like this, the same way, before he went to the War?"

"I don't remember. I guess so. I heard her talking about how he had some girlfriend in Scotland or somewhere he wrote letters to and she found one of the letters from the girlfriend or something. And anyway," he said, as if picking up on an argument he'd started sometime earlier, "so what if she talks about money? Better just us and her, than him, too."

"You think so?"

"You kidding? He *hates* me and Will, can't even stand to be in the same room with us." His usually sweet face was twisted and red. "I'm going back in," he said abruptly. "It's freezing out here."

We crawled in through the window and got mother mad at us because we trucked in snow that melted on the floor and inside our galoshes, soaking our shoes and socks. Overheated inside, Bobby went off to the room we shared and I went to the living room to sit in Daddy's chair and look at the little silver cigarette-paper goblets spitballed by their bases to the ceiling.

Daddy never did make any effort to talk to Bobby and Will. He'd glare at them as if he didn't much like them and most of the time if they asked him something, he either pretended not to hear or made a joke out of their questions, and answered in that piping, mimicking fashion that bothered all of us and made the boys look and feel stupid. It drove Bobby into a state of crimson-faced, clenched-teeth fury. Will would just get up and walk out. Bobby and I didn't have that option. We were too young. When Daddy started to pick on one of us, we were obliged to sit there and take it. Bobby changed, almost overnight, from a cheerful little boy into someone most often silent and easily provoked by our father into a state of rage.

For the most part, Daddy gave straight answers to my questions, which secretly convinced me he preferred me to my brothers. It alarmed as well as pleased me because if Daddy liked me better, Bobby and Will might stop taking me to the movies with them, or to Bellwoods Park, and mother wouldn't take me roller skating anymore at the Strathcona Roller Rink. His direct answers to my questions irked her, prompting her to observe, "You never pay one goddamned bit of attention to the boys! *They're* yours, too, in case you happened to forget!"

Whenever she started in about the boys and how he treated them, Daddy would just go back to reading his newspapers, and pretend she didn't exist. But his face would be dangerously set and a little drum would begin to beat in his temple. A bad sign that, an ominous one. The instant I saw it, I'd go very still, my eyes on that throbbing in his temple; and creep away, if possible, scared.

The first time I heard myself shouting at Jossie in my mother's voice, I stopped so suddenly we were both bewildered. Since then, if I have cause to raise my voice at her, I make sure it's my own and no one else's voice I'm using.

Evidently, I, too, have a look that can make her breath stop. Nothing quite so terrifying, perhaps, as a little drum in my temple. But when I see her wide-eyed reaction to this particular expression, I make my face blank at once and deliver whatever it is I have to say with the full awareness that I'm me being angry with her for some valid reason and not because, thirty years ago, my father terrified and intimidated me with his illogical, unreasoning, permanent anger.

I am angry, though. Much of my anger got lost one afternoon on the beach in Antigua when I was walking with Lola and she stopped, taking her time to say, "You're so angry. The angriest person I think I've ever known." She looked sad, upset, concerned as she spoke.

"Angry?" I repeated. I was thirty-one years old and it hadn't ever occurred to me that I was angry. *Angry?* Was that why so often I flew into gut-wrenching spasms of outrage at the smallest slight, the merest hint of injustice, unfairness? She had to be right. Because Lola has been more right about me, more caringly, oftener than anyone else alive. My very existence is due in no small part to her appearance in my life at a time when I most needed a miracle.

I stopped and looked at her for the longest time, trying to absorb that word, feeling it slide smoothly into place in a lock inside my head and slowly turn.

"You're right," I said, astounded, feeling slightly dizzy. "You really are right. I *am* angry. My God! I really am."

And that did it. Someone I loved very much saying, "You're angry," made me see the reality and acknowledge it. The lock opened and the anger began to seep away because, after that, each time an unreasonable fit of outrage moved to take me over, I knew what it was, could tell myself, You're overre-acting, and allow it to settle, subside. It took so very little to enlighten me, but so many years to fill my secret room wall to wall, ceiling to floor with handwoven, tightly bound bales of it. Most of it's gone now. I feel a bit defenseless at times, without my anger, but infinitely calmer, more capable of feeling and recognizing the happy times when they come. And they come more and more frequently these days.

Summer. With school over, talk had all but ceased at the kitchen table. Bobby kept out of Daddy's way; he'd gather up his books and comics and go sit on the back roof, or wander out in search of friends. Will was out with his friends, or off on dates. I sat downstairs on the step outside the door watching people go in and out of the old North Star until it was dark and scary and better to be inside listening to the radio.

My India rubber ball had been summarily taken from me in June on a preview day of grade one by Miss Clark, the white-haired, stick-thin, imperious, cracked-voice spinster who would be my teacher come the fall. I missed that ball badly, and for some reason my mother wouldn't buy me another one. So I was waiting it out for September when I'd get my old ball back.

But in the fall, I discovered Miss Clark had retired and, the ball forever lost to me, I marched with the others into the classroom of the redoubtable Miss Letitia Love. With basket-

ball breasts riding amazingly high on a wide chest, fullback
shoulders, a face paved in Max Factor pancake makeup, lurid
red lipstick, wild red fingernails, and glittery eyes behind gold-
framed glasses, she was big and tall and had a booming voice.
I was convinced she really was a man, despite the heavy clouds
of perfume that hovered over her.

I wanted to be in school, wanted to learn. I could already
read. I wanted to be able to print, and then to write. But in
order to be there, I had to brave out seemingly endless confrontations with older, bigger kids in the schoolyard. Apparently, I was a natural prey, being younger and smaller. But I
was ready to defend myself with anyone, at any time, if necessary; able to make the big noises and gestures that belied the
terror I felt of being hurt. Hurt physically meant another instantly infected, soon scabbed-over wound that stayed with
me and refused to heal, for months. Both knees and elbows,
the backs of my hands were permanently encrusted or red-raw
with just-healing cuts, scrapes, scratches, bumps, bangs, bruises.
I fell, or walked into walls and doors, slipped, tumbled, came
home day after day to present my newest injury to my mother
who, in time, gave up offering sympathy and became desperate with frustration, saying, "Why the hell can't you be more
careful?" as she searched the ceiling for the god who lived
somewhere up there and who was, she claimed, a witness to
the hell on earth these kids and that old man made her life.

Somehow, I got locked into one of the row of cloak closets
at the rear of Miss Love's classroom by a small group of
maniacally giggling girls. Miss Love stood at the front of the
room brandishing a ruler, and bellowed, "You can just *stay*
in there!" as if I'd intentionally, magically locked myself in.
There I stayed, crouching in the tiny cubicle, and followed the
lesson through the grille in the door, even stupidly waving
my hand around when I knew the answers. How had it come
to be my fault and why did I have to stay stuffed in there
when it had been the others who'd pushed me in and slammed
shut the door, thereby entrapping me? It was very unfair. But
I didn't bother to complain to my mother because, almost al-

ways, she seemed to side with those in authority and not with me. Invariably, she'd sigh and say, "You probably brought it on yourself."

On the last day of school this past June, I went along to collect Jossie and to say good-bye to her second-grade teacher. I was present to witness the exchange of affection between the children and this woman as she shook their hands, kissed them, and thanked them for being in her class for the year. I wanted to turn time around so that I might be one of the grinning children happily returning her kisses and saying good-bye. Impossible, naturally. But I'm deeply grateful for Jossie's sake that she'll never have to know the legion of dragons who terrified my generation of children into learning.

Ceaseless arguments over the kitchen table. Three children without appetite choking down their meals. I spilled the milk. Bobby knocked over the salt shaker. Sudden shouts, whacks across the side of the head. Tears dropping into forkfuls of food lifted to dry mouths.

Teachers who rarely smiled, who patrolled the schoolyards like prison wardens and who smacked small hands with rulers.

"You've always got time to take *her* for a walk but you haven't got any goddamned time to take the boys or me anywhere! I'm sick and tired of hanging around this house. I've got a right to some fun in my life!"

"So what d'you want me to do about it, eh?"

"Let's go the hell *out!*"

"So *okay!*"

Occasional evenings they went out together. My mother beautiful in lipstick, high heels, carefully aligned seams bisecting slim calves. Will argued that he had his own life, things to do, he was no baby-sitter. But he usually stayed. In the living room reading a book or a magazine, he listened to the radio, pulling at the skin on his lower lip. The apartment was quiet but for the sound of slowly turned pages, the muted tinny voices from the big, old console radio. Bobby at the kitchen table did his homework. And I in bed gazed at the red then blue of the drugstore's neon sign making its patterns on the ceiling, or sat by the window studying the TIP TOP TAILORS sign way down by the lakeshore.

A winter, a hot, too-short summer. Bobby had to go to summer camp. He didn't want to go, cried and begged not to. But Will was going to be there as a counselor and mother said, "You'll have a good time, sweetheart," with teary eyes that stated she didn't want him to go, either. Bobby went. He snatched his suitcase and climbed up into the bus without once looking back. She continued to stand there until the bus pulled out. I clung to her hand, thinking I'd have been happy to go away to camp, so why hadn't she sent me.

With a new India rubber ball mother relented and bought me, I spent the summer bouncing the ball against the downstairs wall, or sitting out on the back roof, or on the front step watching the drunk people come and go, in and out the side entrance to the North Star. Slow days, long hot nights of red blue red neon.

Bobby came home altogether altered: silent and angry and no longer quite so beautiful; close-faced, no longer willing to play or talk or answer questions. His curls were gone, clipped to a brushcut at the camp. He was silent, too, and mother went about for a time looking bereft so that I felt sorry for her and angry with Bobby for changing as much as he had. I thought it was the camp's fault and blamed them for the apparently irrevocable alterations wrought in my brother. I couldn't even get him to laugh very often or to play.

But Daddy had a new game: he'd whistle tunes and get me to name the songs. I spent entire afternoons listening to the radio, evenings following the music on *Make Believe Ballroom* so I'd know the answers. When I became too adept, he switched over to words. "Give me a word that means so and so." I started to read the dictionary so that when he looked up from a book of crossword puzzles and asked for a four-letter word meaning thus and such I had a list of possibles at the ready.

I hummed myself to sleep nights, or softly sang songs I'd heard on the radio. Or lying on my right side, I picked at a seam in the crumbling wallpaper, decided that the only one who really seemed to love me was Daddy. Will was never around. Bobby didn't want to play. Mother was busy in the kitchen. But Daddy had some attention to pay, games I found challenging.

I read a book years ago that had in it a girl whose mother told her never to give herself unless the boy/man in question loved her. So the first man who came along dutifully responded to her question of, "Do you love me?" with, "I love you," and she then spread herself out obligingly, having lived up perfectly to her understanding of her mother's rules.

Sometimes, I feel almost as much of an idiot as that girl. I like to hear that I'm loved, that those I love approve of my actions, my abilities. The best way to get to hear it is to tell the people I love that I love them and then they'll fill the needy place in me and say, "I love you, too." But I won't lie down in order to hear it.

Jossie's so sick of hearing me tell her that I love her that not long ago when I did our You-know-what?-I-love-you routine, she screwed up her face to the question of Do you love me too? and said, "Oh, *Mom*! I *told* you the other night. Don't you *remember*?"

Oh, yes.

Four

I'VE HAD to rely on my wits for survival. I've never thought of myself as better than others, or more especially intelligent. If anything, I was convinced the reverse was true. I've just known all along that it was up to me and no one else if I was going to make it through, and I needed my brains intact to do that. One needn't have self-esteem to survive. Anger is just as effective a motivating factor. Or ambition. But when one has survived, a little self-esteem goes a long way toward balancing one's dealings with others. I tell myself to believe in my positive qualities. But no amount of self-telling persuades me that some man or woman is with me because of what I might have to offer. I continue to think how lucky I am someone's interested. I'm still working at believing the opposite could be true.

Grade two brought Miss Fielder, another gray-haired, bespectacled woman, with black lace-up schoolteacher shoes and a stout figure, with a pleasantly mellow speaking voice, an ability to smile upon occasion, and a weapon she called "The Bee." It also brought Marianna, a girl I'd seen and met in the neighborhood and had much admired during the summer when, with her broken leg in a short cast, she'd been wheeled down the street on a wagon by her older sister.

I loved her the moment I saw her smile at me from her seat adjacent mine. Red-brown ringlets, creamy skin, a winsome smile with dimples and a hint of wonderful wickedness in her blue eyes. She wore a blue dress, a most impressive, party-type dress with ruffles and a sash tied in a big bow. I was almost seven, Marianna was nearly a year older.

" 'The Bee,' " she whispered to me, "is just an old chopstick, for Pete's sake."

I turned to look back at Miss Fielder weighing this deadly little stick against the palm of her hand and had to cover my mouth with my hand to smother my giggles.

Marianna lived in a duplex on Tecumseh. Her grandmother occupied one half of the house, Marianna's family the other. Marianna, her older brother and sister, her gentle Italian father and round, always smiling Russian mother were the first complete family I fell in love with. I couldn't resist her mother's quietly accented speaking voice, her father's smiles and obvious affection for his wife and children, her brother's dark, grown-up good looks and wild sense of fun, her sister's womanly but good-natured admonitions to the two of us to behave ourselves when we were alone in the house—which we were most afternoons until at least five when one or both of her parents returned from work.

She and I made a game of waxing the furniture, sweeping up, doing the chores she'd been assigned. At her place for lunch, we'd eat raw hotdogs, or lettuce sandwiches on white bread slathered with Miracle Whip. Out on the top step of the back porch, munching away, we'd work out what we'd do before going back to school, what game we'd play. I wanted to live there, to be her second sister, to stay forever and never go home. This was a family as I believed families should be, with parents who rarely if ever raised their voices at each other, with conversations and laughter around the big kitchen table; with warmth. These people loved and actually liked one another. And me, as well. Every pat on the head or smile from Marianna's mother or father was a positive benediction, small proof of my lovableness. I lived in a state of grace from the moment I entered that house until the moment I left it. I'd fall from that state the instant I skipped down the front steps and walked back along Tecumseh, turned the corner and headed up to Queen. By the time I reached the downstairs entrance to the apartment, I was geared to face the dissension my father would undoubtedly bring home with him to supper.

I ate often with Marianna's family. It was peaceful and the food was extraordinary: Russian dishes thick with sour cream; Italian meals flavored with oregano, olive oil; homemade doughnuts, huge, sweetly leaking apple pies liberally spiced with cinnamon, nutmeg, cloves; enormous bowls of salad. The herbed aromas and mouth-watering fragrances, the platters of delicious food that turned me into a small glutton all conspired to make me feel the worst sort of traitor to my mother. But I was bothered by the unvarying sameness and unimaginativeness of my mother's meals. Hamburgers, mashed potatoes and peas. Salmon patties, mashed potatoes and peas. Hot dogs, or maybe some fish and chips from the shop a couple of blocks over. Lunch and dinner sameness. Most of the time Daddy chose to make suppertime an hour of agony. I preferred to be with Marianna where there was love in the atmosphere and not the tension of a pending electrical storm.

My mother began to go out a couple of evenings a week. To play cards, or to go to the bingo games; claiming Tuesday and Thursday nights as her own. And suddenly, the nights in the apartment were quiet.

Bobby seldom went anywhere, but spent his time reading *Popular Mechanics* in the bathroom, or doing homework either at the battered desk in the living room or, if Daddy happened to be in the living room, at the kitchen table. Both of them in the same room was too potentially explosive, so Bobby worked hard at staying out of Daddy's way. He'd sit at the kitchen table, leaning on one elbow, and gaze down at some book or other spread before him, while he absently ran his other hand over hair that was growing back with none of its former luxuriance.

My mother worried aloud about Bobby's hair, hoping he wasn't going to go bald like the Old Man.

"You mean his hair'll all fall out?" I couldn't imagine it.

"Willie's hair's starting to thin out some on top, too," she went on in that same distracted tone, as if she wasn't really aware of me. It drove Will mad when she called him "Willie," but she seemed unable to remember to call him Will.

"Does that mean," I asked her, "all *my* hair's gonna fall out, too?"

She laughed, and finally focused on me. "Women don't go bald the way men do."

"Are you sure?"

"Sure I'm sure."

"Absolutely sure?"

"Look, you're not going to go bald. Okay?"

"But I'll bet there are some bald women in the world." I started to smile; the mental image of a fully made-up woman with a gleaming skull was very funny.

"I heard Ida Lupino's bald," she said consideringly.

"No, she isn't. When we saw her in that movie, she had hair."

"A wig," she said firmly. "She wears wigs."

I stopped smiling. Maybe it was true.

"How d'you know that?" I asked.

"Poor woman," she said, with a slow shake of her head. "Must be awful."

"How come you know things like that?" I asked again.

"Oh," she said vaguely, "I read it somewhere."

"Well, if she's bald, I could go bald, too."

She laughed. "You're not going bald! Okay?"

Doubtfully, I said, "Okay."

From that moment on, I could never see Ida Lupino without carefully studying her hairline, trying to see if her hair was her own, or a wig. There were all sorts of things my mother told me, snippets of movie-magazine gossip I carried around with me for years, and other items of general information that seemed to have a ring of truth about them. The majority I discarded in time, but it gave me the damnedest feeling recently to read a newly released book on Hollywood and various stars and come across an item that stated that Ida Lupino had indeed worn a wig to disguise hair loss suffered as a result of a bout of diphtheria in the late thirties. I had to smile, and then laugh. A little proof, perhaps, that mothers aren't always wrong.

Daddy teased Bobby cruelly. "Gonna be bald like your old man, eh? What's this here on the floor, hair?"

Bobby turned crimson, raised his fists, then fled from the kitchen. Later, after Daddy had retired to the living room with the second section of the paper, Bobby came back and sat down at the kitchen table while my mother tried to get him to buck up, and told him, ". . . not to let the bastard get under your skin. The son-of-a-bitch just likes to hear the sound of his own voice." It didn't help. Bobby couldn't seem to come out of his anger; he just sat there with his fists clenched, his jaw locked, glaring at the tabletop. I watched, jealous because of all the attention he was getting while I might as well have been invisible.

Home for lunch, I was eating quickly so I could meet Marianna and play for a while in the schoolyard. Around a mouthful of salmon patty, I asked mother, "Where do you go when you go out?"

"Out."

"Where?"

"Just out. None of your business where."

"I was just wondering, that's all."

"I'm going downtown, if you must know, to do a little shopping then out to play cards."

"By yourself?"

"With your Auntie Nell."

"Oh!" Nell was married to my mother's second oldest brother. She had short, thick, black hair, a wide red mouth, a loud laugh and the longest fingernails I'd ever seen. "What kind of cards're you gonna play?"

"Oforchrissake! Poker!"

"You play for money or for fun?"

"Of course for money. Why the hell else would I play?"

"D'you ever win?"

"Sure."

"What. . . ?"

"I'm going out for a decent evening to get the hell away from the bunch of you for a while. Now, if you're finished with that, scram! You're getting on my nerves with all this question stuff."

I hung around for a couple of minutes, while she peeled potatoes for the cold supper she'd leave for Daddy.

"Could I come, too?"

"Jesus! Didn't I just *tell* you?"

"If you loved me,"—dangerous territory and I knew it— "you'd take me with you sometimes. You never take me anywhere anymore, except that time to the park." *We don't ever talk about the park and never go there now because the summer I was five we met with two of my aunts there and I said I had to go to the toilet and she was talking and said go on so I went and there was a man in the women's toilet and no locks on the door but I had to go even though he was there and I tried to hurry but I couldn't hurry fast enough and the man pushed open the door on me and I said what are you doing and he said I'm The Inspector have to check to make sure you wiped yourself properly and touched me between the legs. I hated him touching me I was terrified and blurted out, "My mother's outside waiting," and he ran out. Scared, I got my pants pulled up and ran back up the hill to where my mother and aunts were sitting trying to get my mother's attention but she kept saying, "Don't interrupt when grownups are talking!" and finally after a long time maybe an hour she turned impatiently to hear me tell about the man down there who was The Inspector and touched me that terrible way and then watch my mother go crazy jump up and run away to do something I didn't know what she was doing just put my head down on Auntie May's lap and fell asleep. The police came but the man was gone. And my mother kept asking me over and over, "What did he do to you?" and I kept telling her. And that was the end of it. Except we never went back there and I couldn't go to sleep properly at nights afterward; dreaming about The Inspector touching me, giving me that sick twisty horrible feeling, and my mother not wanting me to interrupt, then listening and going crazy. So we never went back after that.*

"I see you every day of my life," she said, getting angry. "That's enough. I've got a right to a couple of nights out."

Jossie drives me crazy with her interrogations. If I make a telephone call, or receive one, she has to know who's on the other end and the purpose of the call. If I say some name she doesn't recognize, she'll badger me until I either give her a complete rundown of every last detail or else I'll lose my temper and say it's none of her damned business.

With the advantage of time, motherhood, and some definite perspectives, I can readily sympathize with my mother. She had a lot to contend with. And while I'm able—just—to cope with my one child, when I mentally multiply times three, and then throw in my father for good measure, I can understand her exasperation. I know now I was loved by her. It simply wasn't in the demonstrative way I needed.

She went. And in her absence, the apartment was too quiet. Daddy sat in the dusty red morris chair in the living room, reading the paper, listening to the radio. Bobby and Will did their homework, or occupied themselves elsewhere. I roamed about, and ultimately settled at the desk in the living room to play with the new Smith-Corona portable mother had bought for Bobby. "So he can do his homework," she'd explained. The money had come from her winning the Quinella, which I gathered was some kind of horse race.

I poked at the keys for a while, then scribbled nonsense in the small, spiral-bound notebook I liked to carry around with me; I had an inordinate fondness for clean, new notebooks, freshly sharpened pencils, fully filled fountain pens. Finally, I went over to stand by Daddy's knee until he put down his paper and smiled at me, one of the wider smiles of the variety that had the ladies at their machines in the factory melting and glowing.

"C'n I sit on your lap?"

"C'mon." He pulled me up to sit while he smoked one cigarette after another until he'd finished with the newspaper.

He smoked ceaselessly, all through meals, even in bed. Sometimes, wandering down the hall in the middle of the night on my way to the bathroom, I'd pause outside their open bedroom door to see the red glow of his cigarette in the ashtray on the badly scarred bedside table. And a few times, in the mornings, there was a horridly acrid burnt smell and my mother, grunting and swearing, would be trying to turn over the mattress because he'd burned another hole in it and, ". . . one of these times he's going to burn us all to death, crazy-son-of-a-bitch."

"How come," I asked him once I had his attention, "we can't go out, too?"

"Kids don't go out to play cards with grown-ups."

"Why not? I'm good at cards. I can play Casino."

"I'll bet you are."

"Be more fun than being all by myself with nobody to play with," I paused, then significantly added, "nobody who likes me."

"Who says nobody likes you? I like you."

"If you like me," I said, ready with both barrels, "how come I can't get into bed with Mummy anymore Sunday mornings? I used to, before you came back." That big bed was a special place. Times when I'd had a cold, or had run a temperature, my mother always tucked me up in there with my crayons and coloring books and cutouts, and a bowl with an apple, an orange and some arrowroot biscuits.

"That's the only chance in the week I have to get some sleep."

"How come you need to sleep so much anyway?"

"Because I get up at five in the morning, every morning six days a week. One day a week, I deserve to sleep in."

"But you go to bed at eight o'clock, same as me. And anyway, you could sleep if I was there. I'd be very, very quiet, wouldn't make any noise or anything. I know why!" I declared momentously. "It's because nobody loves me."

He laughed: a deep, wheezy, chocolate-brown sound.

"Well, they don't!" I persisted.

He stopped laughing slowly, lit another cigarette and said, "It's time for bed now. Scram!"

Daddy.

A mound in the bed. Smoke smell, husky voice.

At seven, I was very small for my age, and the only one of the three of us children who looked like Daddy. I had my mother's wild, wiry blond hair which was pulled daily, painfully into pigtails while my mother swore, each time, to have the whole goddamned mop cut off. I had my father's large gray eyes, heart-shaped face and dimpled chin. I'd have preferred, I thought then, to look like my mother because she was so pretty; the prettiest of the sisters and they all said so. But Daddy seemed to like the fact that I looked like him and to prove it took me to the park one afternoon and had me pose this way, that way over and over, while he took roll after roll of pictures. It disturbed me somehow, all the posing, and the way he wanted me to stand, or lie down on the grass. And when I said I was getting fed up, didn't want my picture taken anyway and wanted to go home, he put away the camera and marched me home without a word. But when the pictures came back from being developed, he spent a very long time choosing the ones he liked, then put them carefully, with little gold paper corners, into the big album.

Jossie was born, after a series of lunatic foul-ups, by Caesarian section. When I came round from the anesthetic and remembered what I was in the hospital for, I asked to see her. The night nurse broke the rules and, at four in the morning, brought the baby along for me to see. She looked exactly as I'd hoped she would: like her father, but with my eyes.

She's beautiful and rather vain, fond of holding conversations while she eyes herself in the mirror. She's stubborn, and bossy sometimes; she's sturdy and healthy and strong. Her reality is, to me, an exceptional reward for my survival.

Jossie is beautiful, but when I tell her from time to time how special she is to me, it's so that she'll know how it feels, not to be exclaimed over because of her physical features, but to be found beautiful purely by dint of her existence, her lovability, her simply being who and what she is: a child who is wanted and very much loved.

Five

W HEN I was young and thought about marriage, taking
into account what I'd been told and what I'd seen, I viewed
it as one large entity comprised of a number of smaller parts.
First, it was something that occurred much later on in life—
when one was at least twenty-five; and second, it was a form
both of rescue and reward. If you were lucky, you got a
"good" husband—someone of excellent earning power who
could provide you with solid security and who would constantly surprise you with thoughtful and expensive gifts designed to keep you happy; someone so completely besotted
with you he'd never consider glancing at another woman. If
you were unlucky, you got a "bad" husband—someone who
had a lousy job with no future, who only married you because
the girl he'd really wanted couldn't see him for dust, and who
chased after other women and gave up early on in the game
trying to keep it a secret. Marriage, like war, was a state you
entered into for the duration; good or bad, happy or not, you
were in it till the end.

I dreamed of the marvelous man who'd come along, announce I was the one and then install me in a gorgeous apartment, lavish attention on me, dote on the two perfect chil-

dren we'd have, and see me, finally, as both the fine person I really was and also as the ultimate embodiment of all he'd ever hoped for in a wife.

My parents met at a sweet-sixteen party. He was twenty-four, she was just sixteen. She had fine green eyes beneath fair, almost invisible eyebrows, a shortish Clara Bow kind of hair-cut, rolled stockings, and one of those kicky, straight-up-and-down twenties' dresses. He was slim, very dark, with a wide, lascivious grin, I-mean-business eyes, and immediate determination. Within minutes of his arrival at the party, he made his way over to where she was sitting, gigglingly aware, in the company of two other girls, to sit on the arm of her chair and declare, "You're the girl I'm going to marry." Powerful stuff.

"I laughed," my mother told me. "I thought he was nuts. He was so much older than me. I was just a kid," she said with a sudden, very real sadness. "What did *I* know?"

She'd been a sickly child, twice taken by diphtheria; and told me many, many times how her father who did, indeed, sound a kind, deeply caring man, had carried her in his arms to the hospital and, once there, refused to leave her. She'd wor-shipped her father. Hearing her tell of him, I felt I'd have revered him, too. He sounded like a man whose family came first—an example of what a really "good" husband could be.

As the youngest, my mother was cosseted, even pampered by her older sisters and brothers. She recovered from her bouts with varying illnesses to grow, according to the photographs in the album, most healthy and fetching.

She completed grade eight and didn't go on. I'm not sure why. Perhaps she was needed to help at home, or expected to contribute to the family coffers. I don't know.

Daddy finished grade five or six, then went out to work be-cause his family needed the money and as the eldest he was expected to help provide. His father, who'd been some sort of construction worker had, when the children were quite young, sustained a serious head injury on the job. It left him sometimes calm, sometimes given to ungovernable rages. He went on a rampage, striking out, lashing at anything and anyone that got in his way. "We used to take to the closets when he got that way," my father said. They'd stay hidden until it was over. And, he further confided at a later date, the brothers and sisters—all but the youngest—got up to some very sexual activities in those closets.

Daddy looked so much like his father that in one particular photograph of the two of them—taken in a studio, the two men seated side by side on a silver crescent moon suspended by wires in front of a starry backdrop—I couldn't tell them apart. I was told repeatedly, "No, *that's* your father," but the next time I looked through the album, I got it wrong again. Two slim, dark-haired, dark-countenanced men with mustaches, slouch hats, and expressions of brooding menace.

"He wouldn't leave me alone," my mother said, standing by the kitchen window, gazing out. "Kept chasing after me until I didn't know what I was doing. I never wanted to marry him. He was too crazy, too jealous. But he just sort of wore me down. Oh, my mother warned me. She *told* me I'd have nothing but trouble with him. And my father, he was so worried about me."

He used to lock her into the flat when he left for work in the morning, and she'd have to get the landlady to come and let her out. A pretty, eighteen-year-old encountering quiet madness in the first months of her marriage. Why didn't she leave him then? Shame? Intimidation? I don't know. Maybe some of both. Make a mistake, live with it, but don't let other people know.

She was on College Street one afternoon, having been freed, as usual, by the landlady, and there he was strolling arm in arm down the street with another woman. Had he locked Mother in in order to prevent her discovering the other woman? Probably. In any case, it was he who was filled with righteous indignation. And she, I suspect, was already pregnant by then with Will and found herself trapped; too late, too locked in to go home.

When she talked about how things were when she was a girl it made me hurt inside. I loved her and wanted her—all of us—to be happy. If she was happy, she wouldn't become angry, and

I'd be free to sample more and more of these quiet, conversational moments, these occasional times of sad vulnerability that transformed her into someone completely real to me, someone who made sense, who'd had a hard time of it. Life wasn't easy, she often said. Nothing was easy. I knew that. But I couldn't help believing that if she'd only turn to me and Bobby and Will, join with us, we'd make a family.

I spent the first fifteen years of my life trying in the face of hopeless odds to turn us into what I believed a family to be. I refused to give up. There had to be *something* I could say, or do, or think of that would turn it all right, set us on the path forward, finally, as a group of people who loved each other.

I believed in love and families with pathological conviction. It was in every book I read, in every movie, on the radio, displayed by most of the families I'd met. Love was everywhere but in our family. And if I couldn't somehow bring all of us to the realization that we did have what seemed to be the proper ingredients that went into the baking of a family cake, then the fault was somehow mine. It had to do with a feeling I had of having all the answers there inside my head, along with the right set of words and gestures. So *why* couldn't I transmit them to the others?

None of my friends seemed particularly concerned with considerations of the quality of their family life. Later on, in high school, surrounded by girls suffering from acute interior hormonal explosions that rendered them critical of everything pertaining to their families, I was no longer alone in my fears. But that was later on. At seven, I was giving myself headaches, genuine aspirin-taking headaches trying to nail down what last essential element was needed within our group of five too-angry-too-often people to render us at last into a loving, united whole.

I lived for my mother's embraces, and tried to inveigle my way into her rounded arms, up against the softness of her breasts in order to close my eyes and breathe in the scent and familiarity of this woman, my mother; this person who'd surely display love and liking for me if I came back again and again seeking her out.

Sometimes her embraces were gentle, unhurried, immensely comforting and reassuring. At those times, I believed she might love me. But the majority of the time they were quick, too hard, too brief. She was busy getting a meal, or on her way out; she was in a bad mood and still upset from something that, perhaps, had gone on the night before. Yet even these too hasty hugs were acceptable. I was too often in disgrace, however: for having, yet again, talked back; for having dirtied my clothing or lost my hair ribbons; for having spilt the milk or sworn within her hearing; for having come home late from playing. All sorts of things. She'd become enraged. Then, I felt as if I hated her; I'd back out of the kitchen hissing under my breath, I hate you, hate you. It didn't deter me from hoping that the next time I'd be able to go away whispering, I love you love you love you.

Until a few years ago, my mother was the one person on earth capable of sending me into a blind rage within thirty seconds or less. Because she'd been a witness to the first twenty years of my life she seemed to know precisely, unerringly and with true mother instinct, what to say or do that would cause me to roll my eyes, grit my teeth and wonder why I bothered to subject myself to this sort of torture.

In recent years, I've found her an amusing raconteuse with quite an eye for storytelling detail, and something of a genuine and likable eccentric. In the course of a phone call a few months ago, she admonished me to be more patient with Jossie and I laughed loudly, with delight, reminding her, "Do you remember *me?*" She laughed, then sighed and said, "Yeah, I know," then added something to the effect that I'd been hell on wheels. Our conversation concluded with her reminding me to eat because I'm way the hell too skinny.

"*Mother*," I said in my best, long-suffering daughter's tones, "I'm *thirty-eight years old.*"

"Don't remind me, eh?" she chortled.

Daddy.

A mound in the bed. Red glow of a cigarette piercing the

darkness. Thick sleep smoke smell. And his husky voice murmuring, "C'mere, sweetheart. C'mere."

Feeling myself drawing closer, I approached the side of the big, creaky old bed and stared into the darkness, trying to see. His arm went around my waist as he leaned over to crush out his cigarette in the ashtray on the bedside table. The tabletop was a collage of multiple, overlapping cigarette burns.

Being drawn up and in, I climbed into bed alongside him, at once surprised that he wasn't wearing his pajamas; sensing something wrong in this. But it was so gratifying, the warmth beneath the blankets, so reassuring and comforting to hear his throaty whisper scratch light strokes across the sinister darkness. It couldn't really be bad, could it? Yet my mother wouldn't like this—for any number of reasons. An image of a very angry mother stalked my mind, and warned me she'd shout a lot and very loudly if she found me curled so contentedly beside Daddy this way. Especially when he put his hand down inside my pajama bottoms and began to stroke and caress me in a way that was bad wrong, horrifyingly reminiscent of The Inspector in the park, making something twist agonizingly inside me so that I had to say, "*Don't*! I don't *like* it." And he murmured, shushing me, "It's okay, okay," as his voice went on to fill the darkness with distracting tales of his escapades in North Africa during the War, places he'd been; his voice asking me divertingly what I'd like most in the world to have, promising me secret spending money. A little game we'd play, our secret; just the two of us. My brain held an image of the counter in the store across the street from the school where there were stacks of notebooks, boxes of pens, and I was filled with a sudden shamefully greedy need to have brand-new notebooks and fountain pens, bottles of Quink Ink in several different colors, bags of Saratoga potato chips and grape-flavored suckers, the hard kind that really lasted. Notebooks and pens, potato chips and candy. He was promising me limitless treasures.

I don't remember returning to my own bed; in the morning, I decided it'd been a dream. But I do remember the smile that overtook my mouth when I pulled on my mittens in the kitchen—my back to my mother—to discover the coins inside. Money. Two quarters, three nickels and a dime. Skipping off up the street, I laughed. He'd really done it, just the way he'd said he would. He'd kept his promise. And that meant from now on I'd be able to have whatever I wanted. Daddy would get it for me.

"Daddy, are we bad?"

"Bad, shmad. What's that, for chrissake?"

"I don't know. But we are, aren't we?"

"Course not."

"And you really mean it, this is what all little girls and their daddies do?"

"Didn't I tell you, eh?"

"I know. But if everybody does it, then how come I can't tell?"

"Don't you like it just you and me having a secret?"

"I can keep secrets. I'm very good at secrets."

"Sure you are. You're my smart little girl, eh?"

"You think I'm smart?"

"Sure are. Smart as a whip."

"You love me, Daddy?"

"What the hell kinda question's that? Course I do. Nobody'll ever love you better than your old man."

"I love you, too. Wouldn't it be fun to tell . . . ?"

"Now, no! We're not telling anybody, are we?"

"Oh, no. I can keep secrets better than anyone."

"That's my girl."

At the beginning, it was a very special, very secret game the two of us played; hiding out from the others. I'd creep down the hall to the big bedroom those two nights a week my mother was out to play cards or at the bingo; down the hall to play the new game with Daddy. The fact that one or both the boys was usually somewhere in the apartment made Daddy do strange, awful things. One night, he suddenly shoved me down into the bed, pulling the blankets over my head. Terrifyingly, he held me down, keeping me silent, still.

"What's wrong?" I wanted to know, frightened in this hot darkness.

He clamped his hand over the back of my head to quiet me, and kept it there for several minutes before allowing me to emerge.

"Why'd you *do* that? You *scared* me!"

"Be *quiet*!" he hissed. "You want them to find out what's going on?"

I stared at him, feeling comprehension pull itself together in my brain.

"Christ!" he said shakily, as he lit a fresh cigarette. "You almost got us caught."

It really was wrong to have this secret. Wrong, this thing no one was ever supposed to find out about; wrong, bad. After that, I went about feeling jittery, bothered. Yet it was good to be held, to feel warm and protected; to listen to his voice croon huskily in my ear; words spinning out to fill the darkness. I wished I could just stay that way forever: being held, feeling warm.

But he changed it. He took my mother's hand mirror from the dresser, made me open my legs and held the mirror there, saying, "Look, look!" as he put names to the parts of me, put shame into me. I hated looking, didn't want to; felt sick, angry. I hated him for compelling me to look at myself that way, hated the names he said belonged to the all at once horrible parts of me. I felt monstrously ugly, seeing myself; his determination that I see something that, like one of my cuts or scratches, hadn't ever properly healed. An old injury: slotted, unpretty, meant to be kept hidden—for all kinds of reasons. My mother was always telling me to pull my dress down, keep my knees together. "Don't sit that way! *Nice* girls don't *sit* that way!"

I wanted to cry, my throat thick with it. With strength given me by my hurt and anger, I pushed his hand with the mirror away. A voice in my head recited all the warnings my mother had ever issued: Don't get into cars with strangers. Don't accept money or candy from people I don't know. Don't ever again go alone into a public toilet, and never ever sit on the toilet seat in a public lavatory. Dozens of things I was never supposed to do. This was one of those things and she'd never warned me about it. This was the worst thing of all. I knew it. So why hadn't she warned me about this?

Still, come the morning, there were always coins in my mittens or coat pockets. I'd fly into a temper if they weren't there. He only forgot once. After that, never again. My fingertips toyed with the ridged edges of quarters and dimes, slid over smooth-edged nickels as I wondered what I'd buy; yet all the while I felt as I had about the Christmas doll: I didn't really want the money now that I always had it.

I'd go to the store across the street from the school and buy things, everything I wanted. But once I had the notebooks, the colored pencils, the fountain pens and bottles of ink, I didn't want them; couldn't eat the potato chips or candy, and gave them away at random to kids in the playground, with the distant hope these uncaring bribes might make them like me more; scribbled over the notebooks and threw them away. I rid myself just as quickly as I could of Daddy's money, feeling a pressing need to spend it all just as fast as I could. Never mind that my mother was forever telling me to ". . . save your money. That's the ticket. Then you've always got something put aside for a rainy day." I could *not* keep the money. And every day was rainy.

The next Tuesday or Thursday night, I'd be on my way back to Daddy and there'd be more money. I knew where he got it: from day-long gin, poker, or clubbiash games at his club. Or from handbags he took from the factory and sold, keeping the money for himself. He'd taken me along to his club one afternoon, insisting I sit in unnatural silence for the duration of an entire afternoon while he and a group of old war buddies gambled with sweaty, swearing intensity.

Going back to him again and again became something I had no idea how to handle. I didn't dare simply stay in the room

I shared with Bobby, in my own bed. If I did, there'd be trouble of some sort, because since this secret game had started, there was far less shouting and anger at suppertime, less shouting altogether. It was because of me, I knew; because of what I did for Daddy. He'd managed to get something he wanted, so it wasn't necessary for him to exercise himself on my mother and brothers.

I began fervently wishing, even praying to a God I really couldn't believe in—because I hadn't had any training in prayer —that things would somehow go back to the way they'd been, that *I'd* be the way I'd been. But everything had altered and I knew I couldn't ever go back. No matter how desperately I wanted it, I knew intuitively there was no reversing matters. There were too many secrets growing from the big secret, like long thin roots. I had to hide the money he gave me, had to lie to my mother when she asked about the candy or the comic books I forgot to conceal, the sometime magazines or sweet offerings I made to Bobby thinking only how much he'd like them and how much better I'd feel for the giving, and not about the fact that my mother would want to know where the money had come from to buy these things. I had to invent stories to cover the acquisitions—an easy enough job—but found it hard to remember the details of all the stories, and finally, automatically, hid my purchases so there wouldn't have to be any questions I might stumble over answering.

But I despaired of the secret. I hated to tell lies. I'd never done it before and felt shaky in the pit of my stomach at having to lie so often now.

I wanted to tell mother the truth and considered the idea very carefully. But before I arrived at the actual decision to confide in her, Daddy became alarmingly descriptive and specific in his threats.

"Don't you *ever* tell *anyone, ever!*" That ominous little drum beat away in his temple. "You want me to go to prison? They'd put *you* away, too! Whip me. And you, too. You want that to happen? You want to go to jail? Do you?"

So now I knew he'd lied about everything. Other fathers and

daughters didn't do the things we did. Well and truly terrified, I swore never to tell. Thoughts of prison were too dreadful; my brain feverishly supplied the details of cells with steel bars and stone floors; enormous policemen wielding whips, beating me. I could hear the policemen coming up the outside stairs, could hear them banging at the apartment door, could see my mother's bewildered and upset features as they barged past her and came to get me and Daddy to take us off to prison in the terrifying Black Maria. I could see them taking us away to tie us to splintery wooden frames where they'd whip us until all the skin came off our backs. Then they'd sling us into the cells. Rats, damp walls, no windows, bread and water, pain; terror.

I went through the days in a state of permanent and fearful dread, wanting it all to stop, wishing there was someone I could tell about Daddy, someone it was safe to tell who wouldn't just turn around and take the telling back to my parents, someone who'd believe me. But I knew no one would. My mother often accused me of lying, even when I hadn't. And if anyone confronted my father with the truth, with what I'd declared was the truth, he'd simply smile his dazzling, charming smile and lie and lie and lie. No one would doubt him.

But maybe my mother wouldn't believe him. Maybe she'd let them take Daddy away, but keep me. She wouldn't let the police take me away and put me in prison, would she? *Would she?*

Six

AFTER THINKING it over thoroughly, I was on the verge of telling my mother about The Secret when Miss Fielder invited Marianna and me out to lunch. Pleased by the invitation, I carried home her note to get permission. My mother didn't seem to care one way or another and consented.

On the appointed Saturday, dressed in my best outfit—a royal blue jumper with red anchors and white piping, and a pale blue middy blouse underneath—I went along to meet Miss Fielder at the arranged spot outside the Royal York Hotel.

"Unfortunately," she told me, "Marianna isn't going to be with us today, as I'd hoped. So," she went on, taking my hand into her dry, rather papery one, "It's just going to be we two. You don't mind, do you dear?"

I did. There was an oddness about the woman that made me nervous. Not only was she a teacher, but her hands, so dry and hot, her sweetish breath and gray hair scraped into a thin bun, her glinty wire-framed glasses and old-lady lace-up shoes, her clothes that smelled faintly of mothballs all bothered me.

The waiter and she fussed over me, oooing and aaahing at what she declared my prettiness and obvious intelligence. I had no idea what she meant. I was an ugly little girl and not at all smart. If I was, I wouldn't have been there with someone who made me feel so uncomfortable, for one thing; for another, I wouldn't have had any awful secrets to keep me awake long into the night.

I couldn't eat. She didn't seem to notice, but ate an enormous quantity of food. I couldn't bear to watch her, yet was unable to look away as she devoured a chicken pot pie in huge, hungry bites. I felt sicker by the moment, noticing bits of food stuck in the corners of her mouth. It was almost as bad as the way Daddy ate, although not as noisy.

Finally, I asked to be excused and found my way to the ladies' room where I washed my hands twice, then looked at myself critically for a long time in the mirror, hating it. Then reluctantly I returned to the vast dining room, hoping Miss Fielder would be done with her meal.

The waiter was there, hovering beside her, the two of them smiling. They both seemed crazy to me.

"Look at the lovely surprise, dear." She indicated the covered dish at my place, and I lifted the lid to see a half-melted ice-cream mold in the shape of a rabbit.

"Just for you." She smiled madly, her hands clasped before her on the table in a devotional attitude, as if about to pray over my melting ice cream. "Eat it up quickly now, dear, before it melts." I looked at her pleadingly, trying to understand why grown-ups were forever doing things that made so little sense. I knew she only wanted to please me, but I didn't know how to say, I'm not having a good time please may I go home. So, obligingly, I started. After one mouthful, I knew I'd never be able to eat it. Why did she have to pick strawberry, the one flavor in the entire world I didn't like? I took more on my spoon, tried to make myself put the spoon into my mouth, couldn't.

"Is something wrong, dear?" she asked, her eyes round behind the thick lenses.

"No, Miss Fielder." I shook my head and glanced around at the people at nearby tables all talking and smiling, having such a good time. My mother and father would never come to a place like this. I couldn't imagine Daddy here, creating an argument. The man in the black suit by the door would throw him out. But they wouldn't throw *me* out, I decided, as I dried my damp hand on my skirt under the table. When I'm grown up, I thought, I'll eat in places like this all the time if I want to. Quietly. With my husband and children. We'll never yell—not at each other and not at our children. And we'll never, ever order ice cream without first asking the children what flavors they like.

I managed to get down about a third of the rabbit before I gave up, sat back and said I was too full to finish but hastened to add, "It was very nice, though." I watched her eat apple pie with ice cream and a wedge of Cheddar cheese. Crumbs all over her mouth. Why didn't she *know* it?

Done at last with her food, she raised her hand surprisingly gracefully to summon the waiter and ask for the check. That gesture impressed me. All you had to do was lift your hand, move your fingers a little. Click-click. It was recorded indelibly in my mind.

Believing the ordeal to be close to an end, and relieved, I relaxed sufficiently to return Miss Fielder's smile, and suffered her hand enclosing mine as we left the dining room; I hoped no one thought she was my mother or anything. In the elevator, though, instead of pressing the button to go down, she pressed the one for the roof garden and, at this, I panicked, wondering if she planned to take me up to the roof and throw me off because I'd eaten so little of that really lovely lunch. I had no doubt that adults could do such things to children, so it was a distinct possibility that Miss Fielder might just decide to send me hurtling off the roof to my death for my failure to properly appreciate her generosity.

"I've brought you up here," she said ceremoniously, settling the two of us on a settee in the deserted anteroom, "because this is the closest to heaven one can come in this godforsaken city. A great pity the outdoor gardens aren't open today. Still, this is quite comfortable."

Wisps of hair drooped from the small knot at the back of

her neck; her thick, gleaming glasses made her eyes look impossibly large; a few crumbs from the pie still clung to her mouth. I stared at the pale hairs on her chin.

"We must all love God, dear," she went on, "because there's no other way we can survive the evils and temptations of this life."

For a heart-stopping moment, I thought she'd somehow managed to learn The Secret and was now about to offer me an explanation as to why it was necessary for her to open those glass doors over there, escort me out and toss me off the roof.

"Love is God," she intoned. "God is love."

I looked down at my hands, at the infected cuts on the backs of them, and concentrated on trying to calm the wild knocking in my chest; listening even though I didn't want to. I was embarrassed for her, convinced she was crazy. Yet her craziness was fascinating and I couldn't help thinking it was too bad Marianna hadn't been able to come long; if she had, the two of us would've been here now, trying to smother our giggles, clutching at each other's hands to keep from laughing. But Marianna wasn't there. And on my own, with no one to support my thoughts and feelings, I had to take the woman seriously.

"You're an exceptional child," she was saying. "Yes, exceptional." She repeated the word as if it had an exquisite flavor. "One could do wonders with a child of your inherent intelligence and imagination. Those eyes." She shook her head. "One of God's chosen lambs."

Lambs? I tried not to squirm, desperately afraid I was going to start to laugh after all. *Lambs?*

She went on for quite some time before opening her oversized handbag to bring out a small, leatherbound Bible which she presented to me ceremoniously.

"But we're not . . . We don't . . . I'm not . . ." I protested.

"One can always use a Bible."

"But my mother . . . We're *Jewish* . . ."

"It's the *Old* Testament," she said meaningfully. Was there some kind of *new* one? I wondered.

I had to accept the small volume, and took it gingerly into my hands as if it might burn. Actually, it felt cool, and, looking inside, I noted that the print was very very small.

At home, full of relief and renewed spirits, I bounced into the kitchen to tell my mother all about the outing.

"What d'you *mean* she told you about *God*?"

I was laughing. It all seemed so silly now that it was at a distance. "Oh, you know. We're all little lambs of the Lord and I'm a 'special little lamb' 'cause I'm so bright and gifted and one day I'll make my mark on the world." I couldn't stop laughing. Me? Make a mark on the world?

"Gifted?" she repeated suspiciously.

"Yup." I expected her to laugh with me, but privately hoped she'd admit she'd always believed I was very special and, indeed, gifted. At that moment, I'd have thrown myself into her arms and confessed everything.

"For chrissake!" Her features were lifted consideringly, as if she was deciding whether to be amused or offended.

"And then she gave me this." I held the Bible out to her.

She took it, stared at it for several seconds, then exploded. "What the hell does she think she's *doing*, taking a kid like you to a place like that, filling your head with all that religious crap and that 'gifted' garbage?"

Instantly, I was on the defensive. After all, Miss Fielder had picked me and not one of the other fifteen or sixteen girls in the class.

"It was a really nice place," I said. "With lots of nice people, and white tablecloths and flowers on the tables." My eyes were on the old enamel kitchen table, then on the linoleum covering the floor.

"You're taking this to school Monday morning and giving it back!"

"It was a *present*! That'd be Indian-giving!" It was unthinkable to return a gift, even if it was something I hadn't wanted or had any use for.

"You're *taking* it *back*!" she insisted, her temper skyrocketing.

"No, I won't!"

I knew before she did she was going to throw the Bible, and I ducked. It flew across the room and smashed right through the glass front of the kitchen cabinet. There was a long, stunned silence as we both gazed at the shattered glass. She looked amazed, as if unable to believe she'd done what she had. I wanted to get up from behind the table and run, but was afraid to move. I stood up. She bounded across the room and grabbed me by one of my pigtails.

"*What'd you duck for?*" she shouted, and gave the pigtail a hard yank.

"I wasn't just going *to stand* there and *let* you *hit* me!"

"*Look* what you *made* me *do!*" she cried, wrenching my head around so hard that tears came into my eyes.

"*I* didn't throw it! *You're* the one!"

"Don't *answer* me *back! Look at that!*"

"I didn't *do anything!*"

Absently, she let go of my hair and stood wretchedly surveying the mess of broken glass. "Son-of-a-bitch," she said softly, her eyes still on the cabinet.

"You didn't have to *pull* my *hair*," I said accusingly.

She turned and stared fixedly at me for several moments, as if mesmerized; as if she'd never seen me before.

"Well, you *didn't*," I told her.

"Okay, so I didn't," she admitted quietly, then looked again at the cabinet. "Probably cost a mint to get that fixed."

I don't care, I thought. It's your own stupid fault, you shouldn't have thrown it. I took several steps toward the door. She bent down and started to pick up the glass. I kept on going, rubbing my smarting scalp, deciding I'd never tell her anything ever again; not when she could get so mad about something that was *funny*. She'd *kill* me, I thought, if I told her something like The Secret that was really bad.

I have only once—so far—done something to Jossie that was so shameful in its unprovoked lunacy that I wince when I think about it. She was in the shower and I went in to check on her, and ask if she was almost finished. She said she was, nearly, but was having trouble getting all the shampoo out of her hair. I told her to move so she was more directly under the water. She moved about an inch so that perhaps half her head was properly positioned. I told her to move more. She protested, and I went berserk, screaming at her that she was an idiot. "Just move the hell under the goddamned water and get the soap out of your hair!" When she tried to explain, I dragged the shower curtain aside, grabbed her by the shoulders and forcibly held her under the water while she fearfully shrieked and sobbed.

Suddenly, with a sick feeling, I became aware of how little she was, how small her bones felt under my hands. I turned off the water, reached for the bath sheet, got her out of the stall and had to kneel on the floor just holding her very tightly until I had myself back in control. She leaned against me with her head on my shoulder, sobbing, while I apologized and stroked her and told her I hadn't any right at all to do what I'd done to her, nor had I any reason for doing what I had.

After a time, she straightened, and I asked, "Do you forgive me?"

She patted me softly and said, "That's okay, Mom."

I wanted to die.

When Jossie feelingly protests, "That's unfair, Mom," I've got to stop every time and examine all the aspects of what preceded the statement in an effort to be scrupulously certain no unfairness was involved. I hate the idea of it, just as I hate articles about battered children, accompanied by photographs.

I've given away more money to good sob stories than I have to any charity.

Seven

SUDDENLY, MARIANNA was different: thinner, quieter, given to long silences she broke, to my relief, with wide smiles reminiscent of the former girl. But there was a certain dark shadow to her eyes I couldn't interpret.

We got split up the following year, both of us were skipped and sent to different grade-four classes. We saw less of each other—after school sometimes, and at recess. Occasionally, we went to have fish and chips for lunch; we'd walk along the street with our newspaper cones wet with vinegar, eating, talking. Or we went to her house and made our old standby lettuce and Miracle Whip sandwiches. But it just wasn't the same. And I wondered if it was me and not Marianna who'd changed. We simply didn't have the same hysterical, boisterous fun as before. I decided that the fault was somehow mine.

Often, perched outside on the open end of our back roof, my legs dangling dangerously over the edge, I'd look down at the littered, weedy enclosure below, and wonder how it would feel to let go and fall. I'd stare down and find myself leaning slowly forward as if hypnotized. Then, I'd jerk back, settle for a moment, then find myself repeating the process. I was tempted.

Nothing was ever again going to be good, or happy; there

wasn't any point even to hoping. I longed to run away, to get
as far as I possibly could and be happy all by myself. But how
could I? For one thing, I was only eight years old. For another,
there was nowhere to run to. Even if I did manage to get to
somewhere else, no one would give me a job or take me in and
make me one of the family without asking a whole lot of
questions. So how would I live? No. I'd simply get sent to
the nearest police station and, ultimately, home.

I'd have gone gladly to live with Auntie Brenda, my mother's oldest sister, and her husband, Jake. I'd stayed with them
once for a week when I was six and my parents went off for a
week to Montreal. I'd loved it. Still, it was pointless to think
about that, too. My mother would never give me up, for any
number of reasons: because to do so would be to acknowledge
publicly that she'd failed with me or I with her, that our
family wasn't a family at all but rather ongoing warfare between alien tribes. And even if my mother were willing, Daddy
would never allow it to happen. He'd keep me near him for
the rest of his—or my—life, if he was able.

The idea of being whipped and thrown into jail kept me
away from the police. I certainly wasn't about to tell Miss
Fielder who might pray over me before taking me back to the
Royal York, this time to pitch me off the roof after all; or
Miss Love, that frightening Amazon who'd held murmured
conversations with my mother about how difficult a child I
was; or the school nurse with elephantiasis who so frequently
patched me up after schoolyard falls and collisions with doors,
walls and other fixed objects. The woman could scarcely walk,
seemed not even to like children; briskly, competently she'd
swab my latest cut or scrape with disinfectant before slapping
on a bandage and shooing me out. My aunts, uncles, could
I tell any one of them? No. They all belonged to one side
or the other, would ship me home in a hurry and probably
suggest to my mother that she wash my mouth out with soap,
give me a good hiding and lock me up in the closet under the
stairs until I decided I was sorry and ready to come out and
give up lying forever. The school principal? He was a stern,
gray-haired disciplinarian who gave the strap to rowdy boys

and would probably give it to me. I didn't want to involve
Marianna's family in my shame. So, there really was nowhere
to run to, no one to tell who might help me.

I began, nightly, to have the same dream: someone was pulling my mother out through the mail slot in the downstairs
front door while I cried and screamed, trying to keep hold of
her. The wire basket attached to the inside of the door to
catch the mail got in my way and tore my skin. My mother
was always sliding away, going; carried off by some stranger
whose face I could never make out. And at the end I was
left, locked into the apartment with Daddy.

School ended. I was promoted into the fifth grade. Will left
home that summer and Bobby moved into Will's bedroom. My
mother took me along to see the people who ran the B'nai
B'rith Camp to ask for a reduced rate so that I might go away
for six weeks in the country. I felt humiliated, even angry
with her for not being able to pay whatever it cost. I didn't
really believe she couldn't afford the full amount. But I wanted
to go, so I tried not to hear what was said.

There were several reasons why I didn't believe her: because my father turned over his entire pay packet to her every
Friday night and I assumed it contained lots of money, because
my father insisted she had a bank account somewhere crammed
with his hard-earned money, because my father always had a
thick roll of bills and I, therefore, imagined she must have one,
too.

Anyway, off I went on the bus to be violently car sick en
route. I got eaten alive by mosquitoes and returned home with
a huge, suppurating infection on the lower inside of my right
calf that was the result of scratching one of the bites. I'd
watched it grow daily bigger, uglier, wetter and rawer. When
I removed the dirty bandage, the sight of this oozing mess
sent my mother into such a panic that she hustled me out of
the apartment, onto the streetcar and off to the Sick Children's
Hospital emergency room. She was so nervous and upset, she
couldn't seem to speak.

The doctor lifted my leg and pushed gently at the underside
of my calf which, he said, was like a cow's swollen udder,

and swayed heavily, impressively back and forth at his touch. He smiled, patted me on the shoulder and went out into the corridor to talk to Mother. The nurse meanwhile got me off the examining table, into a wheelchair and pushed me into the corridor to wait.

"He's putting you in the hospital," my mother told me, her green eyes larger than ever and tear-filled. She looked very frightened.

"Why?" I asked, watching the nurse drop down, take hold of my right arm and inject a needle.

"He says your leg's ulcerated." Her voice was soft, breathless.

"Oh. Okay." I didn't even feel the injection, I was too captivated by this totally sympathetic and fearful attitude of my mother's. It was as if she were ill, not I; I wanted to comfort her because she was so shaken. "I don't mind," I said, studying her face now as she watched the nurse release my arm and stand up.

She didn't want to leave. And I remembered all the times she'd told me about how her father had carried her to the hospital when she'd been so ill as a child. But I was intrigued by the novelty of the situation and anxious to be left alone so that I might better absorb all that was happening. Finally, she went.

I was installed in a private room off one of the main wards, which was a disappointment because I wanted to be in with all the other kids. I climbed out of bed several times to stand in the doorway, talking to the two unexpectedly friendly girls whose beds were either side of the doorway to my room.

That night, after dinner on a tray—a great novelty—I lay back, and thought about the summer camp. I'd hated it. Six weeks' stay with a cabinful of girls who'd either ignored me or made me the butt of all their gags and pranks because I'd been the smallest, although not the youngest; because I'd been a sick-looking mess of bites; because the counselors had only helped me wash my long, tangled hair once and then left me to get on with it as best I could for four more weeks; because I rejected breakfast since it invariably gave me stomach cramps; because I was the only one who positively would *not* go skinnydipping; because I was there, and no doubt sullen; certainly frightened by the strangeness of it all. Their Friday night religious services were as confusing and alien as their Hebrew singalongs, their Jewish jokes, their Jewishness altogether. I might as well have been a devout Roman Catholic, for all I understood of them.

I also thought that a stay in the hospital meant no Daddy. I'd be left alone. And that was just fine.

The next day, doctors and nurses came and went, trying, they explained, ". . . to diagnose what seems to be the problem." Aloud, as if I couldn't hear or understand, they considered impetigo, but rejected that almost at once. They asked if I had scratched or picked at any of the infections on my hands and legs and I admitted that the bites had itched so horribly that I had. They gave me all sorts of allergy tests, different types of injections and, in the end, were unable to diagnose my peculiar lack of resistance to infection once the surface of my skin was broken and, thereafter, my inability to properly heal; they concentrated solely on trying to treat the ulcer.

My mother was scared to death I had something rare and terrible, or that I might lose my leg. Even after the doctors had assured her none of that would happen, she still persisted in shaking her head fearfully throughout her visits, worrying quietly over when, if ever, the hole in my leg might heal.

It was a peaceful time, even happy. After lights-out, I sang for the kids on the ward. Since I sang in any case to get myself to sleep, I simply sang a bit louder and hoped to put us all to sleep, which I actually did. It was thoroughly satisfying to send my voice out into the still silent air of the ward, with the knowledge that singing was something I could do well and that contained a kind of gentle power. I felt strong when I sang. It gave me a very positive feeling. I'd sing until the night nurse came in and smiled, saying, "That's enough now, honey. You've put all the girls to sleep. Time for you to sleep, too. Like to sing, don't you? Funny kind of low voice you've got for such a little girl."

God! She was so nice, so soft-spoken, so complimentary and kind. She choked the songs right out of my throat, and I wanted to ask her if she had a little girl, did she maybe want one, I'd be very good and help around the house.

There are women who reach a completely responsive area in me. They have both strength and vulnerability as well as a kind of awesome depth of femininity that makes me yearn to put my arms around them and hold them for a long, quiet time. They are, to me, mother and sister, daughter and friend; everything good that's female.

Lola, from the outset, has always instinctively understood this and allowed me to be free with my need to hold her, to close my eyes and breathe in her warmth and softness.

I remember one afternoon two or three years ago, standing in her kitchen in England, talking to her while she did something or other. Then, she turned and touched me on the arm and her touch was so gentle and significant that I couldn't move for several minutes. Stunned, I realized, This woman loves me and her hand just told me so. It was an extraordinary moment, one of total realization. I felt approved, accepted, loved as I'd always wanted to be. Lola and Norman have always known that when words fail to reach me, their touch will inevitably bring me back from wherever it is I've gone. And because of them I've been able to grow, to go out into the world and offer myself with less and less fear.

I stayed in the hospital two weeks, then remained bedridden at home for six more; until a thin film of scar tissue began to reach out from the edges of the half-dollar-sized hole, to join up in the middle. The awful, rotting smell of the open wound went at last; the raw-meat look of it was covered over by papery scar tissue.

Back at school, I found myself the center of attention in the schoolyard for a brief time; gladly I pushed down my kneesocks to show my uncommon scar to anyone who cared to see. No one else had an ulcer scar, or skin that blossomed with infections medications couldn't heal. Even a radical month-long diet of broiled, fatless meats and sugarless, milk-less tea, a diet free of carbohydrates and of fresh fruits and vegetables had no appreciable effect nor produced any diagnosis. I was simply reduced by fifteen pounds and therefore even smaller than before. But I felt fine. I'd been left alone for three entire months. My mother had, with patience and gratifying gentleness, hefted me around the apartment and lifted me in and out of the bathtub—where I sat with my leg propped on the rim while she bathed me. When the leg was at last healed, she looked genuinely happy and, in wrapping me in the bath towel, hugged me. Maybe, I thought, it had taken my being sick to turn everything right again.

But the Tuesday night after I returned to school, Daddy was again waiting for me. And a few days after that my mother got angry with me for something or other. Nothing had changed.

I went back and forth to school steadily feeling sicker and sicker, privately positive Daddy was somehow responsible, until mid-winter when my mother put her hand to my forehead and said, "You feel awful hot. I'd better call the doctor." Tiredly she said, "It's one damn thing after another with you."

While she telephoned, I sat on the piano bench in the living room, doodling over the keyboard, gazing down at the keys through what seemed to be a haze as I strained to breathe. I wondered if maybe I was dying. I sat there in my pajama top, underpants and vest, having argued I was too hot to wear anything more, and thought about crazy Miss Holly who gave Bobby and me piano lessons. She lived in a tiny little house on Bathurst Street with a crippled lady called "Miss Ryder" and two huge black dogs, and gave "Piano, Tap and Ballet Lessons" in her front room. She was little and round, with a headful of bobbing, dyed-red curls and a face painted like a doll's —very white, with round red circles on each cheek. She always wore black-patent tap shoes and fluffy full dresses. When she gave tap lessons, she'd demonstrate the steps and the three or four of us who were there to learn nearly strangled trying not to laugh. Sometimes she'd give me or Bobby ten cents if

we'd run down to the corner to pick up the grocery order
she'd phoned in. She was spooky and so was her house, and
though I'd wanted to have all the lessons—piano, tap *and* ballet—when my mother had offered them, I'd long since lost interest. I'd imagined that after three or four lessons I'd be able
to sit down at the piano and play like a whiz and when it
didn't turn out that way, the twice-weekly lessons became a
chore.

My mother came in in her coat to say, "The doctor'll be here
in a little while. I've got to run down to the store. You stay
put, none of this running around while I'm gone."

The instant the door closed behind her, I sprang up to dance
dizzily down the length of the hall, chanting, "You can't tell
me what to do, to do, you can't tell me." I'd have more time
off school, I thought; Daddy would have to leave me alone
and mother would tuck me up in bed with a little bowl of
fruit and biscuits, and treat me very nicely because I felt so
hot and dizzy, had such a bad cough and it hurt so much to
breathe. After a minute or two, I returned to the piano bench.
Staring at the floor, I tried to catch my breath after my defiant
exertions.

The doctor was plainly unnerved to find me alone in the
apartment. After I'd explained that my mother had gone to the
store, we went into the living room to wait for her. We sat,
in suspenseful silence for a time, until he said, in heavily accented English, "Who knows how long your mother will be?
I have other calls I must make." He proceeded to examine me,
every so often looking about with a wary expression, as if he
expected someone to leap out at him from the closet or doorway. I couldn't understand what was taking my mother so
long, and prayed, as he unbuttoned my pajama top, that he
wasn't going to be another Inspector, another someone who'd
touch me in some awful way or make me do something I didn't
want to do.

"What kind've accent have you got?" I asked, thinking to
keep him distracted so he wouldn't touch me.

"Sshhh," he said, listening to my chest, telling me to breathe
in, breathe out. "Hungarian."

"Oh! Have you been in Canada a long time?"

"Yes, a long time. You have viral pneumonia," he said, re-doing my pajama buttons, not touching me anywhere but where he was supposed to so that the sudden loss of fear left me even dizzier. "A temperature of over one hundred three. You should be in bed. When I leave, you go to your bed, stay there. Give this to your mother, tell her to get it filled. You are to have two tablets three times a day, and the cough mixture four times a day. You understand all this?"

"Yup. What's a viral?"

"A virus is a germ. It means you have an infection in your lungs and should not be here alone, running around with not enough clothes. You should be in your bed."

"My mother told me to stay in bed," I said guiltily, "but I didn't want to."

"No matter," he said brusquely. "She should not go out, leave a sick child alone."

Through the whirl of my dizziness, I studied him: a heavy-set man with dark hair and pale skin, glasses, a worried look. He's right, I realized. I shouldn't be here by myself. But she really did have to go out to get stuff for supper. And there wasn't anybody around for her to ask to come stay with me.

"I must use the telephone," he said.

"It's in the kitchen." I showed him.

After his call, he closed his bag and made his way to the front door, then stopped and asked, "You always stay alone?"

"She'll be right back. There was probably a big line at the store."

"How old are you? Six, seven?"

"Nine."

"Nine," he repeated. The way he looked at me made me feel many things simultaneously: embarrassment, anger with my mother for not being home when she was supposed to be, and the desire to explain that it was okay for me to be there by myself. Lots of times, if my mother had to run down to the store, I stayed alone. And she wasn't someone bad just be-cause she wasn't there right at that minute. Still, his expression stated that he wouldn't leave a child of his alone and he couldn't understand why I had been. He gave a shake of his head, opened the door and went out.

My mother came huffing in with two bags of groceries, complaining about the long wait she'd had in the market. When I told her that the doctor had already been and gone, and what he'd said, she blew up.

"Don't you *ever*," she warned fiercely, "talk about this family! Not to anyone! What we do is nobody else's business! You get to bed!" She hustled me down the hall to my room, and roughly pushed me into bed. "Get the hell in there, and *stay* there!"

"What're you *yelling* at me for?" I cried, dragging the blankets over my head. "I didn't *do* anything. I *hate* you!"

"Okay," she said more quietly, relenting. She sat down on the side of the bed and folded back the blankets, her eyes begging me to understand—what? "Wait," she said soberly. "Someday you'll have kids of your own, then you'll find out it's no picnic, believe you me."

"I won't be *mean* to them," I sniffed.

"We'll see about that. You lie quiet now while I go call the drugstore." She got up and went out.

If you really loved me, I thought petulantly, you'd kiss me, say you're sorry I'm sick and tell me you love me, not tell me what it's going to be like when I'm all grown up and have sick kids to look after.

The pneumonia left me permanently tired. I couldn't get to sleep at night. I lay in the dark and sang to myself, watching the red then blue then red of the drugstore sign, or picked at the old wallpaper, yawning so hard it made my jaws crack and my eyes water; I finally fell asleep long after everyone else. Sometimes I'd hear muffled laughter creeping out from beneath their bedroom door and, through the wall against which I slept, telltale squingy noises I at once identified and couldn't stand to hear. My mother's meaningful laughter and the low, heavy rumble of my father's voice, the sudden silences were ugly, disgusting. I held the pillow over my head, not breathing, until I'd managed to create a thunderstorm inside my skull and had to have air. Surfacing, I again watched the red blue red and, sometimes, the lights of passing cars as they swung across the ceiling; knowing precisely what was going on in the next room because Daddy confided to me things I didn't want to know about or have to hear; I had to tell him to shut up and stop *telling* me. The way he talked about my mother spoiled my feelings for her but I couldn't find the right way to make him see that.

I listened to the loud street conversations, and the drunken fights that regularly took place outside the old North Star, across the road. Tired, I reeled through the school days as if drugged. I'd sit on the school steps and watch the kids play, lacking the energy or the inclination to join them. I'd spend a couple of hours every so often trying hard to have fun with Marianna, but neither of us seemed to have whatever it was we'd had before that had enabled us to find so much amusement in our silly antics.

With the summer, and the end of another grade I'd somehow managed to get through, I walked over to the school each morning with the idea that I'd join in the supervised summer activities programs. But once I got there I'd just hang idly on the sidelines, feeling too aged and weary to make the effort to play. There were black places inside my head, areas filled with things I didn't want to have to think about in the bright sunshine when I was supposed to be playing and having fun. I was a horrible, dirty little girl who did horrible, dirty things for money.

From time to time, I brought along my roller skates and circled the knots of preoccupied children, deeply envious of their ability to concentrate on their enjoyment. I skated round and round the concrete schoolyard, the motions both sickening and soothing, while my eyes were cameras and click-click I took pictures of the schoolyard, the kids, the trees way over there, the softball game; I studied faces, voices, laughter, motion; I felt invisible, like a huge brain on roller skates.

Eventually, I'd head home, skating right down the middle of the road, ignoring the honk of car horns and people who shouted at me to get out of the way, did I want to get killed or something, crazy kid. I didn't care. I knew I wouldn't get killed. Even when I wished as hard as I could to die, I knew it wouldn't happen. You couldn't just die and have everything end because you wanted it. You had to keep on and on, nights and mornings, day after day, forever. If I wanted it to end, I'd have to *make* it end, and the only way I could do that would be by killing myself. I thought more and more about that, but didn't want to do it. I wanted to believe something would happen to change things.

Awake late at night, blinking at the red blue red blue, I'd picture us as a family, the way families were supposed to be. But all the images belonged to someone else's family, not mine.

One of the bonuses of marrying Walt came in the form of his remarkable mother and his four older sisters. For as long as it lasted, being related to those five women was good. There were some highly pleasurable moments in being part of a large, extended family. It still saddens me that while Walt and I are still close, communicating friends, his sisters erased me as if I'd never existed once Walt and I moved apart.

I miss belonging, but I remind myself of all I do have: my friends, and my fine family in England—Lola and Norman, Guinea Pig and Philpa—to visit as often as possible. The distances are sometimes hard to bear—being so far from the people who rescued a mad, sad twenty-two-year-old and offered her a home, and love.

I used to think all the time about returning to live in England in order to be near Lola, her mother and father, Norman. But I've known that the better part of my love for them, and theirs for me, depends upon my continued ability to stand alone. There's always the telephone, the sound of their voices to take off some of the occasional chill, to place music in the vacuum. I know that they're there, that they love me, and that's more than I once ever hoped to have.

Eight

ABOUT FIVE years ago, I came back to Canada from Connecticut to visit old friends and to see my brother and mother. In the course of my stay, Marianna and Joanie—a former roommate—and I went to Chinatown with my brother Will and his lady and his two daughters. It was a wonderful, laughing time; first, because even after all the years away I still found the city of my birth beautiful, inspiring and so charged with memories that, despite its constant growth and change, it would always be home for me; second, because being with old friends, particularly Marianna, was and still is such a fine feeling.

Much later that night, Marianna and Joanie and I settled in Marianna's living room with coffee and slices of her mother's memorable apple pie; we relaxed with cigarettes and engaged in early-morning confessional talk. We were, all at once, very solemn; tired after a long day and evening; tired to the point where truth is able to find an opening.

Joanie had known about Daddy for years. But I'd never told Marianna, perhaps because I'd wanted her to retain the busy image of me I'd created so long ago for her. Marianna has always been interested in my comings and goings, was someone I always wanted and needed to see. I love her. She's beautiful in a most fragile way, and undemanding. Because she makes no demands, I enjoy making her offerings—of words, or gifts; she's a very gracious woman.

I spoke of Daddy, not with my then usual I'm-all-right-now patter but with feeling, with anger and some fear. Marianna listened closely, leaning forward with her arms crossed over her knees, then lit a fresh cigarette and told us what had happened the year she was seven. A seventeen-year-old cousin had raped her in the empty house one afternoon. He warned her that if she told anyone, he'd come back and kill her. She believed him. It drastically altered her life, her thoughts, her feelings; everything.

The irony and pain of it, and my own impotence left me speechless, shattered. All I could think and say was, "If only somehow we could have told each other. Things might have been so different." It seemed monstrously unfair that she'd had to travel through so many years so terribly *afraid*—of men, of life, of herself, of so many things that for a time she drank heavily, and became repeatedly ill. She got almost cadaverously thin because she simply couldn't eat. For years she put off making a commitment to the man she loved.

She did, finally, make it through; she married, had the child she'd wanted, and was able to start structuring a life. Her husband is a soft-spoken, deferential and gentle man who knows and understands her. She has a beautiful daughter, also named Marianna.

I wanted to go out, find that cousin and kill him. Instead, I went home to Connecticut, collected my rage about me and wrote a book about an incident of rape and dedicated it to her. Small recompense. I still feel the anger and protectiveness toward her when I think about that year when we both were seven.

Back in school in a new class with a new teacher, my tiredness grew worse. And along with it came something scary:

I started to hear voices that repeated my name over and over. They started out very low, like leaves rustling in the wind, then got louder and louder until they were screaming my name over and over and over again inside my head. It made me go tight, made me clench my fists and dig my nails hard into the palms of my hands.

At first I looked around, certain everyone else could hear. But, no, it really was only inside my head. If I were to tell people I heard voices, they'd definitely think I was crazy. So I learned to keep my face blank and non-revealing in order that no one would know I was listening to the voices scream and not to the teachers or the kids who sometimes talked to me. Once in a while, the teacher would ask a question and I simply failed to hear, but sat staring into space, fixed on that incredible, frightening interior chorus screaming my name. My marks began to slip.

I couldn't tell anyone about the voices, or about the sensation I had too often that my mouth and throat were stuffed with a substance the consistency of bubble gum so that I couldn't speak or swallow. I knew if I told Daddy, he'd just make up one of his long, convoluted explanations that made no sense and only left me more confused than before. And if I told my mother, she might accuse me of dreaming up new lies just to gain the limelight and get attention.

At the end of a day filled with shrieking voices and a mouth cemented into silence and my heart beating so hard and fast I was sure I was having a heart attack, I was so giddy and exhausted I could scarcely make it through supper before falling, fearfully, asleep. I'd stay awake as long as possible to forestall the return of the dream of my mother being dragged away from me through the mail slot, or the one in which I flew naked over the schoolyard while all the kids and teachers pointed up at me and laughed, or the one where I was in a dungeon surrounded by enormous uniformed men with whips. This dream was both riveting and terrible. Suspended by their wrists and ankles from chains in the ceiling, women hung with their arms and legs spread gapingly and, laughing, the uni-

formed men would shove the thick, stub ends of their whips
up inside the women; howling with laughter when the women
screamed. In the dream, I, too, hung from chains, and studied
the naked bodies, the breasts and tautly spread thighs. There
seemed to be an unquestionable kind of order and justification
about the proceedings, as if this was the sort of thing that was
bound to happen to women and nothing any of us could ever
do would prevent it. It was always just about to happen to
me when I'd make myself wake up.

During recesses, huddled in some sheltered corner of the
schoolyard, out of the wind, I'd nurse the big bubble of anger
that seemed to fill my chest completely; I visualized acts of
revenge and bitterly relished images of myself brandishing a
knife or a gun, seeing my father cowed and fearful; seeing
myself take the big bread knife from the kitchen to stab him
to death. I experienced an overwhelming sense of relief at the
projection of this image, a powerful rightness to the act. I
wanted him dead. Or I wanted him to turn into a father and
love me.

"Why do the two of you always have to fight?"

*"Your mother's a goddamned ignorant, uneducated pain-in-
the-ass peasant."*

"But she finished grade eight and you didn't."

*"Money she understands. Just money. Gimme, gimme, all
the goddamned time. Just gimme, gimme."*

"But you love her?"

"Love. Shit!"

*"You loved her when you met, didn't you? When you got
married?"*

*"Yeah, I guess. I thought I had enough love for the both
of us."*

"You mean you loved her, but she didn't love you?"

"She never loved me. That's why I've got you."

*"Grown-ups are supposed to love other grown-ups. Not like
this."*

"My little lover, eh? C'mere."

"*Don't* call *me* that! *I* hate *it when you call me that! I'm* not *that!*"

"*C'mon, now. C'mere.*"

I hated him, hated his words, his deeds, his promises, his lies, his threats, his money. I loved him, loved it when he was funny, when he'd play word or music games with me, when he proudly took me out to walk and introduced me, with a smile, as his little girl. I wanted him to love me, to be a father.

Auntie Brenda.

She looked and smelled good and dressed beautifully. Her eyes too often told me how dreadful she thought I looked in the cheap sale clothes my mother bought me. Brenda and Uncle Jake regularly made me gifts of clothing and money, and called me their favorite niece. The gifts set pinpoints of envy, even suspicion in my mother's eyes, and caused me to believe she'd have preferred Brenda to have given the gifts to her. But she never said anything. She loved her sister, and envied her, too; impressed by the way Brenda and Jake lived, by their success and money.

My aunt favored me because I was small and a girl; she could play with me like a doll, dress me up and take me out. She staged little fashion shows for me in her living room and put on one new outfit after another so that I might—quite sincerely—admire them; she and I would go through the things in her several jewelry boxes; I would carefully paint her rather stubby fingernails while she praised me. I loved every minute of my time with her.

She was a tiny woman, perhaps five feet, with a full, rounded bosom and matchstick legs. The sight of her bird-like legs bothered me, so I chose not to see them, but looked instead at the professional perfection of her blond-dyed hair, at her clothes, her breasts. She was extremely modest and I was taken aback by this, since my mother's body had always been available to my eyes. Yet here was my mother's oldest sister changing clothes in the bathroom or behind the closed bedroom door, warning me not to come in. She aroused my curiosity, and, in the hope of discovering just what it was she was so anxious to hide, I pushed open the bathroom door one afternoon. She was in the midst of the bathing ritual she performed every afternoon prior to my Uncle's arrival home, and I caught her at it. What she had to hide was a pair of breasts unlike any I'd seen before, or have seen since. She had very fine, very white skin and large round breasts that stood firmly out from a narrow cage of ribs upon which they seemed quite incongruous. Absolutely beautiful. She glanced over, saw me, let out a squeak and pushed closed the door. I went back to the sofa in the living room, glad I'd taken the chance to see. For some reason, I decided then that my Uncle loved her in no small part because of her astonishing breasts.

She wasn't as pretty as my mother, but seemed far worldlier and more attractive. It had to do with her hair and clothes, her splendid taste, and her instinct for quality. I was drawn to her fondness for hugs and on-the-cheek kisses that wouldn't muss her lipstick, to her smiles and soft little-girl voice and her laughter, to her pleasure in hand-holding on outings and, finally, to her opulent and lavish love for her husband.

My uncle was as unstinting with his affections to me as he was to my aunt; he was very fond of my mother and even expressed an appreciation of my father's wit. Well over six feet tall, he was silver-haired, with aristocratic English-inherited features—a distinguished-looking man in custom-tailored suits. He was clean-cut and always wore Pinaud's Lilac Végétal; he had smooth, regularly manicured hands I loved to hold and a lap that welcomed me. He let me light his cigarettes, called me pretty and clever, and patted, hugged and kissed me. He made me *feel* pretty, even lovable, and invariably asked me to sing for the two of them whenever we went out in their zippy red convertible. They never talked when I was singing for them.

• They never argued and never swore. Their quiet conversations were filled with secret meanings, private signals and coded messages; they laughed together and embraced frequently, kissed openly. They were a perpetual ongoing movie I could walk into any time and understand and enjoy implicitly. I was in love with their love.

They took me for day-long Sunday drives in the country, to the movies, to dinner in nice restaurants, for walks window-shopping. I went eagerly, but experienced a definite uneasiness at the relatively innocent physical displays of their love. Hints of sexuality. These two people slept together, did unmentionable things together. Yet they still loved each other. On one level, I admired and approved of them. On another, deeper level, I was constantly afraid they'd do something—touch each other, say, in some too intimate fashion, which would destroy the satisfaction I derived from being with them. They might suddenly turn, scream at each other or strike out. It never happened, but I waited; observing them, studying the way their eyes and mouths and hands met. I longed to be old enough to have exactly this for myself: an apartment like theirs, clothes like my aunt's, elegance and freedom and innate good taste and a sex life that, like a movie, faded safely into an artful dissolve. No details, no nastiness.

My aunt defied her family and everything she'd been raised to believe in order to be with the man she loved. She was five or six years older than he; he wasn't Jewish; he wasn't even earning very much money when they met and fell in love. My mother spoke of her sister both then and now with tremendous admiration and feeling. Brenda was the only one of the sisters with whom she never had a serious falling-out. We three—my mother, my aunt and I—adored my uncle.

Not long ago, Jossie and I were visiting my mother and she took us into the bedroom to show us the progress she'd made on an afghan she was crocheting for me. There's a small gallery of photographs on her dresser and my mother and I stood together for several minutes while I looked at an old photograph of my aunt and uncle. I wanted to laugh and cry at the sight of them. My mother softly said, "I still miss her." Then we both sighed and I replaced the photograph.

Daddy dismissed them with casual disgust. "He's so god-

damned boring and she's a pain-in-the-ass, always giving things,
then going around telling everybody what she gave and how
much it cost."

"They're *not* like that *at all*!" I argued vehemently, so that
he looked up from one of his crossword puzzle books.

"What's this, eh? You think that jerk's better than your old
man? Think you're so hot all of a sudden?"

He had to have something to hate. I wanted to answer him
back, but didn't, afraid he'd find some way to put a stop to my
visits. I couldn't let that happen. I loved them, needed to be
able to see them. Jake was such a kind, fatherly man; someone
who'd never dream of sitting down to a meal in his undershirt; someone who'd never call me stupid or make jokes about
my looks so that I felt ugly; someone who'd never force me to
do disgusting sex things I didn't want to do. No, he-and my
aunt—and I, when I was with them—used cloth napkins, drank
cocktails (I had V–8 in a cocktail glass), played music during
dinner. The three of us sat afterward on the sofa holding
hands, arm tucked into arm, companionably listening to records on their big hi-fi console. And later on, when they got a
set, we watched television.

I spent countless hours in their apartment, waiting in the
living room while my aunt bathed and changed prior to my
uncle's arrival home. I sat on the sofa and went from cover to
cover of the decorating and fashion magazines on the coffee
table, or curled up in Jake's favorite chair and just looked at
everything: the white-painted wrought-iron stand of potted
plants; the thick, fitted carpet; the paintings on the walls; the
heavy glass ornaments on a nest of teak tables; the wall-to-wall
draperies. Everything was immaculate, fresh-smelling, good-
looking. If I closed my eyes, I could easily see myself grown
up, in high heels and a smart dress, moving from room to
room; the place mine.

On warm afternoons, Brenda in a pretty straw hat and pastel
shirtwaist dress would hold my hand as we walked down to
the lakefront to her special spot. We'd sit. She'd remove her
hat, delicately lift her skirt to just above her narrow knees and

place her hands carefully at the edge of her skirt before raising her face to the sun. I gazed out at the water, from time to time turning to admire her. Every detail was absorbed, click-click, and stored away. Tiny pearl earrings, a rope of small glass beads, spotless white cotton gloves embroidered with white flowers; a summer handbag of white straw, fresh gleaming nail polish, diamonds on her wristwatch and on her ring finger; the scent of flowers—Chanel Number Five.

Later on, we'd take the streetcar downtown to the station to meet Jake. She'd buy an afternoon *Star*, a small bar of dark Laura Secord chocolate for me and then we'd go to "our" bench in the vast waiting room. She'd become mildly upset if the bench was already occupied; it showed in the faintest change of her facial expression—a slight turning down at the corners of her mouth, and a sadly remonstrating disappointment in her eyes; small telltale signs I knew. I dreaded ever seeing her displeasure directed at me.

As the time grew near for my uncle's arrival, she'd glance at her watch, then carefully refold the newspaper, wipe her hands on a tissue to remove any trace of newsprint, freshen her lipstick, then turn to inspect me, saying, "Let me just fix your hair, Dear. You know we love to see you looking pretty. Your uncle loves to see his girls looking their best." She'd puff up my sleeves, smooth down my hair, then settle herself, legs carefully crossed, to wait out the final minutes.

Through the crowd, he'd come striding, smiling and waving. There'd follow hugs and kisses, and then the three of us would head for the unmarked door that led to the indoor area where the railroad executives parked their cars. I invariably looked around hoping people saw us and thought I was with my mother and father.

I prayed for disasters, for some event to wipe out my family, leaving me to my aunt and uncle. Or maybe something would happen just to Daddy and then my mother and I could live with my aunt and uncle. Or maybe, finally, my mother and Bobby and I could just *live*. I stared into the neon darkness craving a nice life, with dinners out downtown, and pretty clothes. Maybe, too—miraculously—my parents might at last get divorced and Daddy would decide to turn into a real father and take me to live with him. I didn't care which one of them decided to give me a nice life, just so long as one of them did.

One morning, after her first or second week in kindergarten, Jossie came home to announce, "I *hate* Anne Marie."

I sat down with her, and said, "You really shouldn't talk about hating people that way, babe."

"Oh, but Mom, *all* the kids hate her."

"They do? Why?"

" 'Cause she's ugly, and she's got fat legs, and she eats stones."

"She eats *stones*?" I was convulsed with laughter and so was she.

"Honest, Mom," she said earnestly, taking a breath, "she does. At playtime."

We laughed and laughed until I recovered myself sufficiently to say, "Just say you don't *like* her. Okay? You don't have to hate her."

She thought about it for a moment or two, then went over to turn on the TV set so she could watch The Electric Company. I left it at that, because "hate" for her really means the same as "don't like." I have to keep reminding myself that Jossie isn't a hater. I was. I can still feel the tender residue of it sometimes, but I no longer hate—except in the same purely verbal way Jossie does. It's a relief. Hating takes so much energy, so much concentration that there's very little left to do anything else.

Nine

I spent at least fifteen years going around insisting, "I'm all right. I'm all over it now. I'm fine," when, in truth, all I'd done was develop an ability to touch upon the periphery of my feelings on the matter of Daddy, state what had happened, take a certain inverse pride in the fact that I could even admit it and discuss the details. But I wasn't all right.

I was frightened, furious, and more than anything else determined to prove both to myself and the world how "normal" I really was; normal being what I most wanted to be, what all the people around me supposedly were. For years, I worked at trying to appear "normal," but succeeded only in showing myself to be more and more different.

Then—I don't know why—I decided to try and write it all down. I wasn't a writer, although I'd always written down my thoughts in order to know what I actually believed—the process of putting words on paper seemed to lend order and clarity to my random reactions.

I reasoned that the effort would get the truth out of my system and possibly reach other people. I knew that there were girls and women who'd been through what I had and who, perhaps, hadn't been as fortunate as I in coming into contact with people who insisted upon caring and helping despite my protestations of "all-rightness." I was very lucky. Part of it had to do with my ability to articulate my feelings, thoughts and fears; the rest had to do with what the people who loved me obliged me to see about myself.

Painstakingly, painfully, year after year, I've had to reach down through the layers of me to try to get at the truth, dredge it up and live trying to change it. Always, in the back of my mind, was the knowledge that if I failed, I could open the door marked EXIT and walked through it via pills, or razor blades, gas ovens, or a slow walk into deep water. That EXIT was my secret, long-made reservation with death and if things got too bad, if I proved too unacceptable on too many levels, I could present myself to the maitre d' and make my way over to the door. My feelings on this matter haven't changed in the least. I like knowing I have one irrevocable option at my disposal. It somehow provides me with the courage to take another step, to face the empty house and The Man with the Knife one more time.

I sat down to write about it and pried the scab off my life. It was excruciating to have to go backward, in detail, and minutely examine what happened, and why, and how it had all conspired to see me into adulthood flawed, not really an adult but a frightened, hate-filled, angry child with strong antisocial tendencies, a head filled with dreams and fantasies, and a grinding determination to emerge at the far end of my life as a *good* person.

I was married, pregnant, and secure enough to risk prolonged backward glances, so I went ahead and started to write. I wrote the book over and over and over, but couldn't make it work; first, because I was creating a third-person narrative that had no viable ending, telling the tale of a brash little girl who fought her way through—to what? Second, I simply wasn't ready yet to tell it. I hadn't made enough formidable changes in myself to have the perspective I needed.

But I'd given up singing in clubs and was commuting into New York from Connecticut only three days a week to work at Walt's office, which left me ample time alone, so I kept on writing. After a year, enamored both of the I.B.M. typewriter and of placing one word after another on paper, I set the effort aside and began to write a fictional life story about Helen, who'd been crucially important to me. I wrote the book, sold it in time, and found I'd become a writer. I put *Daddy's Girl* on a shelf and started to produce one book after another. Once or twice a year, I'd drag out the old manuscript and give it another try; each time optimistically sending the newest version to my agent or editor of the moment, convinced this time I finally had it. I didn't.

Fourteen rewrites and nearly nine years later, I knew I was going to have to face it, to tell the truth in the first person, as myself, and hope it would finally be right.

I'm very happy writing. I'm able to live out every dream, every fantasy I've ever had. I can deal with injustice, unfairness, the problems women face; I can say, on paper, what I think. It's illuminating, and almost illicitly pleasurable. I have a home, a career, a child, and a large measure of peace.

Daddy changed jobs. At Christmas, he invited me out for a walk to see where he worked now: another factory where he designed handbags and leather accessories, then supervised the production of these things. He was cleverly inventive and regularly came home with multi-pocketed bags he'd created to my specifications. My bags, wallets, belts and cosmetic cases were the envy of other girls.

He took me into the deserted building and led me up to the third-floor storage area where there were bolts of wrapped fabric stacked to create a sort of rolling, brown-paper ocean that stretched away off down the length of the vast room. Settling on top of some of the lower rolls, he made himself comfortable and beckoned for me to do the new thing: to put my mouth on him. I loathed it. He'd put on one of the little gray balloons he called "safes" that tasted bitter, powdery.

"It won't *hurt* you. Come on."

"I don't like this," I pleaded. "I don't want to."

"Come *on*, eh? I don't have all day."

"Please?"

"Listen, it's Christmas. I'll give you ten dollars." He smiled, then wet his lips.

I looked around hearing a voice in my head say, You know you're going to do it. It was the same voice that told me I'd eat the oatmeal my mother put down in front of me most mornings in winter. Lumpy, like congealed library paste. You know you're going to do it, the voice would tell me, and I'd go ahead and eat, gagging; then I'd spend the morning with fierce stomach cramps. I'd do this thing, too; but didn't know why. I tried to tell myself it was for the money, but it wasn't. I didn't even want it, although it was an awful lot. No, it was something else; like another voice that told me there were no choices. If I didn't do what he wanted, he'd drag me home, infuriated, and create some kind of fight with my mother or Bobby.

So I shut my eyes tight and went ahead, trying desperately not to think about it, instead enumerating all I could do with so much money. But my mind was fixed on the thought of how terrible and terrifying it would be if someone caught us up there. He didn't even seem to care. But it could happen. And maybe if someone did find us, the person would feel sorry for me—only ten years old, having to do these awful things—and make sure Daddy got sent away once and for all. Someone might listen and believe me and not send me to prison but to some couple who didn't have any children and really wanted a little girl who'd behave and keep her room clean and help in the kitchen. How *could* they send little children to prison? I wondered.

It lasted forever.

After, I wandered among the dusty boxes and packing cases, rubbing my fist against my mouth, wanting to cry, to scream. He'd gone to the men's toilet to clean up. Where was I supposed to go? I felt so ugly, so dirty, and wished I could understand why these things were happening. My mouth felt stretched, as if it might split at the corners. My stomach quivered uneasily as if I might throw up. Something wild pounded inside me as I looked down the length of the dim room wishing with all my strength that he'd die; I couldn't stop thinking about the things he made me do, the way he had control of my life. I dreaded Tuesdays and Thursdays, and lived in a state of distracted agitation during the day, wondering what new horror and ugliness the night would bring. And he'd long since stopped pretending to be nice. Now, he paraded out his threats and bribes and lay them down side by side in front of me, and he warned me constantly of the brutal punishments that would come my way if I told anyone.

At night, I'd read under the blankets with a flashlight, holding myself away from sleep so that I wouldn't have to dream he was right there in my bed, pushing himself at me, making me touch him and do those dirty things; caressing me, making me despise myself.

I'd tear myself out of sleep to sit in the dark, my head filled with voices, my mouth clogged with cement, and tell myself these were only dreams I was having. But they weren't. It was all real, all happening. No matter where I might go, or how well I succeeded in forgetting The Secret while I was there, I always had to come home again to the ever bigger horror. I felt trapped, and constantly afraid, with my insides permanently shaking, as if I were standing naked in a blizzard.

I could feel myself splitting, becoming two quite different little girls: one was the sharer of The Secret, who had more money than she knew what to do with, and a strange, almost unpleasant sense of power, too, because of it. She could get anything she wanted. All she had to do was go get it from Daddy. The One was evil, mean, capable of everything bad. The Other was the little girl who played hopscotch and double-Dutch, who romped with Marianna and was in love with her entire family; who was in love, as well, with Auntie Brenda and Uncle Jake; in love with the idea of being grown up. The Other was the role I played out for the world. The Other heard screaming voices, couldn't eat, couldn't concentrate, felt

scared and on edge all the time, and dreamed nonstop of a
nice future, of running away, of having a loving family, of
being left alone. The Other did nothing but act out the role
of good little girl and dream, struggling all the while, for un-
awareness of The One. The Other was the me the world at
large saw. I sent her out on her best behavior, in the hope
someone would see and value her.

Sometimes, the parts of The One overlapped into The Other,
so that, with alarm, I felt a certain awful hardness fill all the
inner cavities of my body. I thought of myself as a small-
sized prostitute, like one of the women who were forever
going upstairs to the rooms of the North Star with some man.
A prostitute. That's what he'd turned me into: a small child
who sold her body for money. To her *own father*.

I fully recognized that the hard something inside me was a
capacity for murder. If I were ever to release the control I
held over the two distinct halves of my self, I'd kill. I'd walk
calmly into the kitchen, pick up the bread knife and kill my
father, perhaps my mother, too. I knew I'd feel no remorse,
but only an overwhelming sense of rightness as I examined
their lifeless bodies and their blood before quietly walking
away from the wreckage and out, into another life. I'd simply
tell the authorities the truth of what had been done to me, to
my life, and they'd understand. I believed no one on earth
could possibly condemn or punish me for an act so completely
justified.

But knowing I was capable of this, I exercised an even tighter
control until it felt as if I were walking at the end of a very
tight leash, straining; strangling. Upon occasion, I was so
choked by unshed tears, I wanted to stand up and scream until
my head burst with the volume and force.

I blamed myself for all of it. Greed for money, for
things, had led me into this, so I had to be just as bad as Daddy.
Except that he didn't feel guilty, didn't—when I confronted
him—seem to think he was doing anything the slightest bit
wrong. He spoke as if it were his ordained right to do to me
the things he did, and I was all "too obviously misguided," not

to mention "seriously deluded" for thinking there was anything at all wrong with any of his deeds. It pulled the air right out of my lungs. How was it possible that he'd worked so willfully at ruining my life and my feelings for myself for three entire years without experiencing the slightest bit of guilt for the damage he'd done? He simply laughed when I tried to reason with him and told jokes to make me laugh so that I'd shut up and stop talking and do what he paid me to do. I was the one who felt guilty. I felt sick with it, eaten alive by it, and fought it by allowing The Other to concentrate on elaborate dreams of the perfect life I'd have once I managed to escape my childhood, and Daddy.

And yet. He could be so convincing, so reasonable when he cared to be, exercising a comprehension of my thoughts and ideas I found irresistible. He *knew* me, cultivated my dreams, recognized my thirst for understanding what I saw and heard and read. Because my thirst was his. He gave me all the knowledge he'd gained in a lifetime of what he called "hard-knocks" experience. He loved me. I knew it. And even though it wasn't love in the way I wanted it, I refused to give up believing I could get his love turned around into what it should have been. Perversely, he used this belief to lead me along the lines of his own wishes; used my appetite for fantasies and my optimism, used everything to bend me to his preferences.

Somehow, I managed to complete grade eight and was promoted to the ninth grade; high school. I couldn't figure out how it had happened since I was convinced I hadn't passed an exam for one single subject.

My mother said, with a wry smile, "They probably just wanted to get rid of you."

It seemed as good an explanation as any.

I was eleven years old, I'd be starting grade nine come the autumn, but at most I looked eight or nine. Something, I was positive, was seriously wrong with me. Four-feet-eleven-inches tall, with a small child's body, I wore the sale-counter clothing my mother provided. And every morning, I checked my body looking for my breasts to be there, more than halfway convinced that my activities with Daddy would keep me a little girl forever. I'd never grow, never become an adult, never get away from him.

"*Why do you tell me the things you do?*"

"*What d'you mean why do I tell you? What do I tell you?*"

"*You're always talking about things you shouldn't be telling a child. You talk to me as if I'm all grown up.*"

"*You're my little lover, eh?*"

"*I'm not! I'm your DAUGHTER! I don't want to hear the things you tell me, or look at those books with the horrible dirty stories, or see those awful photographs! It's not right! Why can't you just be my father?*"

"*Come on, you like it. Admit you like what we do.*"

"*Oh God! I hate it! I hate going to the factory! Don't you understand anything? I hate you for making me!*"

"*Nobody's making you.*"

"*Oh, yeah! Nobody. You're making me! Stop it! Don't keep touching me! Why d'you always have to be after me? Couldn't you even pretend to be a father? You're not supposed to do the things you do. You're supposed to be like . . . a friend. Take me for walks and to the movies, to the art gallery . . . I HATE you for this, for making me. GOD I HATE YOU!*"

Hate you for spoiling everything for making it so I can't have fun anymore don't have friends hate you for making me feel so dirty God so dirty I'm dirty horrible dirty. Hate you for the sound of your voice and the way you eat the way you smell your mouth and your laugh the way you laugh at me make fun of me tease me you think you'll make me laugh but you only make me hate you more I wish you'd die I wish more than anything in the whole world I wish you'd die. Please God make him die I'll never ask for anything else as long as I live if you'll just make him die.

I've never met a man who, on a one-to-one basis, didn't frighten me. I've heard women say that men are unpredictable, capable of pulling about-faces, of making unwanted advances and of persisting with them even in the face of the starkest

NO! Sooner or later all men have some desire to demonstrate their superiority, their greater strength, their capacity to deny or grant pleasure to us, the so-called weaker sex. They know we want to be wanted and needed and they capitalize on our wants and needs and dreams. I believed for years that if a man was with me it wasn't because he was enchanted by my intelligence but because he'd guessed that I was fully programmed to lie down like a good little girl and do as I was told.

That isn't necessarily how I perceive things. Some men fit that category, a lot don't. But I've always wondered why the majority of men I've met seem to have so little desire for friendship. It's something most natural with women, yet seems alien to men. It would be nice to have male friends. But somehow, the inclination is rarely mutual. Sooner or later, his or my sexuality becomes an issue and before we can proceed with the friendship or go off in different directions, we've got to settle the sexual matter. At this point, my intelligence and self-control abruptly leave me. I become a child again and subject to the whims of someone bigger, stronger and adept at games-playing. I've known only three men who were willing to give me the time I needed to become accustomed to them, to feel comfortable before ours evolved into a sexual friendship. The rest seemed to be in a tremendous hurry to demonstrate their control of the situation, their skill, their complicated techniques. And by virtue of my sex, my fondness for good-looking clothes, and some nebulous, perhaps vulnerable, quality to my eyes that they seem to see, I too often find myself on the receiving end of something I don't want, can't handle, and find nearly impossible to forgive. Had I been given a bit more time, seen a display of some fondness, it might, perhaps, have been something we'd both wanted.

In the murk of some bedroom, I can perform with all the passion and intensity and pleasure of a female fully aware of her own capacities. In the light of day and of broken body contact, I'm overtaken by disgust, and contempt for the man in question; I'm more suicidal than at any other time. Mornings are critical. If I'm able to survive the first half-hour in the company of the man I made love with the night before, then there's something between us that may just go on to grow. It takes such a lot of effort and soul-searching and conscious rationalization to accept my own actions and to determine that I don't feel either guilty, or hate-filled, or devoid, once again, of self-esteem.

An alarming number of men seem to think that a woman's thoughts and feelings, all her reactions emanate entirely from the region of her groin; all her talk is simply so much bullshit she's learned from reading too many books, or from getting hyped by women's libbers. It defeats me to spend a good evening's conversation only to find that the man in question considered the exchange of thoughts a kind of mandatory preamble to be tolerated in order to get laid. It doesn't make sense.

Since the age of twenty, I've gone out into the world repeatedly, hoping to find something I feared was beyond my range: the capacity to enter into and sustain a relationship that includes sex. One of the reasons is Daddy. The other is that I haven't met a man willing to accept my supposedly "male" terms: I'll see you when it's convenient; I won't surrender my identity for you; I'll love you but I won't go crazy in love with you.

I've learned not to make impossible demands of myself. When a man says, "I'd like to touch you," and a siren goes off inside my head, I know I'll never be able to eliminate the fear that arises in me to accompany his declaration of desire.

I have fine friends who supply much of the company and approval I need, and a child to hug and embrace and comfort. I have a gratifying career. I'm going to be thirty-nine and I never believed I'd make it this far. I still want all kinds of things, but I actually need very few. It's taken me almost twenty years to learn that my reality is not dependent on any man, but on me. I thought I needed a husband, or a lover, in order to have credibility. It's a relief to know that isn't the truth. The knowledge allows me to feel more at ease with the men I meet.

Ten

Months, years of Tuesdays and Thursdays; hundreds of nights I spent with Daddy in that bedroom. And sometimes there were weekend drives. He'd propose a family outing, then be so unpleasant he often discouraged Mother and Bobby from wanting to come along, making sure I was alone with him for an entire afternoon. I didn't dare protest or refuse for fear of arousing my mother's suspicions.

The car was Daddy's most valued possession. He drove like a madman, with one foot on the accelerator and the other on the brake so that it wasn't so much a drive as a lurching series of starts and stops during which he frequently rolled down his window to curse out some driver who'd committed, according to him, an unforgivable and utterly stupid violation of the rules of the road. He drove so close to the car ahead that I'd clutch whatever was available, and fight down motion sickness, sure our lives would be ended at any moment. On one family outing, I failed to overcome the nausea. Daddy refused to stop the car. My mother told me to put my head out the window. I did, and was violently sick. Daddy stopped then and made me get out and clean the side of the car.

"She's sick, for chrissake! Leave her alone." My mother defended me.

"Clean it the hell up!" he commanded, that drum beating away in his temple. "And you," he whirled on my mother, "mind your own goddamned business."

I'd set off alone with him wanting to believe we'd have a good time seeing the countryside; we'd have lunch in a nice restaurant somewhere, as happened when I went out with my aunt and uncle. But it never worked out that way. Invariably, he managed to find some place to stop. Once, alarmingly, he parked in the driveway of a house just off Bathurst Street north of St. Clair whose owners he insisted he knew, saying, "They're away, out of town," to quell my protests. He said there was no one home, yet he spent the entire time nervously looking around while he made me pay for the privilege of the outing. He pushed my head down to his lap and held a handkerchief in his fist; all readiness. Too afraid to refuse, my head was filled with screams underscored by my interior voice chiding, You're so stupid believing how could you believe when you know he *always* lies you're *so stupid!*

Afterward, on the way home, feeling as if he'd somehow broken all my bones without laying a hand on me, I asked quietly, "Don't you ever feel even one bit guilty for what you're doing to me?"

"What's that? Guilty. What guilty? What'm I doing to you that's so terrible?" Eyebrows lifted, his eyes guilelessly opened wide into that phony look of faked innocence I knew so well.

"Why won't you *understand*?" I begged. "Everything you're doing to me is terrible. You're *changing* me, making me different from other kids."

"Different, shmifferent. You're getting the benefit of an education most girls would give their eyeteeth for."

"I don't *want* to be '*educated*.' I just want a normal, ordinary life, like other kids. You're ruining my whole life. Is that what you want? Don't you want me to be happy, Daddy? *Don't* you?" I wanted to believe that somewhere inside him he had to care about my feelings, my future.

"You don't know how good you got it."

Oh God! He wouldn't hear, didn't care. I gazed out the

car window at people walking along the sidewalks and prayed, *Somebody help me get me out of here please save me help me please?*

I sat slumped in the old wicker chair in the bathroom beside the tub, trying to calm myself sufficiently to face them at the kitchen table for supper. There was a pack of matches on the sink. Daddy always smoked in there. I picked up the matches and then, suddenly moving quickly, unraveled streamers of toilet paper and threw them into the tub. I struck a match and dropped it in. A small *pop* and the tub was filled with flames. I moved back, hypnotized and frightened by the fire; staring at the flames. *Fire I could burn down the world and everything bad in it all the buildings all the people burn it all up kill everyone I'd be the only one left alive.*

My mother pounded on the door. "I smell smoke. You better not be fooling around with cigarettes. What're you doing in there? Open this door!"

"I'm not doing anything," I answered trancelike, and walked over—my eyes still on the fire—to flush the toilet. "I'll be out in a minute." Under cover of the noise of the refilling toilet tank I swished water around the tub and pushed the remains of the burnt tissue down the drain; feeling dreamy, dizzy. I sprinkled some cleanser over the sooty spots, rubbed them clean with my fingers, then wiped my hands on the towel while I gazed at my mesmerized self in the mirror. Blind, unseeing, gone away to somewhere else—a white empty place.

"What were you doing in there?"

"Nothing. Going to the toilet."

She looked around the bathroom with narrowed eyes. "Go on into the kitchen," she said, sniffing the air. "You were sure as hell doing *something* in here."

Still in that strange, distant place, I smiled dreamily and slid into my chair at the kitchen table.

After supper, in a purely evil frame of mind now, I sneaked down the hall to their bedroom and slid open one of the drawers of the bureau to steal one of his "safes." Then I ran noiselessly back down the hall again to lock myself into the bathroom. I held the thing under the faucet and turned on the water, solemnly watching it get bigger and bigger as the water gushed into it. Bent over the tub holding this gigantic gray-white balloon, I started to laugh. I laughed so hard my sides ached, so hard that something wild and uncontrollable began to stir inside my head. It threatened to take the laughter and break it, turn it crazy. I could feel myself lifting into this wild something when the balloon went *plt* and fell limp; the water gurgled noisily down the drain. Sobered, I watched the water go; then again fell into that dreamy, hypnotic state. I sat against the side of the tub for long minutes, breathing slowly, deeply. I could feel the madness going, leaving me weak. I'd discovered two new territories in my brain and wasn't sure how I felt about either the hard-breathing mad place, or the silent, white empty place. Maybe, I decided, I was already crazy. Didn't people always say that really crazy people were the ones who believed they were perfectly sane?

I love to polish my silver serving dishes, the copper pots and pans in the kitchen. I go into a mindless mechanical state where my body functions and my brain sits on hold. My house in Connecticut had no cellar, just a small area beneath what was the old kitchen before renovation. Down there were miles of exposed copper piping. I used to have a vision of myself down in that small place with a soft cloth and a tin of Brasso, happily, brainlessly rubbing away. I knew that if I ever really did go crazy, that was where they'd find me: down there, polishing the pipes.

"You sick again or something?" Mother asked, looking prepared for the worst as I sidestepped her out of the bathroom.

"I'm fine." I smiled.

"You're sure spending a lot of time in that bathroom."

"It happens to be the only place around here where there's any privacy," I said pleasantly.

"Don't you talk back to me!"

"I'm not talking back," I said calmly, quietly. "I'm just

telling you the truth. And don't hit me, eh? Why d'you always want to hit me?"

Her arm dropped; a bewildered look spread over her features.

I could see in her eyes an understanding take shape: I was almost as tall as she, albeit smaller, but I could say things with a certain adult power that temporarily defeated her; say things with an unarguable rationality that would defuse her anger. I'd grown into my brain and was finally able to use it. At that moment, though, all I really wanted was to throw my arms around her and beg her to save me.

"Boy, some kid!" she said, confusedly, and returned to the kitchen.

I stood in the hall a few moments longer, staring into the space where she'd been, wondering if I'd ever again be able to talk with her the way I had when I'd been little, when we'd sat at the kitchen table playing Casino. In my brain, click-click, was a permanent, softly lit picture of my mother with the sun in her hair and her hand curved around a teacup as her eyes searched through her memories and she half-smiled as she told me about her childhood, and her father, and the way things might have been.

I wanted a bike. Mother took me to police headquarters on College Street where they were to auction off unclaimed bicycles. For four dollars we got an outsized woman's bike and walked it home.

Two or three afternoons a week that summer I rode down to the lakefront to visit Auntie Brenda. I'd park the bike in the lobby and lock it with an old combination lock of Will's I'd unearthed, then make my way upstairs to spend an hour or two with my aunt. It was a splendid arrangement and I kept on with it until the afternoon the super came to the door to say the bike was a hazard and shouldn't be left in the lobby where someone could fall over it.

"Nobody's going to fall over it," I began, wanting to argue the issue, but my aunt, flushed and highly embarrassed, shushed me, thanked the man, closed the door and then turned to me, saying, "I can't have people upset. You'll have to leave the bike at home when you come."

"But it's perfectly safe. . . ."

Her look silenced me. It's not fair, I thought, angry with the super for his silly argument, and with my aunt for not supporting me against him. Not fair, I decided, crushed, and stayed away.

When, later on, my aunt and uncle dropped by to visit my mother, I eavesdropped and overheard my mother say, "I don't want her out riding the damned bike in all that traffic anyway," and my aunt respond, "It's too bad she's becoming so argumentative. She used to be such a nice little girl, so polite."

My uncle quietly contributed, "She's still a nice girl, a very nice girl," but no one seemed to be listening to him.

My mother and aunt were agreeing about me. It upset and angered me so much that my visits to my aunt and uncle were never again as pleasurable or as free as they'd been. I knew now I was being judged, evaluated, reported on, when all the time I'd believed they'd accepted and loved me as I was. There were, I now saw, rules to be obeyed, things to be said and done if I were to continue to visit. Awareness of these rules made me so self-conscious about my many faults that I was no longer able to relax and savor their company. My last refuge was gone.

I filled the remaining days of that summer planning how high school would be, what route I'd take to get there; I speculated on the kinds of kids I'd meet, and the parties and proms and dates there were bound to be. My mother began to go on at some length about the importance of a girl's being popular and good fun and lively—all of which she'd been. Popular, pretty and lively; so, at seventeen, she'd married Daddy. Did she expect me to meet someone and be married by the time I was seventeen? The idea that she did scared me crazy. Marriage was one of my better dreams, but it was somewhere off in the future.

Will got married; he'd never be coming home again. Mother received the letter, sat down at the kitchen table and cried over it. Her copious tears confounded me: they were proof that she loved Will and cared what happened to him. I missed him, but found it hard to remember what he looked like and sometimes went into my parents' bedroom to study his graduation picture on the dressing table. He was handsome, grown up, gone; married.

Despite my belief that The Secret kept Daddy pacified, the atmosphere in the apartment began to get worse, and then worse. His temper was constantly on display as he provoked loud, crazed arguments about money, or ranted about his bosses. Rather than listen in silence and allow him—like a strange, mechanical toy—to simply run down and stop, my mother entered into his grievance sessions, turning them into epic battles.

"They're out to get me, the bastards!" he ranted, temples throbbing and eyes widened.

"You're out of your goddamned head!" she told him. "Just shut the hell up and do your stinking job and stop stirring up trouble. *You're* the one who's bringing it down on your own head! They're out to get you," she scoffed. "Why would they bother?"

He had no doubt at all that the younger son of the man who owned the company was after him. This son, a man of about thirty, was shortish, slim and elegant. Whenever I saw him in conversation with my father, he seemed to exercise tremendous self-control in holding back his dislike—not of my father, but rather of my father's practices. And he made this clear.

"Stop mixing in," he told Daddy. "Let the shop steward handle the machine workers' problems. You're not a union man and you just get everyone worked up unnecessarily."

Daddy stood in silence and took it. But after the man had gone lightly away down the stairs, Daddy snarled, "Half-assed punk! The son-of-a-bitch is after my ass."

"But Daddy," I reasoned, "he was just trying to help you."

"Help me? What the hell do you know?"

I shut up. His eyes were bloodshot with rage. I didn't want

it directed at me. If I dared show any resistance to him, either physically or verbally, he retaliated by lashing out even more violently at Bobby and my mother, making all of us miserable, temporarily uniting us in our fear and quiet hostility toward him. The three of us held dozens of hardship meetings gathered around the kitchen table, one by one contributing our complaints. Ultimately, we'd wind up laughing; we'd manage to make such a case against him that it became funny. Then, somehow, Daddy's funnier antics would get discussed and, in near hysterics, we'd go back and forth over other, less recent and less painful, anecdotes until we'd succeeded in temporarily dispelling our animosity.

Nevertheless, it fell to me to try to be the unknown peacemaker. Regardless of my failure to bring my mother around to my point of view concerning the arguments and her part in them, I hated to see her so unhappy, and to see Bobby so permanently upset and grim-faced. I hated the grating misery I felt inside at repeatedly being a witness to Daddy's craziness.

I was also afraid to make him angry with me. He might force himself on me, hurt me sexually. And if that happened, my life would be over. I couldn't and wouldn't keep on living if he pushed himself all the way inside of my body. My mother's seemingly endless warnings—oblique at best, yet pointed enough to strike home—echoed nonstop in my ears. "You start *that* business and you're finished. You think a boy wants a girl who's easy? Nobody respects a girl who holds herself cheap." Was that true? I wondered. What *was* true? What she said sounded like the truth, but it was hard to tell because she never actually told me anything. It was Daddy who set the facts of life and sex in their starkest, most hatefully clinical terms down before me. Had I been dependent upon my mother for this information, I'd probably still be waiting to this day. She assumed, I think, that once I'd attained a certain age, I'd know what she meant when she made her "easy" and "cheap" references. Intuitively, I understood that she found it close to impossible to talk about sexual matters, and rather than being distressed by this, I further understood that women—delicate

and essentially passive creatures—weren't supposed to speak
openly of things that were intended to be kept private.

I was so certain that everything Daddy told me was either
less than half true or perverse that any word with even the
remotest sexual connotation made me squirm. "Breast," even
when spoken of in connection with chickens and white meat,
turned me hot with discomfort. Both the clinical and euphemis-
tic names for the parts of the anatomy distinguishing males
from females made me cringe. As late as my early thirties, I
shrank when, during an obstetric examination my doctor innocently applied the names to the parts of my anatomy with
which he was involved.

Two years ago, armed with a copy of *Our Bodies, Our
Selves*, I steeled myself to explain the facts of life and sex to
Jossie. It wasn't difficult at all. Actually, there was a closeness
between us that afternoon that neither of us wanted to end. We
sat together on the sofa and studied photographs of men and
women. Jossie asked questions and I answered them without
embarrassment, and I felt for the first time both the full extent of the freedom I'd managed to attain as well as a sense of
continuity that existed because my daughter would grow to
be a woman who might have daughters of her own. It was a
lovely afternoon.

I managed to keep Daddy at bay; I satisfied him and allowed him to satisfy himself without totally surrendering my
body to him. No matter what happened, I was determined
never to let him do that to me. I clung to my virginity—
technical scrap of membrane—with passionate tenacity. If it
happened, finally, I believed I'd be lost: no way back, no way
forward. Despite all I knew and had experienced, I still quali-
fied for my mother's interpretation of "virgin." And that
meant I retained a certain purity. I wanted myself intact for the
man somewhere out there who was already discarding one
woman after another because they failed to have my unique set
of qualifications.

But Daddy was always trying to trap me into relenting and
turning myself completely over to him. Bribing me, he'd

wheedle, "Let me just put it in a little way." No, *no*, NO! "I won't hurt you." NO, NO, NO! "In the back then." It hurt terribly. I threatened to scream. He stopped.

We were engaged in a war over my body and I was going to win. If it was the last thing I ever did, I'd win. Even if it meant having him put me down on my belly and suffering his stifling weight while he wriggled and squirmed on top of me, holding my thighs tightly pressed together around him until he finally, sickeningly, finished. Even if it meant lying there with my jaws locked, teeth clenched, hands fisted, eyes fixed on the il-luminated bedside clock while I counted down the minutes and his head burrowed between my legs and inside I chanted, I hate you hate you HATE YOU!; despising everything about him.

Locked again in the bathroom, I'd stare in sobbing disgust at the slime on my thighs, too sickened to touch myself, yet I had to clean it away. Chest heaving in a rage of self-hatred and despair, I scrubbed my flesh with a pumice stone, consumed with self-loathing; and consoled myself with thoughts of my eventual escape one day. One day I'd have freedom and privacy; I'd be left alone to live untouched, untroubled, amid people who really cared, people who'd accept me as I was without laying down a set of rules I'd have to follow carefully in order to receive their approval; people who'd know I was more than a befouled little monster who let these obscene things be done to me for money. I'd scrub my skin until it tore, all the while hearing my voices, and longing for death with a fervor almost equal to my determination to have life; I yearned with every part of me for an end to all this.

On the first day of high school, I rode off on my bike filled with drummed-up optimism, working hard to convince myself this new era would offer friends and big changes, the start of my future. It was a second chance. Pedaling along, ignoring my attendant chorus of voices and quivering stomach, The Other tried to believe it would all be good and new and positive while The One laughed leeringly, and derided my frail hope-fulness.

The homeroom teacher was a short, kindly woman with startlingly green eyes behind wire-frame glasses and a frequent, touchingly shy smile: Miss Redfield. I relaxed a bit, liking both her and the idea of learning French.

The bell rang to signify the end of the class and I followed the other kids out, amazed that they seemed to know where to go without having to be told: to the next class, the next teacher.

As I was about to enter the classroom, I noticed two teachers in conversation just down the corridor. A tall, sternly handsome, gray-haired woman, and a petite, dark-haired one in a red wool suit and high heels, who didn't in the least look like a teacher. She seemed younger, and far more elegantly dressed than any teacher I'd ever met. I'd have continued to stand there, studying her, click-click, but the students behind moved me forward into the classroom.

I took my seat, opened the text and my notebook, uncapped my pen. And by the time the class had ended, I knew I wasn't going to make it. There were too many teachers, too many different subjects all in one day. I'd never be able to remember everything. I found it hard to pay attention; I felt more tired than ever. My eyes constantly strayed to the windows to look at the trees and the sky beyond. I wanted to be one of those sparrows out there and fly away high where no one could reach me; I slipped, unaware, into that strange, silent and enervated place inside where everything was white and the very whiteness and silence took hold to render me still and serene. I went away now on a regular basis, sliding effortlessly into a kind of vacuum where my physical self failed to exist and my mind rested like a bird on the high wires; swaying very slightly but undisturbed.

I did try. The first weeks I dutifully filled my notebooks with carefully done homework. But by October, as I rode home through eddying leaves, I'd lost both my initial interest and enthusiasm. I hadn't made any friends. The kids treated me like a toy, commenting on my size, my age, my clothes, my bike, saying, "Isn't she cute?" as, in passing, they flicked their fingers at the ruffled shoulders of my jumper, and looked down at me, smiling. Part of me knew they weren't intentionally unkind, and part of me believed they thought I was funny, someone to laugh at, not to be taken seriously or to befriend.

I looked enviously at their saddle shoes and thick, white ankle socks, their penny-loafers and felt skirts with billowing crinolines, their sweater sets and Peter Pan dickeys, their breasts and hips and long legs. Only the pony tail was within my grasp. So I brushed out my frizzy pigtails, skinned back my hair with a rubber band and went off to school expecting and hoping someone would notice. No one did. I just gave myself a blinding headache.

Occasionally, I'd catch a glimpse of the small dark-haired teacher whose name I'd discovered and now whispered to myself: Helen. I was captivated by the look of her, somehow cheered simply by the sight of her. And when in passing I heard her laughter, I experienced several moments of undiluted pleasure at the sound of it.

I took note, meanwhile, of how the girls all around paired off with boys, or gathered into little knots among themselves giddily to discuss boys and clothes, teachers and dates; totally excluding me when I attempted to sidle my way into their midst. I didn't fit in. I'd approach a group, they'd all smile and begin to move on, looking back over their shoulders at me as they went off down the hall. I felt like a freak.

The only person who regularly spoke to me was Miss Redfield. She'd pause to say hello, to ask how I was getting on, and sometimes extend her hand to touch me on the arm or hair, smiling. I'd smile back, although the effort choked and made me want to cry, and answer, "I'm fine, thank you, Miss Redfield." Then I'd hurry on my way. There was nothing else it was safe to say.

But when she asked, "How are you getting on, dear?" what I wanted to answer was, "I'd like to be dead, Miss Redfield. Or taken away somewhere. I want someone to save me. Will you? Will you risk your probably quiet and peaceful life by coming to where I live and presenting yourself, properly infuriated on my behalf, to my mother? My mother wouldn't believe a word you had to say and might even get mad and start shouting words you'd probably never say in your entire life. Would you do that for me, Miss Redfield? Would you go to the authorities and defend me, stay with me and then take me to live with you, make me your child and keep me safely away from Daddy so I don't have to do any of those things anymore and I can stop hating myself so hard?"

I could easily imagine the woman backing away, her green eyes horror-filled. Perhaps she'd hurry downstairs to the principal's office to tell him. He'd tell others. These others would go to my parents and confront them with my story. My parents would shake their heads disbelievingly. And my father would lie, his eyes round and wide. Then I'd be arrested, taken right out of one of my classes and trooped off to jail. There was nothing to say except, "I'm fine, thank you."

I was twenty-two and clinging by my fingernails to the edge of my life and my sanity, when I met Norman and Lola and told them about Daddy, praying they'd care because somebody had to. I needed someone to value my life because I didn't feel I could keep on very much longer being the only one who cared if I lived or not.

Norman and Lola and their two daughters were the second complete family I fell in love with on sight and I wanted them to spread their arms, welcome me into the center of their unity and then close themselves protectively around me. Astonishingly, they did. I told them. They responded with appropriate and deeply gratifying horror. I wasn't crazy. It *was* awful. They took me into their home and began patting the shattered parts of me back together; they gave me love and attention and the courage, finally—because I knew they loved me—to get up and keep going.

Lola represented everything I wanted to be: loving, perceptive, sensitive and kind. A small dark woman with a soothingly melodious voice, she tolerated my clumsy, tentative first steps. And Norman didn't think I was too big or too old to seek his lap. "My third daughter," he called me, grinning, "the youngest one, the baby," and let me sit huddled against his chest until sudden uncertainty and embarrassment moved me away—until the next time.

I drove them crazy. I couldn't believe that what they were offering was real and not inspired by dark, ulterior motives. How could they claim to love and want me in their home when I was ugly and tainted and had had everything normal and good burned right out of me?

I dropped a jar of jam on the pantry floor and stared down at the mess anticipating Lola's immediate and loud anger. She laughed, handed me a damp cloth and said, "You'll have to do far better than that to outdo Gail." Gail was their younger daughter and four years old. I cleaned up the mess, then washed the entire floor.

Norman found me a secretarial job at a local factory and I went to work. I helped him polish the children's shoes.

I started my period one morning and stained a pair of underpants. Since there was no time to wash them, I left them discreetly folded on the end of my bed and went off to work. When I came home that evening, they were gone. "I put them to soak in cold water," Lola told me. Obviously, I looked mortified. "I have to wash my own, you know," she said reasonably, with a smile, then continued on her way downstairs. I set the dining table, then insisted on washing all the dishes after.

I was stunted, misprogrammed, and numb. They took on the task of breaking the program, getting me to grow again, and teaching me to feel.

Believing myself to be perfectly rational and in complete control of my actions, I tried to walk out the front door of their home one late and very cold November evening. I hadn't any idea what I was doing. I just wanted to go. I felt I was failing, that I'd never be able to live up to the examples they set for me. Wearing only a too-short skirt and skimpy sweater, I opened the door with the idea that I'd simply vanish into the wet English fog. The three of us did actual physical battle at

the door. Norman shouted tearfully, and I shouted incoher-
ently back at him until Lola at last managed to maneuver me
upstairs and into the small guest bedroom where, as determined
as I, and surprisingly strong, she held on, refusing to release
me, and forced me to cry. She had to force it because by
then I'd sold myself on the idea that no one and nothing would
ever again make me cry. Tears were signs of weakness.

I cried horribly, soaking the front of her sweater, wanting
to be able to speak. But it was impossible to give voice to the
countless fears, the rage and sorrow I felt for the loss of my
childhood, and my choices, and my imagined perfect future.
All I could do was accept the proffered comfort, the wound-
ingly gentle caresses, the caring. It all split me open like some
monstrous surgery performed without anesthetic. It hurt more
than anything I'd ever imagined. But once I was open, breathing shallowly in the dangerous air, the poison began to leak
out steadily, continuously.

I'd fallen in love with a family that had room for one more.
They saved me.

Eleven

My MOTHER'S best friend, Rose, died. Thirty-two years old. She had a brain hemorrhage in the back of the store. I overheard Rose's brother telling my mother how they'd had to hold her head over a pail while blood ran out of her eyes and ears, her nose and mouth. I couldn't believe it. How could someone be alive one moment and dead the next? I'd seen Rose the day before when I'd gone to do the shopping for my mother. How could she be dead?

Pale and devastated, my mother sat down opposite me in the living room, her slim hands quivering in her lap. We sat and looked at each other for a very long time until my mother said, "You want to come to the funeral with me?"

I knew she wanted me to go with her, although I wasn't altogether sure why, and quietly said, "Okay."

Rose didn't look dead. She seemed so lifelike in the coffin that I expected her to sit up and start talking. I remained too long beside the coffin, battling down an impulse to touch her. My mother had to tug on my hand in order to get me away. Rose's black-clad relatives were staring at the two of us.

As we walked home, my mother reminisced about her friend. They'd both grown up on Queen Street and my mother could no more believe now that Rose was dead than I could. I felt grown-up that evening as I solemnly listened to my mother and held her hand as we made our way home. I knew she'd lost something very important in Rose—more than just a childhood friend—and the loss seemed to reach beyond her and into me.

Back at the apartment, she said, "Don't worry. One of these days you'll have all kinds of friends. You won't be so lonely anymore."

How had she guessed that? I wondered, embarrassed by her knowing.

"Oh, I'm not lonely," I lied.

She just gave me a small, sad smile and I went off to bed.

With the first snowfall that November, I had to set out half an hour earlier in the mornings to walk to school. I could have walked over to Bathurst and taken the streetcar, transferred and taken a second streetcar, but I preferred to walk. It was more direct. But the loss of that half-hour of sleep took its toll because I slept soundly and well only just before dawn.

Occasionally, I saw Helen MacKay in the córridors, and sometimes I'd see her and the gray-haired teacher walking off up the street together, on their way to lunch. Miss MacKay would be wearing the red suit, or a gray, or one of the five or six others I'd seen, and upon catching sight of her, I'd step out of the stream of student traffic for a minute to study her before I rushed on to catch up with the class. Something about the sight of her and the knowledge of her existence made my attendance at school bearable.

"What're you going to do when I'm gone?"

"That's not going to be for a good long time yet."

"I'm almost twelve, you know. It's not all that far away. What'll you do?"

"I'll worry about it when it happens."

"You don't think I'm ever going to go, do you? You think I'm just going to stay here for the rest of my life. But you're wrong. I'll go."

"*Yeah, sure.*"

"*What'll you do if I meet someone and fall in love? What if I get married?*"

"*At almost twelve?*"

"*Don't you laugh at me! You know what I mean!*"

"*We'll talk about it when you're in love and getting married.*"

"*You think that's never going to happen either, don't you? Well, I'm telling you right now, one day I'm going away and I'm never coming back.*"

"*C'mon over here, sit on my lap.*"

"*No! What're you going to do? I want to know!*"

"*You think you'll meet somebody better than me? You're crazy if you do.*"

"*You're crazy! Crazy!*"

"*C'mon over here.*"

"*No! You're not going to have me forever. You think you will, but you won't. Soon's I'm old enough, I'm leaving and never coming back.*"

I could never say to him the things I really wanted to. I wasn't ever quite sure of the words, or of the way things were actually supposed to happen in a person's life. What I wanted to say to him had to do with my maybe never being *able* to fall in love because his being on top of my life would never allow me a chance to feel anything for anyone else. I already had trouble dealing with most people. It probably wouldn't get better. He was blocking my way into life like a mountain I just couldn't get past.

As I'd watch him pull money out of his wallet, knowing I was going to give in, I'd hate myself for being weak; I felt totally trapped. I counted down the minutes on the face of the bedside clock and tried not to hear the noises he made or the things he said, or his mustache scratching my skin, or his mouth and hands and hateful body. I loathed him for the insane pleasure he derived from these encounters and for his utter inability to recognize my abject unhappiness.

Once it was over, I'd rush to the bathroom to scrub myself

raw, trying to scrape away the bad feelings; I'd look down at my formless body wanting to kill it. I wanted to murder my body so that I might, somehow, be able to continue on in the world with only a brain. It was my body's fault that this was happening to me. Without it, Daddy wouldn't be able to touch me.

I turned into the class clown. I'd always been able to get a laugh out of my mother and Bobby, my aunts. I thought it might make the kids like me, pay attention to me. The laughs came, but it wasn't the satisfying thing I'd thought it would be. The clown act only detracted from the person I wanted others to know, and I was driving myself into a *third* person with my silly antics. How many people would I have to become before I attained any measure of credibility, before people responded? I despaired over ever being taken seriously, yet something in me couldn't resist an opening or a chance to make what I thought was yet another profoundly witty observation. And the more the pressures were applied from all sides, the more I seemed to see the comic aspect to situations. It was easy to be funny, even though so many times my clever lines fell into the center of silence with the impact of a dropped sack of wet garbage; then embarrassment hotly flared up the back of my neck and made me wish I'd never opened my mouth.

Hoping to create an entirely new image, I volunteered myself as a singer at a tea dance in the gym and sang three songs with the hired trio. Everyone applauded. I did an encore, stepped out from behind the microphone, and was invisible. I tried again and sang at a sock hop. Applause, encore, invisibility. No one asked me to dance, and I yearned to be invited.

I left the gym, collected my books from the table in the lunch room, put on my coat and galoshes and trudged home through the freezing slush.

Before the school year ended, I warned my mother I was going to fail. She was at the kitchen table with a cup of tea.

I watched her remove the teabag and squeeze it between her spoon and the back of the sugar spoon.

"I'm too young," I said quietly, defeated. "I'm going to have to repeat grade nine. But next year'll be really easy." I feigned some eagerness, privately wishing I didn't have to go to school at all. "It'll be a whole lot better," I went on. "The rest of the kids won't be so much older and I'll know what to expect."

"You're probably right," she agreed surprisingly as she put the teabag to one side of the saucer, her diamond engagement ring catching the light and drawing my eyes. "I told them when they passed you out of grade eight you were too young to be going into high school. That skipping business and missing all those weeks when you were sick that time. It doesn't matter," she said. "You'll make new friends."

It was the second time she'd referred to my all but friendless state and, as before, I suffered at her knowing. Watching her sip the tea, I wished more than ever I could tell her the real problem. I held my hands tightly around my glass of milk, searching for some way to get the words out now when she seemed so sympathetic and understanding. But I couldn't. It wasn't safe. She might listen and talk quietly and then, the next morning, come at me in a state of rage, her hands like the blades of a fan, administering blows that came almost too quickly to be seen. It seemed that when she had a chance to consider our conversations, she'd usually decide she didn't like what I'd had to say. She'd build herself up to near fever pitch and, by the time I appeared, be well beyond the point where she could simply say she didn't agree. The anger had taken her into speechlessness where all she seemed able to do was strike out at the source of her disapproval.

Shortly after the start of the final term, a monitor came in with a message. Miss Redfield read it, then beckoned to me. My heart seizing up, I approached the front of the classroom.

"Mr. Jackson would like to see you in his office," she said, her voice even softer than usual so the others wouldn't hear.

It was one of the nice things about her: she seemed to know how children felt. "Are you all right, dear?"

"I'm all right, Miss Redfield."

"You go along down then, eh?"

The office was large and chilly, with portraits of former principals on the walls. I sat on the edge of one of the outsized leather armchairs and waited, feeling lost both in the room and the chair. Mr. Jackson was busy with some papers. I looked around, click-click; every detail of the cold room was absorbed into my memory.

"You're not doing at all well with your grades," he said at last.

"No, sir, I know."

"With an I.Q. of 162 you should be in the top five percent of the entire grade-nine class. The top one percent."

"Yes, sir."

"Is it that you're not trying?" He asked his questions without looking at me, but gazed instead at the contents of what, apparently, was my file.

"No, sir. I have tried. Very hard."

"What then, is your explanation?" He studied his fingernails now as if he'd never seen them before, his elbows resting on the papers in my file.

"It's because I'm too young. All the others are two or three years older. And there's too much work. Memorizing. I can't keep up. I don't even like most of the subjects. History, geography, algebra, Latin. I don't understand them. I don't know why I have to take them—it's not as if I'm ever going to have to use Latin or algebra."

"I see you're doing very well in French, English. Typing."

"Yes, sir. I like those things."

"I see," he said. I didn't think he did at all. He didn't seem to be listening.

"You have some idea of what you plan to do when you leave school?"

"No, sir. Am I supposed to know that now?"

"It does help."

"I don't know. I haven't decided." I wanted to tell him: I'm only twelve years old. Why do I have to decide now about the rest of my life?

"Yes. Well, there's certainly plenty of time for you to consider future careers. But in view of your I.Q. and your grades, we've arranged for you to have an interview with the visiting psychologist. Miss Wentworth is waiting for you in the guidance room. That'll be all."

He hadn't looked at me once. If he passed me in the halls, he wouldn't recognize me. And I was so cold the backs of my hands were mottled white and purple.

Miss Wentworth looked at me though; she stared for so long I found myself becoming scared. It was difficult not to squirm. I knew that psychologists and psychiatrists were very clever people who had all sorts of ways to get you to tell the truth about things. If I wasn't very careful, this woman might get me to admit things I didn't want anyone to know.

"You're very pretty," she said at last.

"Oh, no," I replied automatically, prepared neither for compliments nor the woman's own prettiness. I wet my lips, trying hard not to let my acute nervousness show.

"But you are," she smiled, "very pretty."

I shook my head, speechless.

"Tell me," she said, still smiling. "What would you like to do with your life?"

"I don't know," I near-wailed, wondering if from now on I'd be asked this question over and over until I came up with some answer that would satisfy everyone once and for all. "I haven't made up my mind."

"There's lots of time," she said kindly. "You're only twelve, isn't that right?"

I nodded.

"I'd like you to take a look at these and tell me what you see."

"They're inkblots."

She laughed and said, "You're very literal, aren't you?" She wrote something down. "They certainly are inkblots. Why don't you try to tell me what you see in them?"

One by one we went through the cards. I kept my answers as carefully innocuous as I could, seeing squirrels, dancing witches, lambs, while Miss Wentworth made notes and nodded, saying, "Uh-huh, go on, go on."

These completed, she handed me a sheaf of photographs mounted on stiff cardboard. I was sweating, and wished this were over.

"I'd like you to tell me what you think is happening in each of these pictures."

Fairly conventional family scenes, action shots. I gave more bland answers until I came to a photograph of a young girl with torn clothes, half on, half off a sofa, her expression one of sheer terror. Looming over her was a man, looking fierce, outraged, his arm raised. I stared and stared at it, unable to speak, afraid to.

"What do you see there?" she prompted as she finished writing something in her notebook.

"I don't know." My voice was faint and I felt as if I'd drown in the warm, distracting heaviness of the woman's perfume. I wanted to close down my brain, shut away all the parts of myself that felt so diseased, so ashamed: I didn't see how I could possibly live one more second feeling the way I did.

"There's a girl and a man," she said. "What do you think has happened?"

"I don't know." *Please let me go on to another picture I can't tell you about this one.*

"You must have some idea. Just say whatever comes to mind."

I looked at the blinding whiteness of her shirt, at the soft-looking curve of her breasts, at the gold necklace that fell slightly over her left breast and wanted to cry. I held the photograph, my hands damp, sticky; staring and staring at it. Suddenly I wanted more than anything else to tell this woman, tell the whole world about Daddy. Was I dreaming? I could almost sense the softness and comfort of Miss Wentworth's body. Her perfume filled my nostrils, my throat. I could taste it, could practically swallow the safety and motherly comfort this woman seemed to offer, the security and sanity. This woman wouldn't believe the lies my father might tell. She could differentiate between truth and lies, had special ways of getting to the truth. And that surely had to give her a superior strength. Tell her! The Other cried out in my skull. TELL HER! She'll save us!

"She was . . . um . . . stealing in a store," I said weakly, fighting away the temptation. "Her . . . um . . . uncle . . . ah . . . beat her for . . . um . . . stealing. That's all."

She exhaled audibly, as if she'd been holding her breath, as I handed her back the photographs. She set them aside and said, "I'd like you to take these two sheets of paper and draw a man and a woman for me."

"Who?"

"Oh, anyone at all." She smiled. "Just draw a man on one page, a woman on the other. Take as much time as you need."

Wet with fear, I gazed at her, at her long shiny brown hair. Her skin was so pink, and clean looking. No scars. If I were to touch her, my fingers might sink right into her face. Looking down at the blank pages, I picked up the pencil and began to draw. First, very quickly, a woman, filling the entire page with my drawing. Then I sat and stared at the second blank sheet.

"I'm not very good at drawing men," I offered, hoping perhaps to be told not to bother.

She looked up. "Just do the best you can, dear."

Don't call me dear or say I'm pretty it just makes me want to cry because people who don't even know me call me dear and my mother never tells me she loves me never calls me dear.

I drew a tiny little man in a top hat and evening clothes, a bow tie, and handed the two pages back across the desk, wondering in sudden panic if I'd made a critical mistake. The woman I'd drawn was big, with lots of detail, while the man was teeny-tiny with hardly any detail. I should've drawn both the same size. Oh God! Why hadn't I made them both the same size? I was soaking wet now, the palms of my hands and under my arms, down the back of my neck; all over. My red sweater smelled very woolly.

"Good," she said, and glanced at my drawings before tucking them under her notes. "We haven't talked about your family, your parents. Are they living, dear?"

"Yes." *Why do you call me dear is it because you like me?*

"Your mother? What does she do?"

"She's a housewife."

"And your father? Would you like to tell me a little about him?"

I swallowed. My throat was very dry, hurting dry. "He's alive," I whispered.

"No, dear. I mean what he does."

"Oh! He's a designer. Of leather. Handbags. Accessories."

"Isn't that interesting," she said, one hand playing with the tip of her pencil, the other on the eraser end, her eyes boring into mine. "Is there anything you especially like to do?"

Please don't make me tell you don't ask trick questions to get me to tell you the truth I'm so scared you're very clever and I like the way you look. Lying's so hard for me I hate doing it and you seem so nice and call me dear.

"I don't know. I sing. And write things, draw pictures."

"What do you like to write about and draw?"

"I don't know. Just things. About things." I thought of one of my little notebooks. I'd been about six. I'd put down stuff about my parents, all the things I thought. My mother had found it; she'd torn the pages out of the book and kept them hidden somewhere. Sometimes she brought them out and waved them around, yelling, "So *that's* what you think of me, eh? You'll be goddamned good and sorry one day. 'My mother's my best enemy,' eh?" It wasn't safe to write down true things, so now I wrote only made-up ideas, pretend things about the way I thought and felt.

"I see. Well, thank you for coming in to see me. You may return to your class now."

"That's all?" Now that it was over, I wished I could stay

and tell her everything. Everything. I wanted so much to tell her.

"That's all," she confirmed and smiled again, reaching to shake my hand—something no one had ever done before. "Even though you don't think so," she said, applying a light pressure to my hand, "you really are very pretty. I wish you well, dear."

"Thank you," I whispered, trying to move. I felt very unsteady and brittle, as if I might break into many small pieces.

Upstairs, my books were stacked on the corner of Miss Redfield's desk. "Everything all right, dear?" she asked.

Please no more dears or kindness I can't take it I want it but I just can't.

"Yes, Miss Redfield." Seeing her concerned features, I wanted to climb onto her substantial lap and bury my face against her shoulder; to say, I need someone so badly, Miss Redfield. I *really need* someone.

Instead, I picked up the books and went to my locker to put them away before closing myself into one of the stalls in the girls' lavatory. I lowered the lid and sat down, covered my mouth with one hand and flushed over and over with the other to drown the noise of my crying.

During the seven or so years I spent on the road alone as a singer, I kept journals. I drove here and there with my two guitars and a typewriter, a sewing machine and a record player and books: the ingredients of a portable home. I prettied up dozens of hotel and motel rooms—those places I returned to after a five- or six-hour stint in yet another lounge, in yet another city. I'd sing my sad ballads and slow jazz, play my guitar accompaniment and then return to the motel room of the moment at three or four in the morning to sit down with one of the hardbound journals and try to write out my thoughts. The writing was always shaded with untruths and tinged with distortions because someone might come upon one of my journals, pick it up and read what I'd written. I could only deal safely with truth in spoken words.

But there was no one to talk to. I'd picked the one lifestyle guaranteed to isolate me from all but the lonely men who habituated these bars; men who, like me, needed to pretend this was really life, that there was some sort of future. I saw the plastic sameness of quite a number of these men's motel rooms and faced the dawn of deserted parking lots as I walked to my car, feeling more alone and desperate than before. I was looking for love in saloons and motel rooms and all-night diners. I'd chosen wrong and gone after the easy money yet again; I paid the premiums after-hours, reluctantly giving myself to men I hoped might love me.

I had thought that a singing career would bring me adulation, success, money and mobility. I hoped for mass adoration. What I got was three or four hundred a week and a ticket to ride alone. So, I sat beneath the surprise-pink spotlights in one place after another, creating illusions with the skill of a magician; singing the best and the saddest, the most nostalgic songs—because they were the ones that meant most to me. Poor little, sad little blue Bluesette, jazz-waltzing away when the world was young.

I wrote in my journals, tried to type stories on my portable, composed music and lyrics and filled the hours alone with words in one form or another. Until Rob, through a disc jockey friend, entered my life in the capacity of music publisher/record producer and began repeatedly to tell me I ought to be in New York where it was all happening and not stuck way the hell out in the Midwest in places like Omaha and Indianapolis. Come to New York, he insisted—Porgy and Bess in whiteface—this is where you belong, sister. I finally agreed to move. And things began caving in again.

I was twenty-six and Norman and Lola were too far away to help me. I was doing things I didn't want to do but seemed to have some unknown, interior need to do them. The size, the dirt and the danger of New York terrified me from the beginning. I didn't want to be there, but Rob had promised I'd get more exposure working out of Manhattan. I had to believe *something*, so I chose to believe he'd elevate my career—and thereby, my life. But when I arrived in New York to take up residence in the apartment he'd helped me find, he was away somewhere and wouldn't be back for several weeks. I'd have to figure out the city, find my way around and get started on some sort of life on my own.

I got sick. The doctor at Beth Israel hospital told me it was all in my head and I went a little mad, throwing his psychiatric referral form—there was a sizable stack of them on the corner of his desk—back at him, crying, "If it's in my *head*, then why am I *bleeding* to death? Why are my *insides* coming out?" I didn't bother to stay to hear his answer. My head. What on earth did my head have to do with the four nights I'd had to sleep on the bathroom floor because I'd been too afraid to leave—every fifteen or twenty minutes my intestines had gone into violent spasms that had required all sorts of medications? There'd been rectal hemorrhages and bits of flesh, my flesh; clues to a disintegrating interior. None of that, I insisted, had anything to do with my head.

Of course it had to do with my head. I suspected it at the time, but I despised that doctor with his offhand manner and his complete lack of sensitivity. The internal examination he performed on me was the first of my life. It hurt. As the speculum expanded inside me, I wanted to start screaming. The doctor snapped at me to be still, and I lay in agonized silence until it was ended. I was so offended by him, I wouldn't have believed anything he'd had to say.

I kept on with the belladonna extract and the Darvon, the bottles of pills, and the glue-food, and recovered physically. I signed on with the New York office of Associated Booking —they'd been my agents in Chicago when I'd first come to the States—and took an out-of-town booking. I got sick again. I returned to New York to ask for a local gig. And that was when Noel, my agent, explained about New York A.F. of M. scale. It was a fraction of what I was accustomed to earning —about a hundred and a quarter compared to the three or four hundred a week I made on the road. I accepted a booking on a cruise ship, sold my car and hoped I'd get more unusual bookings like this one that would pay reasonably well—two-fifty a week—until Rob turned me into a star.

After six cruises back and forth to Bermuda and the Virgin Islands, during which I lived on a diet of Dramamine and Coca-Cola, the job ended. I accepted the offer of a gig in Hartford, rented a car, went to work and got sick again. It was no good. Obviously, my sickness was somehow tied into performing in clubs.

I was frightened. Something unknown and dark that had been chasing me for years had started to gain ground, and was catching up. I was frightened into immobility: a rabbit on the highway mesmerized by the glare of oncoming headlights. Every time I left my apartment, I felt invisible. The overpowering height of the buildings and the crush of people sucked the air out of my lungs and had me walking against the lights into the oncoming stream of traffic; the sight of happy couples entering restaurants made me want to cry. I was starting to think about death again, considering ways and means. I wanted to run away but didn't know where to go.

I got a job in an office and, ignoring the fact that he was married, threw myself at Rob. When I learned that his marriage was breaking up, it inspired me to become what I thought was the sole entrant in a one-woman relay race. The prize was Rob. He had no intention of being won, but he wanted me. And to keep him wanting me, to continue on as the beneficiary of his skilled advances, I threw out all my dignity, my self-respect and my precious small bit of hard-won self-esteem and, like Mickey Mouse in *The Sorcerer's Apprentice*, went wild trying to play Rob like a twenty-six-piece orchestra. I was positive I could make him switch from, "I love you, but I'm not in love with you," to, "I love you." At that point, I'd have won and would be able to let the entire insane game come to an end, because I didn't even *like* him all that much. I spent the majority of my time with him fervently wishing there was some man who really loved and valued me.

The longer our relationship went on, the more out of control I slipped. I tried to reason myself out of the quicksand depressions, but I just kept sinking in more deeply.

I was alone. I had no friends and few acquaintances. I had a job-job and earned about a hundred dollars a week instead of singing and collecting the three to four hundred I was accustomed to and needed in order to pay the backlog of debts I'd somehow managed to accumulate. I was living in a two-room, roach-infested rattrap walk-up on East Nineteenth Street. Going crazy. Because the only man I'd met and been attracted to who'd ever displayed any interest in me didn't really want me. He just happened to like my body and the way I dressed and undressed it. I was drowning and couldn't seem to save myself.

I went back to writing lies in my journals.

Twelve

IT SEEMS that each time in my life I've come right up to the edge, prepared to let go and fall over, someone has come along and allowed me to value myself. Walt did that for me. After Rob and Rob's women—his wives, ex-wives and countless girlfriends; after Rob's drinking and dinners at eleven when I was well beyond hunger; after his talk-to-you-soon, and his calls from the China Song—where he hung out—drunk and wanting to see me; after allowing him to come and go, rummaging about in my body like some depraved scavenger looking for a prize, Walt was like a step straight into the heart of normalcy and sanity.

I'd worked in the office with him and his partners, learning the insurance business, for eight months. In that time, he'd shown himself to be quiet, gentle, kind and wonderfully funny in a very English, subtle way. He was from Hartford, had attended good schools and was an insurance broker, like his father. He was forty-four, a long-time member of Alcoholics Anonymous and impressively humble on the subject of his past drinking and the mess it had made of his early life. He'd never been married, and lived alone in a garden apartment on East 74th Street; he was still friends with most of the men who'd been boys with him during his years at St. Paul's. He didn't assume, nor did he play games or use pressure tactics. Six-feet tall, barrel-chested, dark-haired, dark-eyed and shy, he'd long since come to terms with himself.

At the urging of his two younger, married partners, I invited him to dinner. A week later, he asked if I'd be interested in a weekend in the country. I accepted. Three weeks later, we got married. In the wedding photographs taken at City Hall in New York, we both look startled, nervous and uncertain. We were. We weren't in love, but rather two friends —one who needed looking after and one who needed to do some looking after. I thought it would work. But it wasn't the way I'd always thought it would be. Walt was fine; he adapted easily and settled into being a married man with enviable alacrity. During the first six months of our marriage, when we lived in Manhattan, we had a good time going out to dinner, to movies, to visit friends. But by the time we'd moved to Stamford and I'd arranged the furniture and accustomed myself to commuting into New York to continue my job for Walt's company, I felt claustrophobic and depressed. The routines that quickly evolved were like invisible ropes that tied me to several paths that led to the office, to the stove, to the bedroom. There was no visible magic in being married, no sudden change in my reactions. Once the strange newness of being called Mrs. Allen had worn off, I became restless and started to look at the walls and ceilings, at the faces of our fellow commuters, in an effort to understand why I'd always believed that marriage would save my life. Where once I'd thought only of how good it would be to have someone around on a full-time basis to share the days, I now began to resent my loss of privacy. It was confusing. Why couldn't I enjoy this when it was what I'd waited for for so long?

But I did learn from Walt. His hard-earned, deeply believed A. A. philosophy began to rub off: get through a day at a time, don't worry about what you can't control, strive for serenity. My desire to write came as a surprise to us both but he encouraged me and, unexpectedly, I began to grow; not into the marriage as I'd hoped, but into my own self. The interior child commenced an accelerated growth, moving to fill me inside. My skin seemed to fit better.

When we moved from Stamford to the house in Darien—the very first place that satisfied all my prerequisites, with its sixteen-foot cathedral ceiling in the living room, its skylights and its odd, erose walls—I was spending five or six hours a day at the typewriter and resented Walt's or one-year-old Jossie's interruptions. Disenchanted with marriage, I was anxious to remain in the paper world I was constructing in an ongoing, silent frenzy. Walt loved me, and I loved him, but mine wasn't the kind of love strong enough to support a marriage. Why hadn't anyone ever told me that marriage was cooking when you didn't feel like it, was doing someone else's laundry and taking out the garbage? Why hadn't I known that being a mother and a wife took so much time and energy? I began to see that I'd viewed marriage as a series of still photographs —immobilized smiling group portraits—that revealed none of the static and frequent tensions. Nevertheless, I wasn't ready to throw in my hand. Through the years I'd read any number of books and stories about women who'd married and, after the fact, learned to love their husbands. I did love Walt. It was our marriage I disliked. I didn't want to hurt him but I began actively to want an end to the life-style we'd structured. I was spending eight and ten hours a day at the typewriter.

For six months, I went frantic trying to justify to myself my need to escape. I couldn't. We simply had to talk about where we were headed. So we talked and I tried to explain the mounting desperation I felt. Walt was crushed, but gracious, and we agreed to live apart. The marriage was over. I took long, deep breaths, battling down the fear that I was back to where I'd started without having made any gains. Then I eased off on the number of hours I spent at the typewriter and tried to deal rationally with the situation.

Life became easier, so did Jossie, who was, by now, two years old. I could cope. Walt was still in my life, still my friend and he didn't hate me. I had sold three books and had a contract for four more. Perhaps next time, I thought, the new man and I would live out the happily-ever-after dream.

It's taken five years for me to understand that no marriage, ever, could do what I'd been led to expect it would; that marriage wasn't the inevitable end of the story, or even—of itself —any sort of answer.

Helen.

The first morning, the second time around in grade nine, I walked into my assigned classroom to experience a shock of recognition and pleasure. Helen MacKay, the small dark-haired woman with the beautiful clothes was my new homeroom teacher. I slid into my seat unable to take my eyes off her, filled with a curious expectation.

It wasn't that she was the most beautiful woman I'd ever seen. Miss Wentworth had been younger and more magazine-ad beautiful. But there was something about this woman that drew me so magnetically it was all but impossible for me not to stare at her nonstop throughout her classes, something about her that had me offer up carefully done homework and the right answers to in-class questions in order to garner whatever praise might be given. I wanted that woman to find me special, to find me.

Her clothes were the subject of much discussion among the girls. She wore elegant high-heeled shoes and suits of soft wool worn over blouses so silky they seemed to glow, of fabrics that looked as if they'd be wonderful to touch. Sometimes —I felt my eyes grow wide the first time I saw this—she wore the suit jackets without a blouse underneath so that when she leaned forward over her desk, it was possible to see the tops of her breasts swelling above scallops of lace-trimmed silk. Even her underwear was beautiful. At this first viewing, a shock of panicky excitement tore through me; my mouth was suddenly dry, my eyes filled inexplicably with tears. The sight of her was so pleasurable it was like pain. I wanted to close my eyes, open them and find myself inside the circle of her arms, being held against those swelling breasts, while she stroked my hair and murmured endearments.

She ignored the school formality of surnames, preferring to address her students by their given names. It seemed a most intimate, even daring thing for her to do—as if admitting to us that she was aware of our individuality and saw us as more than simply another pack of young bodies filling space.

She seemed happy, serene. It showed in the way she moved up and down the aisles during an assignment—unlike other teachers I'd had who'd remained at their desks and poked pencils into their wispy gray buns while preparing the next, fiendishly difficult lesson with which to torment us—and paused here and there to look over someone's shoulder. She'd speak in a confidential, encouraging undertone, and let her hand touch a student's arm or shoulder, before moving on. Sometimes she stopped before the windows to gaze out, a half-smile on her lips, her eyes locked onto something only she could see. Her movements and speech were calm, inspiring in me an extraordinary longing to disappear inside her; to *become* her. The first time one of those small, graceful hands fell lightly on my arm, I felt its penetration all through me so that I wanted to take hold of her hand and press it to my cheek.

"Why can't you leave me alone? I don't want to. Please! Please? Just leave me alone. Can't you understand? I don't want to. I hate this! Oh God I hate this! Why do you make me? Why can't you just leave me alone? Please?"

I sat in the old wicker chair in the bathroom—the only room in the apartment with a lock on the door. With the light off and the reflection from the streetlight across the road rendering the far corners of the room less ominous, I stared out at the night feeling that my lap was full, heavy with the debris of too many years' accumulation of shattered wishes and hopes. My disgusting body. The smell of him in my nostrils; my mouth sore; I wished I could be dead. Or that I could be Helen. *I love you Helen love you.*

If I ever got a chance to grow up, if I didn't die before I was twenty, I might someday have serenity, elegance and a

brilliant smile. I might actually get to be a woman, with breasts
and hips, and thighs that would gladly enclose some man;
with height to lend me a measure of authority. I might be a
woman whose opinions would carry weight, one capable of
placing a gentle hand on the arm of someone young and unhappy; I might be kind.

After a gym class volleyball game midway through the
term, I hurried back to the locker room to change. I was
expected at my aunt and uncle's for dinner and quickly
stripped off my blue gymsuit, anxious to be on my way; anticipating a pleasant evening. Perhaps we'd go out for dinner,
or take a walk along Bloor to look in the shop windows.

Sensing an unnatural silence and stillness in the room, I
turned to see Marie, whose locker was next to mine, standing
stiffly as she stared unblinkingly at me.

"What's wrong?" I asked her, tensing.

"I had two dollars in here," she said in an accusing tone,
holding out a battered wallet. "It was in here when we went
into gym and now it's gone."

"Did you look in the bottom of the locker?" I peered
around the side of the open door. "Maybe it dropped out or
something."

"It didn't drop out," she said loudly, brandishing the wallet.
"It was right here!" Her voice rising higher, she declared,
"*You* took it! You were the first one in here, all alone in here."

I looked at her red, angry face. This was shaping up like
one of the stormier confrontations with my mother, where all
the sense lay on the side of the accuser.

"Why would I take your money?" I asked softly, my heartbeat accelerating. A nightmare was about to happen.

"You must've! You were the only one who *could've* done
it!"

"You're crazy!" I laughed a thin sound, strange to my ears,
as I looked slowly around at the faces of the other girls who
were all, in various stages of undress, watching. White bras-
sieres, nylons and garter belts. I looked like a grade-sixer who'd

wandered in by mistake in my cotton vest, underpants and knee socks.

"*Don't you call me crazy!*" Her hand clutched at my shoulder as she near-screamed and waved the empty wallet back and forth in the air between us. I winced, flinching at the noise, the menace, abstractedly thinking that there'd be bruises on my shoulder tomorrow.

"Listen," I said, fear pulsing in my throat as I tried to shrug off her hand. "I didn't say you were really crazy. I'm just trying to tell you I didn't take your money. Why would I?" I felt very afraid. She *was* being crazy—like my father when he ranted on about how his bosses were out to get him.

"Just give it back and I'll forget it," she said, her foot tap-tapping impatiently, a hand on her hip, the other still waving the wallet.

"I didn't take anyone's money," I said in an appeal to the others, my eyes on their faces. Surely someone else had to see how crazy this was.

"You *were* the first one in here," one of them offered.

"Because I'm going out," I explained blindly, to all of them. "To my aunt's. For dinner. I didn't *take* any *money!*"

"Well, if *you* didn't, *who* did?" Marie asked and took a step back, some slight doubt edging its way into her eyes. A very tall, thin girl with stringy brown hair, bulging eyes, and an Adam's apple bobbing in her throat, she was a good eight inches taller and thirty pounds heavier than I.

"I *didn't* take it!" I insisted, my heartbeat gone wild now; heat rising into my neck and face.

"Why don't you just give her back the money?" another voice lazily suggested.

I glanced around to see who'd spoken, but all the faces looked the same: closed. Against me. Why? What had I ever done to any of these girls to make them believe me a thief? Something seemed to snap all at once inside my head.

"What *is* this?" I challenged them. "Some kind of game? Why're you all ganging up on me? Just because my locker happens to be next to hers. I *haven't done* anything!"

"Just give me back my money." Marie refused to budge. That hint of doubt was gone from her prominent eyes and she was back to being sure of herself.

I broke.

"OKAY!" I shouted, slipping out of control. "Okay, *okay*, OKAY!" My voice was smashed, unrecognizable. "I didn't take anybody's money, but you all want to believe I did, okay!" I started to cry; my voice jerked up and down; humiliation and anger sent a red film over my eyes. "I'm not a thief! I'm *not*! I don't need anybody's damned money!" I was shouting into my locker as I snatched up my bag. "HERE!" I cried, and pushed some money into the shocked girl's hands without looking at it. "HERE! Take it! *You take it!*"

Silence.

Trembling, hands shaking, I let the bag fall and threw myself against my locker door. My back turned to them, I sobbed uncontrollably, my nose streaming and my brain racing. *I'll run away and never come back here never.*

Miss Bennett, the phys-ed teacher, came in from putting away the gym equipment and stopped to see what the commotion was all about. The girls dispersed. I remained where I was, aware of the sweaty stink of sneakers and gymsuits and the salty not-so-clean smell of females; I wished I could die, disappear, die. I heard the girls leaving and their whispers as they went; felt their eyes burn my back through the hateful cotton undershirt. I was so ashamed, caught there in my kiddie underwear, and didn't move until the last of them had gone. Then I went to splash my face with cold water. I no longer wanted to see my aunt and uncle and wished I could go to the movies, wished I could hide somewhere dark or lose myself in a crowd; get away from me forever. But if I didn't go . . . all the explaining . . . I couldn't face it. I'd have to go.

Miss Bennett appeared in the door of her office, dressed to leave.

"You okay, babe? How come you're still here?"

Miss Bennett.

She was the youngest woman on staff; big, not fat, with

powerful muscles in her arms and shoulders and thighs. She could run faster and farther than most of the boys in the school, could throw a football farther, hit a baseball harder, and sprint more hurdles better and faster. She had a plain but appealing face and Indian-black hair tied with a shoelace at the back of her neck. With warm brown eyes and a gruff-hearty way of talking, she wasn't a bit like a teacher.

"I'm okay," I answered. "Just a headache."

"Okay. Get a move on, eh, babe? They'll be coming to lock up in here."

Heavily and stiffly, feeling a thousand years old, I got dressed.

On the streetcar, I stared at my reflection in the window, hating what I saw, and wondered why nothing ever seemed to show on my face. I looked the same as ever: an ugly little kid.

My aunt asked, "Do you feel all right? You're awfully quiet, and haven't eaten a thing."

I'm breaking all the parts of me breaking I want to go away somewhere or die cry hide somewhere dark.

"Your forehead's kind of warm," she said, pressing the back of her hand to my cheeks and forehead. "Maybe your uncle should drive you home. And you'll go straight to bed. We don't want you getting sick."

"I guess I'd better. I'm sorry about not eating."

"Never mind. You just go right to bed." She looked very apprehensive, as if fearful I'd become sick on her carpet. My aunt couldn't deal with weakness, illness. They frightened her.

In the car Uncle Jake stroked my hair, hugged and kissed me, then held my hand in his for a long moment before saying, "You feel better now, honey. You know we love you." I wanted to cry, but I didn't. I hugged and kissed him back, said good-bye, got out and went inside to our apartment.

"Some girl Marie's been calling you," my mother said. "Says she wants you to phone her right away, no matter what time you come in. What's going on?" she asked, her eyes narrowed and suspicion collected in the corners like tears.

"I don't know." With heaviness bending my shoulders, I looked at the drab sameness of the kitchen: the gas stove, the sink, the pantry-closet with its shelves that went all the way to the ceiling. Daddy had once brought home a puppy. I'd been about five. The puppy made a puddle on the kitchen floor. While my mother and father argued, I hid in the closet with the quivering puppy and hoped they'd forget we were in there. Furious, Daddy had thrown open the door, grabbed the puppy from me and stomped out. My mother had said she'd enough to do with three kids, she wasn't going to look after any dog. I always wondered who had my puppy.

"Aren't you going to call her back?" she asked me.

"I don't feel like it. I'll see her at school tomorrow." Thinking about the puppy led me to recall how, when I'd been little, if my mother and I were out together and she saw a stray dog coming down the street toward us, she'd take my hand and hurry me over to the far side of the street. She was terrified of animals. Her terror had infected me.

"The girl said it's important," she persisted.

I was so tired, all I wanted to do was go to bed. Barely able to focus, I dialed the number Mother had penciled on the back of an envelope. Marie answered at once, as if she'd been waiting right beside the telephone.

"Listen," she said urgently, "I've been trying and trying to get you. I guess your mother told you. See, I, uh, found my money. You know? I forgot. It was in my coat pocket and I, uh, forgot I put it there. You know?"

"Jesus!" I had to bite my lower lip to keep from exploding. She'd caused so much trouble, for nothing.

"Well, I thought I'd better call and let you know. You know? And say I'm, uh, sorry."

"Don't you think it's a little late for that?" I said. The hardness of The One was overtaking me, and a murderous anger building. I might take the bread knife to school in the morning and cut her throat before classes started.

"Oh, don't worry," she said quickly, brightly. "I'll tell everybody what happened. I really am sorry. Honestly, I am.

I'll give you back your ten dollars first thing in the morning. I shouldn't," she admitted, "have said you took it."

"Just forget it." Without bothering to say good-bye, I put down the receiver. The sudden loss of anger had left my head so heavy I wanted to rest it on the thick telephone directory and go to sleep.

"What was that all about?" my mother asked, from the kitchen table.

"Nothing important. Some girl in our class lost some money and she called to say she found it. That's all."

"Why'd she call *you*, of all people?"

"How should I know? I don't know. I'm going to bed."

"Did you take the girl's money?" she asked, as if she believed I'd done it.

The exhaustion and anger I felt battled each other for ascendance. The anger won out. "No, I didn't take that girl's money!" I snapped. "What's the *matter* with you? You're always ready to believe the worst about me. Like that time the money was stolen from the meatmarket and because I'd been there doing your shopping, the manager calls up wanting to know if I'd been going around flashing a whole lot of money. And what do you do? Instead of telling him, My kid doesn't *do* things like that, mister!, you drag me down there and make me tell the man myself I didn't do it. Why'd I have to get *you* for a mother?"

"Listen to the mouth on it!" she said, looking thunderstruck. "I ask a simple question and listen to what comes out!"

"You didn't ask me any *simple question*. You made it sound like you believed I'd stolen the money. Oh, leave me alone!" I cried. "A mother's someone who's supposed to stand up for her kids, not always think the worst of them. Everything *about* me's wrong where you're concerned. Nothing I ever do is right. Why did you *have* me if you didn't *want* me?"

This last line struck home. She looked properly wounded. Feeling both guilty and justified, I ran down the hall to my room, to lie on the bed in the red blue red dark. My head pounded with a migraine as the red blue red turned liquid and I whispered to the ceiling, Please God, get me out of here!

Marie was near the lockers the next morning, waiting. She handed me the money, stammering, "I'm really sorry. Really. Just tell me what I can do to make it up to you. I'll do anything. Really anything."

I looked at her skinny arms and drawn, worried-looking old-lady face, and sighed. "Forget it. Just forget it. It doesn't matter."

She wavered uncertainly for a few seconds, then went on into the classroom.

I hung away my coat, collected my books and headed into the homeroom. I wished I didn't have to be there so that Helen could see me in such a worn-down state. I had deep circles under my eyes. Some mornings, I was an ugly, skinny kid, and others, I was an ugly, fat kid. This particular morning, I was ugly, fat. I had on the short-sleeved red sweater I'd worn on the day of my interview with Miss Wentworth. I'd made it all stinky-sweaty that day because I'd been so nervous. Now, when I wore it, I stole some of my mother's Arrid because I hated to have to smell myself.

Several of the girls smiled and said hi as I walked up to my first-desk-in-the-row seat. I disliked having to sit at the head of the row, but had been assigned front-row desks since that year of the ulcer, the tests, and the dizzy spells, when I'd had to go for visual therapy for more than six months in order to strengthen my eye muscles; I'd put lions into cages day after day so I'd stop seeing double. But I *liked* seeing double. It meant I didn't have to see things exactly as they were. Involved in my fatigue and the aftermath ache and nausea of the migraine, everything seemed to be happening at a great distance. I opened my zipper case to get a pen, sensed movement, and turned to see Lexie Anderson in the aisle beside me. I felt myself gaping stupidly at her and wondered what was going to happen now.

"Hi," she smiled, showing small perfect teeth. "I thought I'd ask if you'd like to come home for lunch with me today."

"What?" Was it some kind of trick? Was she another one come along to snap off one more piece of me?

"Can you? I'd really like you to."

"Is this part of yesterday?"

"No, really. I'd like you to come."

"Well, okay."

She smiled again. Mystified, I turned to watch her go back to her desk. She was the best-looking girl in the class, the best-dressed and, it seemed to me, the most popular. Popular—what my mother wanted me to be, why she'd financed all those lessons with Miss Holly. The word made my teeth ache. It was something, I knew absolutely, I would never be.

My bag of sandwiches abandoned to the trash, I met up with her at midday; as we walked toward her house, I asked her, "Why?"

"Why what?"

She had a beautiful face, lovely features, and short, dark, curling hair. A tall, tawny-skinned girl with a kind of effortless grace, and very long legs.

"Why'd you ask me to come?"

"Oh," she smiled, nodding. "I was going to ask you ages ago. I just haven't had a chance. I guess 'cause you're different, not like everybody else. I wanted to get to know you."

"Different how?" I thought perhaps she'd be able to pinpoint it with specifics and I'd then be able to stop being so different.

"Oh, I don't know. I've watched you sometimes. You look as if you're trying harder than anyone I ever saw to be just like everybody else. But it only sort of makes you more different. I don't know. It's hard to explain."

"But different *how*?"

"Just different," she said, becoming a little exasperated at her inability to offer me a satisfactory explanation. "Not ordinary. You should be glad, you know. I mean, boy, I wish I wasn't like everybody else."

But she wasn't at all. She was taller, prettier. I couldn't understand what she was trying to say.

"How," I pursued it, "do you decide what's different about someone? Clothes? The way they look? What?"

"Just seeing someone who stands out, who isn't sort of just another face. It's *really* hard to explain." She paused for a moment. "Okay," she said, brightening. "Like Miss MacKay, for example. She likes you. I've noticed her looking at you sometimes. And she didn't ask any of *us* to go downtown to the French Tourist Office to get new posters for the classroom. She asked you."

"That's just because it was late . . . I was still by my locker . . . I mean, I said I'd be glad to go. So she gave me the letter and I went down on my bike and picked them up."

"You don't have to explain why," she said seriously. "I mean, I think it's really nice . . . the whole thing. And you picked out terrific posters, too."

"But it was just an errand."

"No, it wasn't," she disagreed quite strongly.

She was right. I'd felt as if I'd been entrusted with a sacred mission. With Helen's note in my bag, I'd gone downtown on the bike and returned with the tube of posters. And Helen had praised my selections and at once removed the old posters from the walls so she could put up the new ones.

"She isn't the same with any of us," Lexie went on. "I've seen her a couple of times during assignments, sitting there looking at you when you didn't know she was going it. With this really interesting look on her face. Anyway,"—she smiled again—"just forget about that idiot Marie. She's really creepy." She shuddered effectively. "I was going to say something yesterday but then you got so mad. I've never *seen* anybody get so mad."

I'd stopped listening. I was thinking about Helen looking at me when I didn't know it. It gave me the oddest sensation both of gratification and alarm. If I succeeded in getting her attention, what would I do with it?

I used to wonder if it were possible for someone to become so angry she could have a nervous breakdown. I didn't know precisely what elements constituted a "breakdown," and very much wanted to know how it worked, what happened when you had one; I thought of it as if it were some sort of course I might take to perfect the ultimate escape.

Try as I would, I couldn't seem to break down. I wanted to badly. But although part of me often felt as if it were slipping right out of control, another, stronger part of me stood its ground, refusing to allow any such thing to happen. So, at best, I was only ever halfway broken down.

That was my emotional state when, at twenty-two, I was employed as a social director at a rather seedy hotel in Cornwall, England. I sang three nights a week and ran myself ragged during the day making arrangements for that evening's bingo, or dancing, or entertainment. And, in between times, I babysat the children of the guests. Luckily, there weren't too many children at any given time.

I met my first genuine case of anti-Semitism as a result of my sudden friendship with a family who were guests at the hotel. Norman and Lola were Jews, and because I was with them as often as possible during their two-week stay, it became understood that I was, too. I had never attempted to hide the fact, nor had I made a point of announcing it; it simply didn't seem relevant. To be a Jew, I'd always understood, involved a comprehension of one's Jewishness, as well as of the religious significances involved. I hadn't any of that. I was a Jew simply because my mother was one, just as Lexie was not a Jew since her mother was gentile. It was all mystifying, but these were the rules as I'd been given to understand them. Whatever it meant, I was a Jew and because of it, I found myself cornered by the couple who owned the hotel in the storage room where the bingo game, among other things, was kept.

"Jew, dirty Jew," they called me, closing in. "We want you out of here *now*, *today*!" I went. Somehow, my skeleton was not in contact with the fleshed parts of me; it rattled and shook inside, an independent thing.

I went to the only place I had left: to the home of two people I'd met a few weeks earlier who'd said, after my strangled truth-telling, "If you need somewhere to go, come to us.

We mean that. Not that 'ships in the night' business, but for real. Come to us."

The parts of me all disconnected, my thoughts as scattered and jumbled as the contents of a child's toybox, I went. They opened the door, smiled out at me, and said, "Come in."

Norman worked with his father in their interior-furnishings business at the shop in downtown Leamington Spa. And Lola tended the house and took care of their two little girls, Stephanie and Gail. Externally, they seemed ordinary people. They were anything but ordinary; that they were capable of expressing such interest and sympathy in a stranger elevated them well beyond that.

I was poised at the edge of a breakdown and they drew me back to solid ground and anchored me there with their love so that I couldn't fly away. I'd have preferred to fly away. It was terrible to have to stay and to learn, like an autistic child, that the reward for my tears and fears and slow-emerging truth was a soft hand on my face, unlimited embraces within arms that were willing to hold and shelter me. Their kindness was a blanket I could wrap around myself, warmth I could carry into the world with me.

They were two people with problems of their own who, from a depth of caring and quietly unshakable personal and religious conviction, were willing to take on a cripple. To justify their incredible and revitalizing belief in me, I had to prove I could walk.

Thirteen

MISS BENNETT said, "Hey, c'mon in here for a minute, talk to me," and held open the door to her office off the girls' dressing room. I followed her inside. "How come you didn't tell me what was going on here the other afternoon?"

"It's okay."

"The way I hear it, they really went after you. You don't have to put up with that kind of stuff, you know, babe. Ganging up. I can't stand that!"

"It's all over now."

She looked at me hard. "You don't have to prove anything, you know."

"No, I know."

"I don't think you do."

"It really doesn't matter, honestly."

"Okay." She shrugged seeing that I wasn't willing to pursue it. "I need some help. How about teaching an extracurricular beginner's swim class? I think you could handle it. Do you?"

"I guess so, sure."

"Great."

I turned to go.

"Babe?"

"Yeah?"

"Don't try to tackle the world single-handedly. It's no sin to ask for a little help. Puts a little less strain on, you know? And it doesn't make you less of a person."

"I know. Thanks, Miss Bennett."

Two afternoons a week I could stay in the low-ceilinged pool room, breathing in the muzzy chlorinated air, tank-suited, going over the strokes with my attentive flock of students. I got an automatic passing grade in phys-ed for the effort. It was enjoyable to walk back and forth along the side of the pool, with the silver whistle around my neck; good at something, finally. I thought it might be quite rewarding to become a phys-ed teacher, but rejected the idea almost at once in view of all the additional years of school involved. Still, it was an agreeable pastime.

Marianna moved up north, a good hour away. We talked a lot on the telephone but no longer saw each other very often. I spent more and more time at Lexie's house, a place right out of one of Aunt Brenda's decorating magazines: filled with teak furniture Lexie's mother had had made in Finland, hand-hooked rugs and wall hangings; café curtains on the kitchen window and copper-bottomed pots on the wall. Upstairs was a bright, yellow-painted sunroom with pots of African violets on a shelf that ran along three walls. The entire house smelled pleasantly of wax and spices.

Saturday nights, we'd sit up in the sunroom, munching potato chips and drinking Pepsis. We'd experiment with makeup or play records; I'd listen to Lexie's plans to become a veterinarian, and her outpourings of misery at being ignored by a boy she really liked who didn't seem to know she was alive and suffering due to his failure to notice her. "If he doesn't ask me to the dance," she wailed, "I'll *die!*"

Not only had I long since given up hope of ever being invited to anything, I also never for a moment doubted she'd be asked to the dance.

Her mother made her a white, mid-calf length, strapless formal; an exquisite dress, quite unlike the *Seventeen Magazine* tulle and taffeta numbers with stiff boning in the bodice that were popular. Lexie's gown was of a soft cottony fabric with thick bands of luxurious lace, and not a bone anywhere. I saw the photographs after: she looked very grown up and beautiful in that dress.

I was intrigued by the fact that the girls I knew fixed their sights and hopes on some boy whose looks or voice or athletic prowess appealed to them, and then dug in and began trying everything conceivable to get that boy to notice and fall in love with them. It didn't make any sense to me. It seemed like a process of talking yourself into caring for a boy with whom you had nothing in common, then driving yourself half crazy in an attempt to *create* common interests. I tried to picture myself at random selecting one of the boys in class and pursuing him; I couldn't make the picture come clear. For one thing, none of the boys struck me as all that interesting, and for another, I had no idea what I'd do with a boy if, against all odds, I managed to get one. It seemed some sort of silly game and I truly couldn't understand how someone as intelligent and imaginative as Lexie could take it as seriously as she did: replete with crying jags, mooning looks, and fits of agony at seeing the boy she liked dancing with another girl at some sock hop.

No, the way it really ran—I privately believed—was that some man who'd admired me for a time and had gone to the trouble of finding out who I was, presented himself to me and the mutual attraction was immediate. I didn't do the looking or deciding, *he* did. I'd just wait and when the time was right, the perfect man would arrive and we'd go off together in silent but complete understanding.

I was, I decided, probably abnormal in all sorts of ways. While Lexie went on about the boy she adored, I thought about Helen and wondered how it would be to go to her house, knock at the front door, have it open and be welcomed inside. I knew why I wanted this, and wondered if

Lexie knew why she wanted that boy. I suspected that if I admitted to my feelings for Helen, I'd be labeled queer. So I revealed only a bit of my tremendous interest in her to Lexie. Happily, Lexie was very sympathetic and claimed not to think it the least bit strange that I admired Helen to the extent I did. "Everybody likes her," she said. "And I think it's really *nice* the way you feel about her. She really likes you, too."

How, I wondered, was Lexie able to make these observations? What in her noticed the differentness of people, was aware of the acts beneath the acts? She seemed more aware of nuances, of subtlety, than anyone I'd known. She displayed, I thought, an exceptional comprehension of the reasons why people did things, and their need to do whatever they did. And yet, coupled with her captivating intelligence was this somehow unworthy yearning for things that seemed so trivial.

Lexie's mother was a strange, diffident, distant-seeming woman of exceptional talent. She knitted Lexie's sweaters and sewed her clothes, even her overcoats; she took herself and Lexie off on trips to Boston and to New York where they went to the theater, on shopping expeditions, exploring. She hooked rugs, embroidered complex pieces that were framed and hung on the walls of the house. She could, it seemed, make absolutely anything. Yet Lexie didn't seem particularly impressed. At least she didn't display any great desire to agree with me when I commented on how lucky I thought she was.

As for her father, she didn't care to discuss him. She appeared not to like him. I didn't find that hard to understand in view of my undisclosed hatred for my own father. Lexie was my first high school friend and I felt lucky to have such a perceptive, good-looking companion. It eased a lot of the loneliness.

I sat down at the kitchen table one morning with a non-allowed cup of coffee and wrote a letter to Helen.

I wanted to write to you but I don't really know what I want to say. I just wanted to say something. I think about you. This is crazy and I probably won't even give it to you. But I did want to write. Because sometimes I can say things, write things down, that I can't say out loud. This is crazy and I won't give it to you. You look so nice to me. The things you wear and the way you look. I won't give you this. I only wanted to know how it would feel to write to you.

I didn't bother to reread what I'd written but put it in an envelope, printed her name on the front, then dropped it into my bag. I knew it was an idiotic thing to do. I wouldn't give it to her. Yet, why not? Why shouldn't I? The world was an insane place. Why shouldn't I be just as crazy as everybody else?

Feeling like a spy, or a secret agent—someone definitely sneaky—I darted into the school office before the secretary arrived and pushed the letter into the box marked "Helen MacKay." Then, my neck and ears on fire, I fled outside—panic threatening to overturn my stomach—to wait for the bell to ring. When I saw Helen arrive and enter the building, I decided I shouldn't have done it. I'd gone too far. There'd be trouble. You weren't supposed to do things like that. God! She might read the letter out in front of the entire class. They'd all laugh and make a joke of it: this girl in love with her teacher. They'd think I was queer. But I wasn't; I just loved her and wanted her to love me.

The bell finally rang and I went leadenly along to the classroom to face the inevitable consequences of my rash act; I sat through the hour bent over my textbook waiting for something to happen. Carefully, I wrote out the vocabulary in my best handwriting, putting in the accents and running up little French sentences in my head; waiting. Nothing happened. I risked looking up and was relieved to find she wasn't looking back at me. Nothing was going to happen. The class ended and the kids started to file out. Helen smiled at me. She wasn't angry, didn't think I was crazy, hadn't shamed me.

Two weeks later, I wrote another one.

Things are never the way I think they'll be. Different. Or worse. I like September best. The way it smells and sounds. It feels like the beginning of something, makes me want to live in

the sky, or run away somewhere. I keep writing things down all
the time because there are so many things I can never say. If I
write to you, it's me talking but it isn't me. I guess I sound crazy.
I probably am. But when I write things down, then I know what
I really think. You always look so nice.

Again, she smiled at me. It was okay.

A few weeks later, there was a postcard for me in the morning mail; on the front a picture of boats silhouetted by a ra-
diant sunset. And on the back: "We were here for the weekend. Thought you'd enjoy this view. Too cold for sailing, but
beautiful. Helen MacKay."

I stood and held the card, reading it over and over until I
could see the words, her strong, straight-up-and-down handwriting when I closed my eyes. It was all right.

Again, we exchanged smiles.

And I wondered, Are we really saying something to each
other? Is there a meaning here? I don't know anything about
people, nothing at all; how to talk to them or care. Maybe
I'll never be able to care, or to love, fall in love. It feels all
empty inside me, as if nothing's there. Only my needing you;
I need you to approve of me. Please like me, think me special.

Almost thirteen. I'd arrived at a point where the very sight
of my father made my insides clench, where the sound of his
noisy eating robbed me of my appetite. To allow him to touch
me, I had to close down my mind, make my body wooden. I
viewed both of us with revulsion, and suffered his grotesque,
unnatural caresses. My head filled with shrieks as he indulged
himself; a buzzing, pressing anguish crowded my chest. I despised him so much I was barely able to contain it. Since it was
impossible to express my loathing for him, I turned it back
toward myself.

I couldn't look at myself in mirrors. Repelled by the sight
of my own face, I brushed my hair with the help of any dis-
torted reflecting surface—the side of the toaster, the backs of
spoons—so that my image returned to me as misshapen as I felt,
as ugly as I believed myself to be. The compliments my aunt

and uncle or Lexie paid me upon occasion I received with total disbelief and denial. I was so unrelentingly ugly that the inadvertent sight of my face in a mirror filled me with black depression and a raging desire to rip my face off.

I developed a terrible, irrational fear of closing my eyes when I stood at the bathroom sink washing my face each night and morning. The instant my eyes closed, something immense and violent slunk up behind me and my heart went crazy, panic shot through my veins. I'd throw down the washcloth and whip around to confront the empty bathroom, positive I'd saved myself by mere semi-seconds. Had I not opened my eyes at that precise moment, something would have wrapped itself around me and torn me to pieces. The Man with the Knife had taken up residence in my brain.

It was the same, and even worse, at night, so I kept the venetian blinds of my bedroom open to the reassuring red blue red constancy of the sign outside to avert the dangers lurking in the dark. I knew I was losing my mind. Normal people didn't walk around hearing voices, weren't terrified of the dark or of closing their eyes when they washed their faces. Normal people didn't find the sight of their own faces revolting, or abhor their bodies, or feel a continuing, barely suppressed need to scream. I wanted to go mad and viewed my projected descent into madness with a great sense of relief. It would be my release, at last, from life; perhaps even soothing and restful. I'd just let go, relinquish my sweaty grip on those frangible dreams of the future and on my waning private small feeling of specialness. After all, they were just dreams, slight feelings, and nothing more. It would take so little so let them all go fluttering and drifting away, like tissue paper caught by the wind; my insubstantial, weightless dreams.

One evening in early December, while Daddy waited for me in the bedroom, snap-snapping his lighter and coughing the special cough that meant he was getting impatient, I looked up Helen's address in the telephone book, found a street that sounded right, tossed on my coat, gloves, hat and scarf and ran out. I grabbed my bike and set off in the direction of her house.

I knew I was risking Daddy's anger, but I didn't care. He could go ahead and kill me; it no longer mattered. He might do me a favor by killing me. I was unconcerned with what he might do. I simply had to get away from him.

It was miles away, much farther than I'd imagined. By the time I finally found the place, I was breathless and overheated, my face frozen, my legs numbed with cold, and inside my coat, stickily hot. I leaned the bike against a nearby tree and walked slowly past the house, my breath huffing out in urgent clouds. A large, beautiful house, it sat regally at the top of a hill; its lawn sloped down to the cross-street below. It was, I thought, wonderfully appropriate that someone so important should live in such a fine house.

I hung on the scrolled wrought-iron fence that ran along the front of the house and looked up at the brightly lit windows. Helen walked into view. Followed by a man. My heart jumped. What was I seeing? I leaned farther over the fence, click-click, to see more clearly. I couldn't make out the man's features. He was a not-too-tall, wide-shouldered man in a plaid sports jacket, shirt and tie. The two of them stood talking while I watched, breath held, wishing I could hear what they were saying. Click-click: I captured the images quickly one after another. Helen, with her head to one side, was listening. Then she smiled suddenly, brilliantly; her hand lifted—the gold bangle on her wrist catching the light—as she began to say something.

I watched them, riveted; my mittened hands holding onto the spiked rails. Then suddenly, alarmed, I realized that if either of the people up there should happen to turn and look out, they'd see me. What on earth would they think? With a last look at the house, I retrieved the bike, turned it around and headed home; I traveled back all those miles until, with everything sinking inside, I was within sight of the apartment.

During classes, I debated the issue of my possibly being queer, feeling as I did about this woman. I had no craving for her body, the way Daddy did for mine. No, it wasn't anything like that at all. I had no desire to touch her in any sexually explicit way. The idea of that was actually upsetting, knowing, as I did all too well, what the sexual ways were. There was something else I wanted, but didn't have a name for. It went beyond love, beyond my ability to define.

I sat and doodled in the margins of my textbooks, filling the pages of my notebooks with drawings and ideas, instead of homework. For a time, I forgot my earlier resolve to do well and get the highest possible grades, and worked at minutely detailed sketches of nude females with large round breasts, tiny waists and long perfect legs: all the womanly attributes I failed to have. Drawings of complete, beautiful women, with penises aimed at them like cannons. In my mind, I called them "things," deeply offended by the very thought of them. Stabbing the point of my pencil through the drawings, I dragged the point back and forth until the images were gone, the page shredded. My women though, being beautiful, I left unmarred. Women could be motherly and kind, like Miss Bennett and Miss Redfield; they could say things to me that wiped out the pain for a time. And some men could be kind, too. Uncle Jake was. All men weren't bad. It was Daddy I was stabbing, shredding; the parts of Daddy that made me gag.

I sat one morning, completely absorbed in my drawing, unaware that I was being watched—by two people, I later found: Helen and Lexie. Lexie was watching Helen and Helen was watching me.

She spoke my name and every head in the room lifted in the broken silence; except Lexie who, guiltily, lowered hers. "Would you come here, please?" Helen said. "And bring your notebook."

Swallowing hard, hands trembling, I picked up the book and walked to the front of the room. A loud roaring, rushing started up inside my head as the voices began frantically to whisper my name; getting louder and louder.

"The rest of you continue on with the assignment," she said, and held out her hand for the notebook as I approached the desk.

My body molten with fear, I held my hands at my sides and watched her open the notebook and expressionlessly study each page of drawings and writing before turning to the next, and the next; she kept on turning the pages while I stood paralyzed, too afraid even to attempt to imagine how all this had to appear to her: the women, the slashed out men, a whole page of "Helen MacKay" written in columns, and on the last page, my first name and her last, also in columns, in six different styles of handwriting.

I gazed at the top of her head, noticing the way the hair came down and curled around her ear. Pearl earrings. I saw things at this close range I'd never before had an opportunity to examine: the well-defined angle of her jaw, the faint sprinkling of freckles across the bridge of her nose, the length of her eyelashes, the smooth-looking skin of her neck and throat, the perfect whorl of her ear. Praying I'd die, I stood and breathed in her perfume while my eyes fixed on the sight of her motionless hand holding the notebook. A small, unblemished hand with red-lacquered fingernails. On her wrist was the gold bangle which had, I saw, a tiny gold-link safety chain.

Finally, she closed the book; her hand rested flat over the top of it. She turned and looked at me; gold-brown eyes penetrated mine for several long, painful moments. I couldn't read her eyes and felt only a sick shame, a clutching fear, but was unable to look away. Her eyes searched mine, probing.

She wet her lips and picked up the notebook and, her voice not quite right, said, "You may return to your seat. Please get on with the assignment." She held the book out to me, her eyes still fastened to mine, a pulse beating visibly in her throat. Stunned with relief I took the book, astounded that nothing had been said or done. I started unseeingly back to my seat and collided with the edge of the desk. Automatically rubbing at my thigh, I sat down trying to understand what had just happened. Still caught in the grip of fear, I glanced up without lifting my head to see her staring unblinking down at her desk; she leaned on her elbows, the fingers of her right hand lost from view in the depths of her hair, the fingers of her left touching against her lips. She seemed very far away, lost in thought. I averted my eyes guiltily, knowing I'd destroyed the dream. I'd never be invited into that beautiful house, never be what I'd hoped to this woman. Why did I have to do the things I did? Why couldn't I stop it when, seemingly of its own accord, my hand would reach out to begin drawing or writing?

I gazed at my scarred hands, her perfume still in my nostrils, wanting more than anything else to dissolve right into Helen so that there wouldn't have to be any more me but only her with the gold-brown eyes and soft-looking mouth, the elegant clothes and long red fingernails. It would never happen. I could dream it so well I could almost feel it happening, but the dream always had to end and I was still just me: no hips, a flat chest, scars and scabbed infections on the backs of my hands, on my elbows and knees. There was no way I could ever become anyone else. But what would I *do*? I couldn't live being me: I hated myself too much. I *had* to become someone else. And I'd wanted it to be Helen. No matter what I did or where I went, in the end, I still had to go home; I was still the child who got bought and paid for twice a week and sometimes oftener.

Do you really like me? It's hard to tell because you're so nice to all the kids, not just me. You were very kind that day, not saying the things I thought you would about my notebook. I feel sometimes that you like me and when I think that maybe you do, I feel so happy. I don't know why I keep on writing these letters. I know it's crazy. I do so many crazy things. I really think I am crazy. But you're really nice. And writing is easy for me, not like other things. When I write, I don't have to be me. I'm just someone writing. It makes me feel almost strong, writing. As if, if I could write all the things I wanted people to know, I'd be able to have everything the way I want it. I probably won't give you this one either.

I received a more meaningful smile for this effort. And as I moved, on my way to the next lesson, I sensed she wanted to say something to me. Seeing her mouth opening, I paused for a moment. Then I ran. Scared. So scared I had to go to the girls' lavatory and lean against the wall until the dizzy fear went away.

I lived in England for almost three years, from shortly after my twentieth birthday until just before my twenty-third. Before I left Canada, I took everything I valued in a big box down to the cellar. Helen's cards and all her letters were carefully stored in a square tin box. It was my intention to keep these things always and even if the house burned down, I knew they'd be safe inside the tin box.

The same afternoon I returned from England—obliged to stay with my parents for three insane and claustrophobic weeks until I could find a place of my own—I ran downstairs to the cellar to look for the carton. It was gone.

"Where are my things?" I asked my mother in the kitchen.

"What 'things?'"

"The box with all my papers and stuff."

"Oh, that crap. I needed the space, so I threw it all out."

"How could you *do* that?" I cried. "You *know* I wanted to keep those things!"

As always, when confronted with my displays of emotion, she shrugged and turned away. I nearly reached out to wrap my hands around her throat. Instead, I slammed out of the house and marched down the road to try to calm down; sobbing over the loss of all the tangible evidence I'd had left of Helen and over the stunning proof of my mother's absence of feelings for what was important to me. I couldn't help but believe she'd known how much the things in the box had meant to me. Yet she'd called it all "crap," and trashed it. I felt as if she'd torn off long strips of my flesh.

Three weeks later, I moved out into my own apartment. It was a terrific place, in a lovely old house at the corner of St. Clair and Spadina Road that had been broken up into apartments. The living room had rows of windows on two sides and a fieldstone fireplace, newly refinished wood floors and a high ceiling. There was a good-sized bedroom, a tiny kitchen and a bathroom. Best of all, it was mine; the first place that belonged entirely to me.

I joined the Toronto Musicians' Union, Local 149, and started to sing in clubs, playing my own accompaniment on guitar—which had been taught to me by an American girl I'd met in London. I signed on with an agent and started going out on the road—to Peterborough, to London, to Gander, to places that kept me away from Toronto for weeks at a stretch. When I was home, I wanted to relax and savor my independence, but I couldn't. Daddy kept telephoning. Several times he made drop-in visits. He wrote long, yearning letters. I threatened him with everything I could think of to get him to stop. And he did.

But when I wanted to visit my mother, or to talk to her on the telephone—I enjoyed my telephone chats with her, we always seemed to laugh a lot—I first had to get past Daddy. Soon he began a renewed effort to see me privately. I felt hounded. Finally, the pressures applied by him were too much. The only way I was going to get away from him would be to leave my home and the city I loved.

I emigrated to the States to place as much distance between myself and Daddy as I possibly could. But he was still there—in my mind, in my memory, in my cold-sweat nightmares, in my numerous fears. I began actively to pray that he'd die so that I'd be free to go home again.

Fourteen

JUST BEFORE Christmas, I was racing up the stairs at school one lunch hour to the third-floor landing—usually deserted at this time of day—planning to eat my sandwiches and to think. I ran straight into Helen who was on her way down. Hard. A collision into scented softness. Startled, we leaped away from each other, her handbag falling. It slithered down the stairs, opening in the process and spilling its contents along the way.

"Oh no!" I exclaimed. Instantly upset, I stared at everything strewn on the stairs. "I'll pick it all up. I'm sorry. God! I'm really sorry." I put down my books and lunchbag as she leaned against the handrail watching me. Frantically, I collected the fallen articles, overtaken by the strangest sensation in handling her personal belongings. I wished I could stop, sit down on the steps and examine every item carefully. Instead, I pushed things back into the leather bag, click-click.

"Here you are." I handed her the bag, still apologizing.

"It isn't that serious," she said, accepting the bag with a smile. "But try not to run. Much as I admire and envy your energy, you might hurt yourself. Or," she added, the smile growing wider, "some daydreaming pedestrian." She snapped the bag closed and continued on down the stairs.

Jesus! I was such a clod, so inept, graceless and clumsy. Watching her go, my fingers could still feel the warm-soft leather of the bag, the cylinder of lipstick, the ring of keys, the lace handkerchief, the small bottle of smelling salts. Smelling salts? Was she someone who fainted? The idea of it bothered me.

The perfumed scent of the bag's contents was still on my hands as I sat down on the top step of the landing and unwrapped one of the sandwiches. I took a bite and couldn't chew, replaying the incident, seeing that small bottle. I put the sandwich down on the step, my throat closing. The softness, the scent; it hurt so much.

The following Saturday, I went downtown to Simpson's, then made my way home considering how I'd deliver the gift I'd so carefully selected. The bike was out of the question: the streets were snowbound and too icy. I couldn't go by streetcar; it'd take hours. I'd have to ask Daddy if he'd drive me there.

He said he'd be glad to. "It'll be good to get the hell out of here for a while," he said. That seemed reasonable, and he didn't ask any questions but waited in the car while I hurried up to the front door of Helen's house. It seemed to take ages before anyone came, but then the door swung open and she looked so flushed and pretty that I felt giddy and uncertain, intimidated by my boldness in presuming to be there.

"What a lovely surprise! Come in!"

"I really can't. I just wanted to give you this. My father's waiting in the car and I can only stay for a minute." I thrust the gift-wrapped package forward.

"At least come in for a moment. It's awfully cold out here." She stepped back from the door expectantly. Casting a quick glance at the car, I followed her inside and watched her close the door, then examine the box. With an almost impishly pleased expression, she asked, "What is it?"

"You'll have to open it and see." I laughed soundlessly and looked around, click-click, unable to believe I'd done it: I was actually inside her home.

"It's lovely!" she exclaimed, plainly surprised as she lifted the cream-colored leather wallet from its box. Her eyes for a

moment were filled with the question of how a twelve-year-
old could afford an obviously expensive wallet. "Absolutely
lovely," she said, examining my eyes, her smile intact.

"I wanted to get . . . something you needed . . . something
you'd like."

"I *do* like it. It's exactly what I've needed for ages. But
how did you. . . ?" She laughed suddenly, understanding. "I
see. Fortuitous collisions. Well, thank you. This is just wonderful. Will you stay another minute and meet Mother?"

"Yes, all right." I wondered if Daddy was getting impatient
out there and if he'd ask a lot of questions I wouldn't want to
answer.

Her mother was a smaller, older version of herself who
came smiling down the hall, wiping her hands on a paint-
smeared apron. She was, I knew, quite a well-known artist and
I felt honored in being asked to meet her.

"So, this is the little girl I've been hearing about," she said,
and extended her hand to me. "A little girl who likes to give
presents and run about doing errands, among other things."
Her hand closed firmly around mine and stayed there. "She
has a good, solid handshake, too, Helen." With her free hand,
she tilted my chin up and searched my eyes as Helen had done
as she explained, "That's a sign of strong character, my dear.
What extraordinary eyes!"

Speechless, I was unable to do more than simply stand there,
caught in the elderly woman's very blue, piercing gaze. Pe-
ripherally, I could see Helen nodding, as if the two of them had
assessed me and arrived at satisfactory conclusions. Had Helen
told her about me? Did that mean something?

"You must come again and stay longer," Mrs. MacKay said.
"Pity you're in such a rush. I'd like more of a chance to talk
to you, dig around inside this head." She tapped one finger
against my temple. "You come again," she repeated.

I turned to see that Helen was smiling in agreement. The
two of them were saying they were happy I'd come, and that
I must come again.

"I . . . I really would like to. The house looks so beautiful . . . what I've seen."

Helen stood watching her mother and me and I looked at her, wanting to throw my arms around her, to hide my face against her shoulder and ask her to have her mother call the police and get them to come take away the man out there in the car.

"Next time," her mother said, "we'll have Helen give you a Cook's tour. It's a fine old house. We've lived here since before Helen and her brother were born."

Stupidly, I said, "I didn't know you had a brother."

"I do. And you have *two* brothers, haven't you?"

"Yes." I was anxious to go, fearful that Daddy might, at any moment, decide to climb out of the car and come lumbering up the steps to the front door to find out what was keeping me. I didn't want these people to see him, to know I had a father like him.

Seeming to sense my anxiety, Helen opened the front door, and said, "It was good of you to think of me. You're very generous. Too generous. Wish your father a happy Christmas from us, won't you? And do come again. Perhaps next time Mother will show you some of her work."

"Love to," her mother said, as she went back down the hall. "You come back, eh? I want a better look at those eyes."

I stepped outside.

"Have a good holiday," Helen said. "And thank you for the lovely present."

With enormous reluctance, I went down the front steps and got into the car. I was so lost to wishes and dreams I didn't hear him the first time Daddy suggested we stop somewhere for a bite to eat before going home.

"To eat?" I was amazed he hadn't said we were heading downtown to the factory where he'd push my head down to him, extracting payment for the ride.

"You don't want a hamburger or a sandwich or something?"

"No. I mean sure. Okay."

Settled in on opposite sides of a booth, he said, "Tell me about her, this teacher of yours."

Forgetting myself, I rattled on for several minutes, then was stopped by his furrowed expression and my own indiscretion.

"I wouldn't," he said seriously, "get too carried away about her in front of your mother, I were you. She'll probably put the kibosh on you going there."

"But why?"

"Your dear mother, number one, has a dirty, suspicious little mind. And, number two, she can't stand to see anybody enjoy something. She'd put it together there was something going on with you and this teacher. So take my advice and keep your trap shut."

"What d'you mean 'going on?'"

"You know what I mean."

"God! Why would she think *that*?"

"Listen, you and me, eh, we know what's what. But your old lady's liable as not to put it all together back-asswards and come up with something dirty. So keep quiet about it and everything'll be fine."

"You mean you think Miss MacKay's a *lesbian*?"

"Hey! Did *I* say that? Jesus! Not in this world, she isn't." His face melted into too familiar greedy lines, a hateful wet-lipped smile lifting his thick lips at the corners.

"Don't you *talk* about her that way!" I cried. "Don't you *ever talk* about her at all!"

"What'd I say?" he asked, with a face of assaulted innocence. "All I said was . . ."

"I *know* what you *said*, what you *think*! It's you . . . You're the one who doesn't want me to see Miss MacKay anymore, not my mother. Why do you always have to *spoil* everything for me? Why can't you *ever* let me have anything the way I want it, without ruining it for me?"

"Hey!" He reached across the table trying to touch me. I jerked away.

"Don't! Leave me alone!"

"Okay, okay." He backed off. Doubtfully, I looked at him. What did this unexpected move mean?

"One day," he said, again serious, "you're gonna be one beautiful woman, anybody takes the time to stop and really see."

"I'm ugly," I said, my voice flat and uninflected. "I'll always be ugly; short, fat and ugly."

"Who the *hell* ever told you that?" He looked genuinely shocked.

"Nobody had to tell me. I know it, that's all."

"You listen here to me, let me tell you something," he said firmly, in a voice I'd rarely heard before. "You're never going to look like all the rest of them. So what? Who the hell cares? But I'm telling you, anybody can't see you're beautiful just isn't looking."

It only made me start to cry again, because it was always safer to believe the reverse of whatever he said. Yet, for that entire week I was off school, he left me alone; he was good-natured, funny, engaging—even with Bobby. He gave all of us nice Christmas presents—I got saddle shoes—and he took me downtown to the movies and out for something to eat after. In the restaurant, he talked about an article he'd read in *Punch* about British humor and explained it to me. Throughout the week my mother kept looking at him as if he'd finally lost his mind altogether. Bobby merely kept out of the way. I think I must have spent the time looking at him the way my mother did, because I didn't believe this display of good natured benevolence could possibly last.

I received a letter.

Thank you again for the wallet. It was very thoughtful of you and exactly what I'd have chosen. I hope you had a good Christmas, a pleasant vacation. Helen.

I carried the letter and her postcard around with me everywhere.

In January, a week or so before my birthday, I went to see her again. It was a rare, snowless day and I pedaled hard into the icy wind, trying to keep my face down. I parked the bike in the driveway, went up the front steps and stood there for quite some time before finally ringing the bell. I heard heels moving over a wood floor, then the door opened. She smiled; her hand reached out to draw me inside. Her hand was warm, melting something inside my chest; it turned to liquid and ran warmly, like oil, through the interior hollows. I was being welcomed in. She'd really meant it when she'd asked me to come back.

"We're just finishing lunch," she said; withdrawing her hand to close the door. "Come, take off your coat. You look frozen. You didn't ride all this way on your bicycle?"

I nodded.

She shook her head disbelievingly, then took my coat. She folded it over her arm, saying, "Come along in here," and led the way to the living room. "You won't mind waiting? I'll be with you in a few minutes. Please, make yourself comfortable."

I stood there motionless. She smiled again, turned and walked away. I could hear her voice lifted in explaining tones from the dining room, but couldn't distinguish what was actually being said.

I sat down, still cold, on the edge of one of a pair of armchairs positioned opposite each other beside the side windows and, click-click, looked at the cozy living room, at the glowing remains of a fire in the grate, then out the window at the people walking at the bottom of the hill. I took a deep breath and closed my eyes, frightened. The mingled scents of wood smoke, roasted meat and traces of perfume made me hungry, but I'd never dare eat in front of these people and risk having them see how clumsy I was because my mother had given up when I saw six or seven trying to teach me to use a knife and fork properly. I was so hopelessly left-handed, she'd shrugged her shoulders and said I'd have to teach myself; she couldn't figure it out. So I learned by studying other kids and people in movies, but I probably didn't do it right.

Helen returned after a few minutes and sat down in the chair opposite. My perspective was suddenly dimmed by that same drowsy fear that had overtaken me during the interview with Miss Wentworth. I gazed, unable to tear my eyes away from the sight of this woman's smiling mouth, the smooth column of her throat, the narrow planes of her knees and the slight show of white lace where her legs were crossed, her fingers curving over the scrolled ends of the chair arms, polished red fingernails, the gold bangle on her left wrist.

She was so feminine, so attractive. Why hadn't she ever married? Why were none of the female teachers married? Did you have to stay single to be a teacher? Was it possible, I wondered, that someone like this, with adulthood on her side, with full breasts and a small waist and slim legs had never opened herself to some man? That couldn't be. It didn't fit my dreams. In the course of five or ten seconds, I ran through an entire scenario wherein it was nighttime and she welcomed a man into the house. They embraced and then, slipping to the floor, made love in quick, wild abandon. Very possible.

Throughout my inspection, she sat, perfectly composed, waiting; a slight smile on her lips and her eyes on mine.

"Would you like something?" she asked. "A glass of milk, or a Coke? Something to eat?"

"No thank you." My voice emerged hoarse. *I'm here with you I could put out my hand touch you you must think I'm so ugly how can you stand looking at me?*

"Mother's just had a most successful show. It quite wore her out, I'm afraid, so she won't be in to see you. But I have some photographs here." She opened a drawer in the small table beside her chair. "Perhaps you'd like to see them?"

"Yes, I would."

"These are two of the larger pieces." She examined the photographs for a moment before passing them over, again watching me closely as I looked at them. I had the feeling that a great deal hinged not only on my behavior, but on my responses to her mother's paintings as well.

"Mother's very fond of boats," she said and leaned forward to tap the top photograph with a red fingernail. "That one was done at the marina near our summer home."

"It's beautiful," I said. It was. Her mother's water colors had a kind of delicate boldness, I thought, because a lot was left to the mind of the viewer and the rest implied by strong washes of color.

"It is, isn't it?" she agreed, going now through a sizable stack of photographs in her lap. "I don't know how these got in with the others," she said, nevertheless handing them to me. There were four or five black-and-white snapshots of a woman in a white one-piece bathing suit. It took me several moments to realize who the woman was.

"Is this you?" *My God why are you showing me these pictures you might as well be naked I don't know how to react to what you're showing me.*

"Mmm, let's see." She came forward again to look, then sat back to go on with her sorting. "Last summer," she said. "A friend took those."

The friend, I guessed, was a man. Perhaps the one I'd seen that night. I looked at the photograph again. On tiptoe, arms outflung, she looked much taller in the snapshot than she actually was; she appeared long-legged and slim, her upraised outflung arms lifting her breasts from the top of the swimsuit.

"You look so different here," I said, searching for a way to compliment her, "so . . . young."

"I'm flattered," she smiled, "to have anyone think I look young, even in a photograph."

"But you are. I mean . . ." I knew how old she was: almost forty. It didn't seem old. If anything, it seemed to me a perfect age.

"You're so serious," she observed, her eyebrows lifted slightly.

"Am I?" How, I wondered, could she think me serious when she'd seen me leap into openings at least a dozen times in order to get the class laughter?

"You are. Very serious."

"But things are important. I mean, things *are* serious."

"Not that serious."

I waited for her to elaborate. She didn't, but simply passed over more photographs. This continued for nearly half an hour, until I raised my head to find her looking at me with an intense expression that said, Tell me! Talk to me! I know there are things you want to say to me. It's why you came here, so why not tell me?

I looked down at my lap, taking care to shape the photographs into a neat pile which I then returned to her.

"They're wonderful paintings," I said politely. "Thank you for showing me."

"You like them, do you?"

I nodded.

"Why?"

"Because . . . I don't know anything about art."

"That doesn't matter. Why?"

"Because they feel—strong—I guess. And I like the way she makes things real with just a little bit of color, the white spaces. I just like them."

"Remind me," she said, setting the pictures aside, then recrossing her legs. "How old are you again?"

"I'll be thirteen on the nineteenth."

She gave a slight shake of her head. The fingers of her right hand were poised tips-down on the arm of her chair.

"Mother's a very fine artist," she said. "I've always somewhat envied her talent, wished I had some."

"Oh, but you . . . you're a good teacher. That's a talent."

"That's a craft. Talent's something much larger, more important."

"But it's important to be a good teacher. I mean . . ." I didn't know what I meant. I was bothered that she'd have any negative thoughts about herself, especially when I found her perfect.

"What an odd child you are," she said slowly. "In some ways, you seem so old you remind me of Mother. She's right: there is something about your eyes, the way you look at things. And the observations you make aren't the sort one expects from someone your age. I find myself forgetting every so often how very young you are."

"I don't feel young," I admitted. "I feel really old. If I look into a mirror, it's always a surprise to see . . ." I stopped, reminding myself to be careful of what I said.

"See what?" she prompted.

"That I'm not really old."

"Why did you write those notes?" she asked.

"I don't know why."

"Of course you do."

"I guess you think I'm crazy, doing all the things . . ."

"No."

I think I'm crazy, I thought, and felt myself succumbing to the dreaminess, to that enervated heaviness in my limbs, my brain.

"What would you like to do with your life, do you suppose?" she asked, her head slightly to one side.

"I don't know yet. Something." *What I'd like. To run away and have life, just have it. I'm going to fall asleep right here in this chair my eyes all of me so heavy.*

"You're not ugly, you know," she said quietly.

"How can you *say* that?" Wide awake again, I stared at the backs of my hands.

"You think you are, though, don't you?" she persisted in that same quiet voice.

"I *know* I am," I said and tossed my head back as if to fully reveal the totality of my ugliness.

"Your thinking it doesn't make it so," she disagreed.

Don't! I'll break. So many different ways to break losing pieces here and there always breaking little parts of me maybe I'll never be able to find all the pieces of me put them back where they belong I love you so much I'd give my life if you'd hold me.

"Would you like to see the house?" she asked, preparing to rise. "Yes? Come along."

I followed her up the stairs feeling I was suffocating. I wanted this house, wanted to be able to move from room to room and look out this window or that one; I wanted to be grown up and capable of controlling a situation, the way she was controlling this one. I had no idea what she thought of me. I thought she was unbelievably kind and indulgent to make it seem as if she actually wanted me here.

"This is my room," she said finally, having shown me several others, and stepped aside, noting my reactions.

It was a wonderful room, peaceful; with a fireplace and a

chaise longue set at an angle before it, an afghan thrown across one of the arms. Against the far wall was a bed, and in the bay between the two front windows was a wide antique desk with a polished brass lamp on the left-hand corner. Bundles of examination papers sat in the middle of a blotter. There were several textbooks and a fountain pen lying atop some papers, a telephone. Click-click.

I didn't seem able to make myself accept that this was real. It felt like a movie. This is a movie I'm in right now, I thought. I'm playing a part and the invisible camera is over there capturing everything I do. I could turn and smile, make the camera think I'm happy if that's the part I want to play.

"Everyone's a movie," I said, tracking this elusive concept, unaware for a moment of how bizarre it might sound. "Every single person, we're each our own movie. We can run it in our minds any way we want, backwards or forwards, slow-motion or all speeded-up and funny, the way they do sometimes. Like Charlie Chaplin movies. Fast." I laughed a jangled sounding laugh, then hurried on. "I'm a movie. I'm my own story. I can be . . . I can be . . . happy. If it's part of the story, the part I'm supposed to play, I can be. Anything I want, I can pretend to be. If I act a certain way, that's the way people have to see me. And I only have to let them see what I *want* them to see." I turned to look at her, finding it easier now to meet her eyes. "You're a movie, too," I tried to explain, ignoring her bemused expression. "Someone could be over there with a camera filming everything you do. So, if you think about it, you could be your own camera sitting over there, watching what you're doing over here. I do it all the time; I film everything, or take photographs in my mind. And then, maybe at the end of the day, or at night when you're in your bed, you can run your movie of all the things you said and did and see how you like it. I can do it. I can be over here and watch myself from over there and I'm two separate people."

I closed my mouth abruptly, convinced that what I was saying was completely crazy. "I don't know what I'm talking about," I said and tried to smile.

She made a gesture toward me, her expression one of concern. I flinched and her hand drew back. She looked as if I'd hit her.

Dón't I want to tell you I might and it'd spoil everything.

Distraught, I said, "I think I'd better go now." I *can't* tell you! My parents will destroy you if I do and I'll have nothing left. I need you here. *I can't tell!*

"All right," she said easily, and turned to lead the way back downstairs. "Next time you come," she said lightly, "perhaps Mother will show you some of her latest pieces. I'm sure," she said, presenting me with my coat, "she'd be most interested to hear your comments. Sunday's always a good day to come," she said, watching me struggle into the coat. "Come again," she invited. "Sunday's always good."

She looked as if she wanted me to stay. I risked a last look at her, said, "Thank you very much," then escaped out the front door and ran down the steps, after a few moments hearing the door close quietly behind me.

Pedaling home, blinking against the bitter cold that seemed to slice right into my eyes, I knew I'd go back; I'd keep on going back there for the rest of my life. I thought about the photograph, and saw it play against my eyes like a damaged film sliding into focus again and again until the image of the woman's body was permanently etched into my brain; click-click: a photograph of a photograph.

I imagined that man, the one I'd seen in the window; I saw him bend her back, down on that bed in her room, down on the white pillow. Pressing his mouth to hers, he wound himself around her naked body like a snake. Her thighs opened to him. Slowly. I could see his mouth on her throat, breasts, belly, thighs; could see his hands weaving through her hair, passing up and down the length of her body. Then, he pushed himself into her. A cry, sighs, soft sounds, motion. Exquisite lines of arching throat, enclosing arms, flattened breasts, flexing thighs. Muted colors, sibilant whispers. It was Helen's image, but I was the woman inside her. It was me, in her form, being willingly bent open to passion.

After my marriage came apart, it was Jossie who kept me

firmly anchored to life. I had responsibilities to her, so I couldn't go back to England to live as I might have liked. I couldn't run away from this as I had from every other unpleasant experience in my life. I had to stay and begin trying to come to terms with a lifetime of rash acts, impulsive decisions, obsessions, fears, and ambition.

Walt was always there, willing to help. But I also had to stop leaping in to make his decisions for him before he had a chance to make his own, allow him the courtesy of deciding for himself at his own speed.

When my first book was published, I wanted, more than I'd ever wanted anything, to be able to call Helen and say: "Helen, I've been married and divorced; I've got a little girl and I'm an author." I constantly want to call her, but can't.

A number of editors who read earlier versions of this book wished to know why I was skirting the lesbian issue, avoiding it. And I reacted each time with surprise and dismay, because what I was and am writing about wasn't a sexual relationship but one based on *love*. And if people see, in the totally innocent relations between a grown woman and a desperate child something covertly sexual, it makes me wonder if love hasn't been lost sight of somewhere in our hot pursuit of sexual freedom.

I *loved* her. I wanted to *be* her. To my mind this was a great compliment: the wish to emulate what is good, wise and mature in an adult. I certainly had no desire, beyond the constant one to embrace her, for her body. The idea of that was abhorrent to me.

Helen was the only person in my life at that time who had no strings, no snags or hooks, no special requirements of me. She welcomed me into her home, glad every time to see me. It was never a bad time for her, never inconvenient, never an imposition. She simply accepted me precisely as I was, and expressed pleasure in my decision to be with her. She never probed too deeply or pried cruelly. She never criticized unkindly or speculated aloud on the reasons for my attachment to her. We were friends. It was the first time in my life that someone gave me equal status, placed me on a secure, recognizable footing. I've had few gifts in my lifetime of like quality.

I did, however, wonder for years if I didn't perhaps have strong lesbian leanings and was simply refusing to acknowledge them; I liked women, admired them, derived pleasure from the sight and sound of a beautiful, elegantly-turned-out woman.

Several years ago, I had an encounter with a woman that was, in any number of ways, no different from those I'd had with a lot of men. I was wooed and pursued in much the same fashion; I capitulated with my usual trepidations but with both tremendous curiosity and also a desire to satisfy the question once and for all. It wasn't dreadful. Rather, it was onanistic. And if I was going to make love to myself, I preferred to do it quietly, in the privacy of my own room, without a witness. I discovered, finally, that I wasn't gay. It was both a relief and enlightening, yet the experience provided me with different and better insights. I'm not sorry. There were elements of comfort and safety in being with another woman that I can't deny, as well as indisputable moments of pleasure. It simply wasn't a strong preference in me.

Helen occupies an entirely different place in my mind. It's a place free altogether of sex. Enshrined, perhaps, in pastelled memories. But colored primarily by love.

Fifteen

DURING THE first years of her life, I had all kinds of fears for my daughter. I watched Walt with new eyes and wondered if this man I thought I knew was capable of harboring an unnatural desire for his daughter. I studied him through days and nights, closely observing his behavior with Jossie until I was completely satisfied he was incapable of harming her. All the men who've come and gone in my life have been subjected to that same close scrutiny. I had nightmares when Jossie was three and four and five that someone had taken her from the house without my knowledge and raped her. I awaked from these nightmares terror-stricken and unable to get back to sleep.

I've lived almost half my life with a stark firsthand knowledge of how nightmares transcend the sleeping state and play themselves out; perhaps that's why I'm so acutely aware of the harm that could befall my child. I want nothing to happen to her that would be a dead weight she has to carry with her on her trip through life.

My fears are less morbid now. She's almost eight; each year she grows that much more aware, and secure, and capable of defending herself. I'll never entirely stop worrying, fearing for her safety, but I realize that this residual, ongoing fear is part of the territory that came with my motherhood.

Sharing my life with Jossie has compensated for a lot. I've been able with her, and through her, to savor the enthusiasms, the fads and the joys that comprise her childhood. It's been a second chance, in many ways, to enjoy things I missed.

Sometimes I'm overindulgent. Sometimes I'm sharply critical of her. I try not to go overboard either way. Often I have to stop and tell myself, "What you just did, that's the mother part. But this other thing you did, that's your fear. So stop that, don't do it anymore." It's a long, ongoing process of ciphering out what's motherly, and what's prompted by the child in me and hasn't anything at all to do with Jossie.

This ciphering goes on in every area of my life. I haven't one simple set of reactions, I've found, but two: the child's, and the woman's. At times, the child is instinctively, intuitively right; the woman has to acknowledge this and go with it. At other times, the woman is right and the child has to be suppressed. I'm not an easy person and I know it.

I faced myself some time ago, swallowed the bad news and, with the help of people who cared, got on with trying to improve and grow, to become the person I wanted to be. I can't afford to be dishonest with myself. I had over ten solid years of nonstop lying; more than enough. I have a memory that's too retentive as it is to clutter it up with half- or partial truths, so I go at truth as I go at everything: head-on, prepared for brilliant success or absolute disaster.

I'm calmer now—less angry and frightened than I was even two years ago. I've discovered the pleasure of simple things and I feel happy at being alive. Old neighborhoods, places where I once lived, and people who once seemed threatening, no longer have their former impact.

The house on Indian Valley was a sanctuary, a place where I could reveal the best of myself and be praised; a place I could go when things seemed bleakest. I went back again and again and was never made to feel anything but wanted. Just come as you are, there's your chair, let's talk. Helen always seemed to be expecting me, was always prepared to offer food or things to drink. We'd sit facing each other in the living room, talking abstracts while I tried to make myself say, I love you.

I knew she'd long since guessed something was critically wrong in my life. It showed in her eyes, on her mouth, in the questions that remained unasked month after month, for years. I'd sit there wanting to tell her, but too frightened to risk it.

Occasionally, her mother joined us; she'd make cryptic comments and observations I pretended not to understand, although all three of us knew I feigned my lack of comprehension. She made light remarks alluding to my visits—how regular, how welcome they were—or to my abilities—I'd sung several more times at school, primarily in order to have Helen hear and comment favorably, which she did—and to my continuing confusion about my future. She'd spend an hour or two from time to time showing me her latest paintings, or her exquisite pieces of pottery; she'd explain the glazing technique, or how she'd effected the particular mood she'd created in a painting, all the while studying me carefully. I felt utterly transparent with her: it was as if she'd managed to bypass the growing-thicker-daily veneer I'd constructed to render me less vulnerable to the people most capable of harming me; she was able to see the someone in me who longed for everything beautiful. The Other was predominant from the moment I rang the doorbell until I left that house. I was clean, pure in mind and spirit; allowed to enter into a state of grace as I had those times I'd visited with Marianna's family.

With Helen I felt, in equal parts, both at peace and at war. She took what I had to say seriously and evaluated my words as she'd have done those of a peer. There seemed to be no danger in voicing my opinions on any number of matters—as long as they were a safe distance from my private life. When I sensed or, more accurately, felt the questions begin to build in her, I sank into a trench of fear and sat huddled inside it, mute.

I visited. She went off on vacations, trips, but in her ab-
sences there were always postcards or letters, one or two a
week: from Cuba, Haiti, different West Indian islands. I
hoarded, reread and studied—front and back—for hours, everything she sent. There was a person in the world who loved
me, who had no evident wish to change me. I loved her with
complete devotion and would have done absolutely anything
she asked. She asked nothing.

The summer between grade nine and the start of grade ten,
I got a job at Simpson's-Sear's typing orders that rolled past
my desk on an assembly line. I spent most of what I earned
exercising my employee's discount privilege on clothes that I
hoped would make me look the sixteen years old I'd said I was
in order to get the job.

Upon returning to school, I had an entire day of undiluted
panic at discovering Helen wasn't there. I had to find out why
and approached Miss Redfield in the corridor to ask circui-
tously about Helen to learn that, ". . . she was called away
unexpectedly. But she'll be back in a few weeks." Miss Redfield's green eyes were as kind as ever. I thanked her—completely unconvinced by her story—and that evening rang the
house to speak to Mrs. MacKay who said, "Helen will be
away for two weeks. You sound upset."

"No, no," I lied. "I was just wondering."

It was a prepared story. I wasn't being told the truth. Something was going on and it felt all wrong. I remembered the
bottle of smelling salts and it struck me as a telltale, even ominous sign of some sort of weakness. Helen was going to die
and no one wanted to talk about it.

Two weeks later, I saw her in the corridor and was so
overcome by relief, I became a little hysterical; I ran from
her approach to hide in the girls' lavatory and cry silently
behind my fist, trying to control the convulsive shaking that
had overtaken me at the sight of her, looking unchanged, walking toward me. I'd thought I'd lost her, but I hadn't.

On my next Sunday visit, I was more tongue-tied than ever
—something that happened only with Helen. Elsewhere, I

chattered on, but with her, words had so much more significance that I didn't care to waste any. I wanted to be able to tell her of the fear I'd lived with during her absence when I'd been convinced she was dying or even dead and no one would tell me. But it was months before I could summon sufficient nerve to ask.

I was with her in the living room, watching her drink tea from a delicate porcelain cup, when I casually inserted the loaded question into our conversation.

"What happened in September?" I asked, my eyes on her gold bangle. "When you were away."

She seemed to pull herself back from somewhere remote as she turned from the window and set down her cup. "Nothing at all." She smiled and I knew she wasn't telling the truth.

"I was so worried about you," I admitted, feeling a flush of heat rise into my ears, "afraid something had happened to you."

"You were worried about me," she repeated, then let her head fall back against the chair so that the line of her throat appeared too whitely exposed. She sighed and turned her head once again to look out the window. Then, enigmatically, she said, "Thank you," and removed her glasses so that her face seemed suddenly naked. "Do you know," she said, "that people choose their lives? We *choose*." Her head came slowly forward; her eyes fixed on mine.

"We do?" I had to look down—first at her Owen's & Elm's black-leather high heels, then at the skirt of her red wool suit.

"You'll make your own way," she said. "Always. You're a very strong, resilient little girl. So strong, it's sometimes exhausting to be with you. That's not a criticism, but simply an observation. Do you know that?"

I didn't know how to answer.

"Do you?" she asked again.

"I don't know what you want me to answer to."

"Do you know you're strong?"

"I . . . think so."

"You have such a good brain, such a fine intelligence," she

said, her bright red lipstick drawing my eyes. There was a tiny smear of lipstick on one of her front teeth and I wanted to reach out my finger and wipe it away. "It's all there," she said. "All of it. But it's always going to take you far longer to accomplish what you want than you think it will. Because you go headlong at things, and because you're impatient. That's the hard way." She looked almost angry with me, I thought, and wondered why. "Most people," she said with a sigh, "including me, instinctively search out the easier routes, the faster ones. But you don't. It seems you constantly have to battle the headwinds. I don't know why. I've seen you do it again and again. But you'll get whatever you go after. Do you know *that*?"

"Are you mad at me?" I asked in a small voice.

Her chin came up and she looked surprised. "I'm not mad at you. I'm asking you a question. Do I seem angry?"

I shook my head.

"*Do* you know that?" she asked again.

"I know it," I answered in that same small voice, bewildered by her sudden, rewarding smile.

"Good!" she said, and lifted her teacup. "It's important that you know yourself, your strengths."

"I know myself," I said. It was true at that moment. There were times, like this one, when I knew exactly who I was and what my future would be; but they were only periods of a few seconds out of months—like glimpses of the faces of pedestrians viewed from a passing bus. Most of the time, I actively played at being different versions of me, in the hope of being recognized.

Now, as if to confirm my doubts, she finished the last of her tea, returned the fragile-looking white cup to its saucer and said, "You know about the parts that'll get you through. And I know something of the parts you don't, perhaps, think you show. But you'll get along. You always will." Again, she looked out the window. Was she bored with me because I was being so stupid?

"Did you always know you'd be a teacher?" I asked, wanting her to be the way she always was: smiling and pleasant and receptive.

"Always? No. At a certain point in time, I knew. My father was a teacher. It interested me. Eventually, you'll know what you want, the direction you want to go in." She spoke without turning and I thought, *If you stay that way and don't turn, I'll say I love you. The words will come; I'll say them. I love you you're the only part of my life that's beautiful the only reason I haven't thrown myself in front of a streetcar or off the back roof.*

She turned.

I looked away.

Now that I was no longer in Helen's class, there was no reason to make an effort and my grades slid steadily down. I loved the *idea* of school, but disliked being there. At fifteen, I looked fairly much as I had at eleven: just about five feet tall, and as hairless, breastless and hipless as an infant. I weighed eighty-two pounds, because I couldn't eat. The sight and smell of food, combined with the sounds of my father's noisy eating, deprived me of my appetite.

Lexie had grown high, round mounds of breast, attained a height of five-seven and was being asked to school dances by the boy she'd liked for ages. I'd never been invited out on a date, or ever been asked to dance at one of the sock hops and tea dances I kept attending in the blind hope that somewhere in that school was a boy I hadn't previously noticed who was on the lookout for someone like me. It never happened because, I knew, I was short, fat and ugly. And no mirror could ever show me otherwise.

I was giving instruction in surface dives one afternoon, enjoying the class as always, treading water as I explained how it was the powerful downsweep of the arms through the water that brought the body around and straight down. Believing myself still in the nine foot depths, I spread my arms to illustrate. My body plunged down hard and fast, bringing my face into a stunning, sudden collision with the floor of the pool. I let myself drift back to the surface, feeling about my face with my fingertips, hearing my students making shocked sounds. Blood poured down my arm; the water around me swirled pink-red.

"C'mon." Miss Bennett was at the side of the pool beckoning to me. "Let me give you a hand out."

She lifted me from the pool as if I were weightless, directed me out through the locker room, and into her office.

"Sit down there and let me have a look at you," she ordered, grabbing a handful of tissues to blot up some of the blood and water on my face. "What a mess!"

"I got down to five feet. I thought I was still at nine."

She shook her head, standing hands on hips, the sodden blood-stained tissues crumpled in her hand.

"Do you think my nose is broken?" I asked her.

"Does it feel as if it is?"

"I don't know," I said. "I've never had a broken nose." This struck me as funny and I laughed. Pain shot through my head.

"Want me to run you over to the hospital?" she offered.

"Oh, you don't have to do that. I'm sure it's all right."

"You sure?"

"I think so."

"Well, okay. At least let me put a bandage on it. You really did quite a job on yourself, eh?"

When I got home, my mother said, "What next! D'you break it?"

"I don't know," I said in a pained whisper.

"Maybe I should take you over to the hospital. Jesus," she smiled sympathetically, "I never knew a kid in my life had more accidents than you."

"If it's not better tomorrow, I'll go," I said. I had something else in mind. It was going to be expensive and I was sure she'd say no, but I went ahead and asked anyway. To my amazement, she agreed.

The doctor was very soft-spoken. He asked my mother to wait outside; he wanted to talk to me. He put his fingers up inside my nostrils, looked into the upper interior of my mouth, touched my face all over with hands so gentle I wanted to cry.

"It's cracked, not broken," he said, at last.

"Could you change it?"

"I could, of course. But you're only fifteen; your bones are still forming. And why would you want to change it?"

"Because I'm ugly."

He said nothing. He touched my face again for a moment or two, then went to call my mother back in.

My mother said, "She wants it done. She's got this bug in her ear she's ugly. And her father's always picking on her, making jokes about the way she looks." She looked at me, while she talked, with an expression that seemed to be apologizing for my father's treatment of me. Before that moment, I hadn't realized that she knew how his jokes made me suffer. I loved her for defending me now, for offering me this chance to stop him from teasing me in public ever again.

It was her sad, quiet remarks about my father that decided the doctor to go ahead.

I didn't want Helen to be concerned, so before I left school I said only that I was going into the hospital, but not why. It surprised me when she asked for the specific dates and made a note of them, an inscrutable expression riding her eyes.

I went in and the surgery was performed. A pinprick in my arm, a strange rush of chemical-tasting fluid in my mouth, and then there was whiteness from which I awakened many hours later with blood leaking into my mouth and down my chin; to hear my mother's voice saying, "If I'd known she'd come out all bandaged up this way, after all those hours . . . I'd never have done it." She said something more but her voice faded and I slept again. When I awakened a second time, it was to see flowers: lavender-colored chrysanthemums. From Helen. My first and only call from the hospital was to thank her, in a murky baritone, for the flowers.

"You sound *terrible*!" she exclaimed. "*Why* are you there?" Breaking into tears, I said, "I cracked my nose on the bottom of the swimming pool." It sounded silly even to me.

"Jenny Bennett told me," she said. "She said it wasn't a terribly serious injury."

She'd talked to Miss Bennett about me. How odd, how gratifying to know that she cared. The whole tone of this conversation was unlike any other we'd ever had. She sounded angry and upset; she sounded like a mother. And I liked it, but felt guilty without knowing why.

"*Why?*" she asked again. "What are you *doing* there?"

"I had to change the way I look," I wailed. "I'm so ugly!" I couldn't say anything more, didn't trust myself not to go completely hysterical. I held a wad of tissues to my eyes, then to my nose, then stared dully at the bright red blood on the tissues as I waited for her to say something. I could hear her breathing, could sense her upset in its volume.

"You are *not* ugly," she said at length. "I can't think what . . ." She paused, took a breath, then asked, "Were there seven?"

"Flowers?" I glanced over and counted, then answered, "Yes."

"For good luck," she said, sounding agitated and more and more unlike herself. "I don't understand why you're doing this. I *wish* you'd explain it to me."

"I had to! It's too late anyway . . . it's already done."

"Do you feel as dreadful as you sound?"

"Oh no! I feel really all right. It's just the bandages making me sound this way."

"My God!" Her voice was truly horrified now. She took another deep breath before saying, "All right. I'll see you after Christmas. I hope you feel better."

We said good bye and I hung up to lie there crying. Her caring could crack open my chest and touch all the need in me, but it wasn't strong enough to force me into the truth which, I believed, would inevitably harm her.

On my first day back to school, when I least wanted to see her—or, more accurately, to have her see me—we met unavoidably in the all but deserted late-afternoon corridor of the third floor. I wanted to turn and run, but she stopped me; her hand on my shoulder held me still while she looked at the bruised circles under my eyes, at the battered, anemic look of my face. Almost inaudibly, sounding grieved, she said, "You really didn't have to do it."

Swallowing the knot of anguish in my throat, I argued, "Yes, I did. I *did*!"

"No, you *didn't*!" she said strongly, her hand firmly fixed on my shoulder. "There was nothing wrong with the way you looked. *Nothing*! You were a very pretty girl. You've hurt yourself for no reason." There were several seconds of pulsing silence, then she removed her hand but continued to stand there looking at me. "You *really didn't* have to do this to yourself."

Was that the truth? No, no. I couldn't allow it to be; not after all the pain.

"Yes, I did," I whispered, and fled, looking back as I turned the landing to see she was still there, watching me go, wearing the unhappiest expression I'd ever seen on her face. I tore down the stairs, nearly falling, and arrived at the bottom with my heart gone wild, trying to catch my breath. I'd made another mistake: I could change my face but everything else remained exactly the same.

Tennessee Williams knows something. When I was in summer stock years ago, I did several readings of Blanche from *A Streetcar Named Desire*, and choked over her lines: I *do* depend upon the kindness of strangers. And when it comes, it's a shock and a comfort every time—something I feel in dire need of, yet unworthy to receive. I yearn for people to be kind; I hope for it constantly. And when they are, it blinds and stuns me, renders me speechless. I respond to its display with complete trust. Someone who is kind will not hurt me, or tap-dance on my dreams, or shout with laughter at my thoughts. Kind people have room inside them for one more. They're not afraid other people will think they're foolish. They're simply not afraid.

For the most part, whatever kindness I possess instinctively usually directs itself toward females. Perhaps it's because *I* know something: all the different ways in which, intentionally or not, unkind people can hurt us.

Who I am is often subject to whom I'm with. If I'm with someone who makes me nervous—and unfortunately, most people do—I'm the me I like least. When I'm in the company of someone with whom I'm relaxed and at ease, then I'm someone else—the best and realest person in me. I have people inside to meet whatever situations life presents. I have bravado, if it's needed; confidence, too.

Not in how I look, though; I don't know if that'll ever come. I'm five-five, weigh a hundred and eight pounds and when I look in the mirror, all I see is fat. If I didn't love food and the preparation of it, I'd have been anorexic. As it is, I'm dangerously close: if I eat even an extra cracker, I feel guilty. I've stopped talking quite so much about it now, people think I'm just plumping for compliments.

My friends long ago accepted my peculiarities, but strangers think I'm plain looney. What is really nice is that it no longer totally undermines me to have people think I'm bats. I'm nervous, optimistic, trusting, suspicious; I'm shy, curious, bold and timid; somewhere mid-chest I have a small calm area, and very little upsets that hard-won, sweet, interior balance.

Sixteen

IN APRIL, that same year, as I rode home from Lexie's house one Saturday night, the front wheel of the bike hit an icy patch on the road. I lost control and flew forward over the handlebars to find myself lying on my left side in the middle of the road, with a piercing pain in my elbow. Struggling to my feet, I walked the bike the rest of the way home, knowing my mother would go wild. Another accident would confirm her belief in my troublemaking, troublesome qualities. Maybe, I began to think, she's right. Maybe there's something about me that's terribly wrong.

At the emergency room at the hospital, my arm was X-rayed, then put in a sling. Told it was only a hairline fracture, we were sent home.

Mother was cheerful about it all, and said, "God help the guy marries you! He'll go broke paying the medical bills."

"It was an accident."

"It's always accidents with you. You want me to help you get undressed?"

"No, thanks. That's all right. I'll do it."

She stood by while I grappled one-handedly with my clothes. I looked down at my underpants. Rust stains. From the bike. God! No. Not rust stains. "It's finally happening," I said. And looking quite wistful, smiling, she went off to get me a belt and a pad.

Later on, in the dark, I sat in bed plummeting into the depths of a depression so thick, so dark I didn't think I'd ever be able to climb up out of it; I knew with certainty that everything was going to get worse. Because I was finally a woman. And Daddy would become even more determined than ever to make his way into my body now that it had proved itself normal after all.

What I hadn't anticipated, though, was the sudden, quite violent awakening of my sexual responses. The caresses I'd received so passively for eight years now created sensations, reactions I had to struggle to conceal. Mindlessly, I'd find myself enjoying the stimulation of his attentions. And then, appalled, my self-hatred assuming newer and bigger proportions, I began a concerted effort to stifle my responses, bury them; rejecting them one by one, until nothing he could do made me feel anything at all. I was wood. I was concrete. I could effectively segregate sensation out of my body, controlling it and my feelings with deadly determination. I would allow nothing to move me from the stiffly inflexible posture I maintained throughout our sessions.

The effort totally exhausted me. I sleepwalked through the days feeling drugged, drained. A wool sweater next to my skin made me want to scream. Any article of clothing that I thought didn't look good on me filled me with panic, and even more of a desire to scream. Having to wear bulky pads between my thighs kept me on the verge of hysteria for four or five days a month. Without warning, I'd choke up and start to cry. I awakened most mornings to find myself in tears. Night after night I stared at the red-blue-red of the ceiling, and wondered if there was any chance at all that this would ever end, if I'd ever somehow manage to get away. I thought constantly of dying. And I fought down something inside me that jumped up in a rage at the slightest hint of unfairness or injustice. I felt like a seething, jittery mess of hot wires. Anything at all might blow my circuits.

By now, I had a full-scale smoking habit. On lunch hours, with my cigarettes hidden behind the lining of my handbag, I'd walk a block or two away from the school to smoke. I was the only girl in the class who smoked. I didn't do it, as Lexie initially accused shortly after the start of our friendship, ". . . to be different. That's the only reason someone starts smoking." I did it, I'd explained, "Because it's mine and it makes me feel better. If you don't want me to smoke when I come here, I won't. I'll understand."

"It doesn't matter," she said indulgently. "I was just wondering why. I should've known you'd have a reason. You always do."

"Why do you say that?"

"Because you do. Everything you do, if someone asks you why, you've always got a reason. As if you're right there ready, in case someone wants to know why."

"Is that bad?"

"I don't know. I don't have reasons for everything I do. Sometimes I wish I did. Maybe it's a good thing to know why you do the things you do."

"But I just do the things I . . . have to do."

"Well," she'd said philosophically, "at least you're different in that, too."

"Because I know why I do what I do?"

"Because you wouldn't be you if you didn't."

I finally began to grow, getting taller, then taller. And at last I had breasts. Small ones. Which was disappointing in view of the premium placed, by everyone around me at school, on big ones. Big breasts somehow translated into desirable, sexual. I was automatically eliminated, displeased on the one hand, uncaring on the other. Rather than being reassured that I had not been damaged, I was more frightened than ever. Particularly when Daddy commented approvingly on the changes, as if he'd created me, his personal machine, and I was at last taking shape according to his specifications.

I tore away from his hateful inspection to lock myself into the bathroom, quaking with anger and the steadily building need to escape. I dug my nails into the palms of my hands, despising all the female parts of me because he approved of them. I grabbed handfuls of my hair and pulled until I was conscious only of the pain.

I began to resist in earnest, saying no, simply not being available on a Tuesday or Thursday night. I believed I was risking my life as well as testing the perimeters of a small new freedom I'd taken for myself when I went out to ride aimlessly around town on my bike, or to visit Helen—but not too often because I was afraid to overdo it. I'd just go out—anywhere —as long as I was out. Eyes click-clicking, I was searching for something, someone, somewhere. I stepped through the door of the house on Indian Valley like a fugitive; never questioned, never questioning.

That spring, when I was sixteen, upon receiving a notice from the landlord that he was going to increase the rent, my mother announced, "Over my dead body! I'll *buy* a house and to hell with this whole renting business."

A house of our own? I went off to school with my head filled with all the pictures of the lovely rooms in all the magazines I'd ever seen. I was going to live in a proper house with a beautiful room of my own.

I couldn't believe how quickly it happened. A few weeks later, my mother announced she'd bought a place. She and Daddy came to pick me up after school near the end of May, to take me to see the new house. I sat in the back of the car, my eyes closed to discourage motion sickness, filled with a thumping anticipation, excitement.

The new house.

Miles and miles away, so far north of the city that the pavement on Bathurst ended and we drove along on dirt for several more miles before turning off onto a treeless street lined into infinity with identical bungalows on either side. Monuments in an outsized cemetery. I knew later on exactly what Malvina Reynold's song, "Little Boxes," was all about. I'd lived there.

"You didn't *buy* this!" I cried, unable to keep a tremor out of my voice; and at once felt guilty at the look of smashed pleasure creasing my mother's face. I knew this house meant a great deal to her and I didn't want to spoil it, but I couldn't contain my welling, bitter disappointment. "It's really awful! Why didn't you at least wait until we all had a chance to see it? How could you just go ahead and buy something like this without even asking us if we liked it? I have to live here, too."

My room: about ten feet square, one window, one closet; a box within the box.

I wanted to be able to like it, to say all the things that would make her feel satisfaction in her decision, but I could only believe that her determination not to spend one unnecessary cent was taking us into this tiny cage where we'd all have to live pressed up tight against each other like prisoners.

Until the end of the year I was going to have to try to catch the one bus an hour and commute downtown to school.

I wouldn't be able to see Lexie anymore, except during school hours. Or Helen. There was no way I could possibly ride my bike the forty-odd miles back and forth to her house. No movies, no sidewalks, no paved roads, no trees, not even sewers.

I leaned against the living room wall while my mother and father went to have a look around down in the cellar, feeling cheated, beaten; depression a black bag over my head. Cement in my mouth, screams howling inside my skull. *I'll die here I'll never make it out of here they'll bury me in that little back-yard beside the septic tank.*

I kept wanting the world to turn beautiful, to surround myself with soft things, green things, good-looking things. My parents kept erecting new and shinier lines of barbed wire to hold me in.

Daddy with his neverending demands, his meaningful looks, his whispered commands; Daddy constantly grumbling about his bosses and all the people who were out to get him. My mother despairingly complaining about *his* complaining. The sound of their voices, raised in argument, was like a long nail being slowly driven into my skull. I wanted my mother to

cross her arms over her chest and at last tell him to get out and
never come back. When I asked her once why she didn't do
it, she looked at me as if I'd just landed in a spaceship and
said, "Sure! And what would we live on?" Unarguable logic:
we couldn't survive without Daddy's salary.

Bobby and I both—at different times—offered to quit school
and go to work so that we'd have a means of support, but
she simply smiled sadly and said she wished we could, but two
kids couldn't bring home much, certainly not enough to live
on. "And what would I do?" she said. "I'm not trained to
do anything."

We could have done it. I was convinced the three of us
could have worked and lived together in a state of relative
peace. But I understood, finally, that she was afraid. And I
also understood that shame was a factor in her considerations,
because a woman got married and was provided for by her
husband. What would her sisters think if she threw the old man
out, let her two kids take jobs and even took a job herself?

From the first moment we moved into that tiny bungalow,
everything became more nightmarish. On the two evenings a
week we were alone there, Daddy began to whistle for me,
scratching at my bedroom door; he summoned me like an ani-
mal, calling me like a good dog, come! I begged, pleaded,
shouted, wept, and tried to reason with him, but nothing,
nothing would persuade him to stop. And every time I heard
his fluting whistle, or his fingernails rasp on my door, I felt
sure I was losing my mind under the pressure of my revulsion
for him, my clawing need to scream. I knew if I ever started
to scream, I'd probably never stop.

I braved the eyes of that face, my face, in the bathroom
mirror with hate steaming out of my nostrils on every breath.
Jaws locked, I grabbed a handful of my hair and the scissors
and started to hack my way through. The basin filled with
my hair and overflowed onto the floor; hair everywhere. Until, out of breath as if I'd run several miles, my hand with the
scissors came to rest on the rim of the basin and I blinked at
the transformed reflection: a someone with short curling hair

and huge, staring eyes in a pale face. A prisoner of war. Blinking, I looked down and let go of the scissors, to scoop up my hair. *My hair oh my God my hair what did I do!* On my knees on the bathroom floor holding an armload of hair matted with tears I couldn't stop crying.

My mother said, "You did a pretty good job. It looks kinda cute."

"If you don't stop I'll kill you! So help me God I'll kill you! Stop it! If you want me, call me, knock at my door like a human being. I swear to God if you don't stop I'LL KILL YOU!"

He'd just grin, eyes slitted, before shuffling off to undress and wait for me. I looked around at the too-close walls of the house with rage surging inside me; I wanted to smash down the walls with my fists and explode out of that house like a rocket. Powerless, hopeless, I got up and went into the bathroom to wash between my legs.

I used some of the money he gave me to take driving lessons and get my license, then suffered through several additional bargained-for hours in the bedroom in order to have the use of the car one or two evenings a week, and on Sunday afternoons to go see Helen.

During the last weeks of school, I rode downtown each morning with Daddy, and counted license plates in order not to have to hear what he said. Once, parked at the St. Clair loop waiting to pick up my mother and aunt after a bingo game, I counted all the bricks in the face of the church in front of which we were parked so that I wouldn't have to listen to him. What he said invariably had to do with my body: what he wanted to do to it, long-range plans he had for it. He believed he was going to have me forever. I'd simply stay in the house, continue on at school or at work, and dedicate my life and body to him. He was insane. I wanted to rip his throat out, silence him permanently.

When he changed the subject to his only other theme—the matter of his job—with that drum beating away in his temple,

I heard his words rattle against the cage of my indifference with foreboding; I knew he'd soon be out looking for a new job where he'd be appreciated, where he wouldn't have some asshole on his back all the time, out to get him. He'd had three jobs since coming home from the War. Between the first and the second were quite a few years, but between the second and third was not a lot of time. And he'd only been at this third place for a few months. My mother was living in a permanent state of panic, constantly trying to tell him that if he'd just shut up and do his job he wouldn't have any problems. But he didn't listen. He'd shout at her, or slam out of the room.

He'd started the skid. A long, loud decline.

On the last day of school, I went to an employment agency, advanced my age two years to eighteen—knowing they'd never bother to check—handed in an error-free typing test at a hundred-and-six words per minute and secured a job that same afternoon with an engineering company, to start work the following Monday.

There were just two of us in the secretarial cubicle: Tracy, the woman who'd hired me and who ran the office, and me. There were twenty odd draughtsmen and engineers at drawing boards in the main body of the office. The building was on Yonge just north of Eglinton, quite a distance from where we now lived in Downsview. One of the partners lived even farther north than I did and offered me a ride to work each morning. He picked me up on Bathurst at the corner of my street and we drove along in silence to the office. I knew him to be a kind and loving family man, yet I expected, every time, that he'd pull over somewhere and throw himself on me. I expected it of every man with whom I found myself alone, even the husbands of the women I sometimes babysat for. They'd run me home at two or three in the morning on a weekend and I'd sit as close to the door as I could, shivering so hard that I stuttered when spoken to; just waiting for them to stop the car and rip my clothes, expose themselves briefly before yanking apart my thighs and murdering me with their deathly little clubs. Any one of them could have done it, and in perfect safety, because I wouldn't have dared to tell. I believed that men could do just about anything to women and we'd simply bear it.

When I imagined something like this happening to me, I had a vision of madness so complete in its detail that I could almost feel it. All it would take to turn that vision into reality was some man forcing himself into me, scalding my interior with his body. Even when I was alone with my Uncle Jake now, I found it hard to speak coherently. His every gesture was suspect. I loved him. Why was I afraid of him? I knew him, knew he'd never harm me. But there existed between us a tension that kept me out of the embraces he sought to offer, and I was reluctant to accept his affectionate kisses. The inner shuddering would start up if I found myself alone with him —or any man—and nothing I could tell myself stopped it.

I liked the job, gladly turned over half my salary to my mother, and spent my lunch hours in the library around the corner from the office. I was intrigued by the English librarian who often stopped to smile and comment on the books as I checked them out.

"Interested in the theater, are you?" she asked.

"Movies, really. I like to read about these people."

"Do you?" She looked approving, and I warmed to her.

Pamela.

She was in her late thirties and had short brown hair, an unusual but appealing face with an exceptional, beautifully defined mouth that was perfect even without lipstick. She was, I learned quickly, eccentric in a self-deprecating fashion, with a wonderfully nutty sense of humor, and appreciative of my attempts to make her laugh. She was forever knitting something that never got finished because, halfway through, she'd discover some error she'd made several inches back and tear the whole thing out, to begin again. She had a pleasant, theatrically trained speaking voice, a passion for health foods, for brown sugar in her tea, and for bread she called "natural" that was on the verge of turning green. She fascinated me.

I wrote her a note, pushed it across the counter as I was checking out some books one afternoon, and she looked up, surprised.

"It's for you to read later."

"Thank you, sweetie." She played out the little charade, slipped the note furtively into her pocket, and saw me on my way with a smile. I liked her enormously—she was different. I was beginning to understand and appreciate what Lexie had tried to tell me that day we first had lunch together.

Sitting on one of the benches outside the library, Pamela asked, "Do you always present yourself by letter?"

"I don't know. I guess, now that I think about it, I do. It's easier to write down what I want to say. Then I know I won't make a mistake, say the wrong thing."

"It's charming," she declared. "Absolutely charming. You're so refreshing after all that frightfully stale air in there." She indicated the library behind us.

"Don't you like working there?"

"It's just a job, sweetie, with some dreary women. Now,"—she crossed her legs and settled herself on the bench facing me —"tell me about you. What do you do? Are you studying theater?"

"Me? I'm still in school."

"Ah!" She nodded sagely. "I thought you looked rather young."

"I'm not young," I said soberly.

"No," she agreed, "you're not, are you, sweetie?"

I loved it when she called me that. It meant she liked me. And I liked her. She was so interesting, so pleasant to be with. We began to meet regularly for lunch. She told me she'd studied for the theater, and had been in the Oxford Repertory Company. I was entranced. Perhaps, as Lexie had tried to explain, there was something of value in being different.

On one of my Sunday afternoon visits, it was Mrs. MacKay who came to the door and not Helen. At once I sensed something was wrong.

"Helen's in the garden, dear," she said, and led me by the hand through the house and out a side door to the grassed area between the house and the garage.

Helen was in a wooden garden chair, her head resting against the back, eyes closed, her hands lying loosely on the arms of the chair, fingers slightly curled. I slipped into the chair opposite, reluctant to disturb her. Something was happening here. The sensation became more pronounced by the second. I put my handbag down on the grass and looked at her, thinking her asleep; wondering if I shouldn't wait inside the house, or perhaps go home. I was deciding to get up and go when, her eyes still closed, she said, "I spent hours yesterday and today tidying my closet, the dresser drawers. It was awful!"

"Why did you do it then?" I asked, finding it odd to be talking to her without being able to see her eyes. Despite the fact that it was difficult for me to look directly into people's eyes, and easier to follow their mouths when they spoke, it was disconcerting to be having this conversation with her and not have her look at me.

She laughed and opened her eyes.

"What," she smiled, "if I were hit by a truck or something? I'd be mortified to think of people ploughing through that mess of accumulated trash. A good twenty-five years of it."

"You shouldn't say things like that." Darts of alarm were striking my chest, eyes and throat.

"Nonsense!" she said gaily. "You're always so serious. You'd have said it yourself if you'd seen the clutter I'd managed to create up there. Let's go inside, shall we. I think I've had enough sun for today."

"You're very tan," I said, caught by a mental picture of her standing unmoving in the middle of a road and a truck bearing down on her.

"I've been sitting out here quite a lot. I love the sun."

"It makes me feel sick, sunbathing. Sunshine makes me sneeze, too."

She laughed.

She looked lovely, I thought, in her sleeveless bright green

dress of some silky fabric. I admired the shape of her bare
arms, the smooth slope of her chest, the soft matte look to
her skin. Nothing had changed: I still wanted to be her. What,
I wondered, did she think when I stared at her this way? She
was plainly aware of my eyes, but remained still until
I looked into the somehow glowing brown of her eyes. Then
she turned and walked across the grass.

Inside, the house was dark and cool after the heated glare
of the garden. She stopped in the dining room with her hand
on the kitchen door.

"I'm going to have something to drink. Will you join me?"

"Yes, all right. Please." Everything was the same, but different. Did she realize it was the first time I'd ever said yes
to one of her offers of food and drink?

"Go along into the living room," she said as she pushed
through into the kitchen. "I'll be with you in a minute or two."

For a change, I sat on the sofa in the bay of the front windows, and turned to look out at the street. The trees were
brilliantly green; the street itself looked bleached by the bright
sun. Over everything lay a glaze of hot stillness. I turned back
slowly to look at the room, loving this place, watching—as
if from a distance—as she came in and sat, unexpectedly, beside me on the sofa, handing me a glass of iced tea. It was the
first time we hadn't taken our usual seats by the side windows.

"Cheers!" She smiled and put her mouth to the glass, looking at me over the top of it.

For some reason, I thought about the picture she'd shown
me of herself at seventeen. I must have asked about her childhood or something. She'd gone upstairs and come back with
a large portrait that had been taken upon her graduation from
high school: a girl with long, softly curling hair and a pure,
pretty face. I'd studied the photograph thinking she looked
like someone who would have been friends with me, no matter what age she was. I'd have liked and admired her as much
at seventeen as I did now at forty-three.

"You seem so . . . happy," I said, returning her smile. What
is it? I wondered. What's happening here? The air was confused.

"Why not?" she said with a light shrug. "It's a glorious day."

Apropos of nothing, except that I'd always wondered, I said, "You have a middle name. What does the A stand for?"

She set down her glass, tucked her legs under and, with her arm along the back of the sofa, sat facing me. It was the closest we'd been since our collision on the stairs at school, several years earlier.

"It's a perfectly hideous name." She smiled, showing her teeth; her eyes still held that same indefinable something. She seemed playful, I decided.

"What is it?" *You're so close I could touch you why can't I let myself touch you I want to so much your face your eyes all the dozens of times we've sat together here talked to each other all the times I've wanted to tell you how much I love you but haven't had the courage.*

"Guess!" she challenged, and ran her fingers through her hair, grinning now.

"Okay. Alice?"

"No."

"Amanda?"

"No."

"Alison?"

"That's quite a nice name. I wish it were."

"Annabel?"

"No."

"Agatha?"

"That's dreadful! That's even worse than mine."

"I give up. What is it?"

"I'll give you a hint," she said, plainly enjoying the game. "In it's short form, it's quite a popular name."

"Now I'm really confused. I can't think of a single name like that."

"I want you to know," she said, more seriously, "that I *never* tell anyone my middle name. *You* have one. Tell me yours!"

"It's awful," I protested, flushing, unprepared for this turn about.

"Well, then," she said, "you tell me your awful name and I'll tell you mine."

"That's not fair!" I argued, having fun.

"But of course it's fair. It's absolutely fair."

"Oh, all right." With a groan, I told her, then covered my eyes with one hand.

"Now that is a perfectly *nice* name," she said. "Not awful in the least."

"It's *horrible*! Yours *couldn't* be worse than that!"

"It is, I assure you."

"Well, *tell* me then!"

"It's—Abigail. *Abigail!*" She grimaced, throwing up her hands in a gesture of hopelessness, and said, "It's really hard to forgive Mother for that. Gail would have been nice. But Abigail?"

I looked at her, trying the name out in my head.

"Well?" she said.

"It's not so bad," I lied.

"You're lying!" she accused, pointing a red-tipped finger at me.

"You're right," I admitted, wanting to laugh. "It's about the worst name I ever heard." The laughter erupted out of my mouth; tears spilled from my eyes with the force of it.

She put her hand over her mouth and began to laugh. We sat rocking with laughter, our eyes wet with it; laughing, so close together. Her hands moved through the air between us, reaching to touch. One hand touched mine for a moment and our eyes met. *Don't touch me please God don't I want to put my head on your shoulder feel your hand on my hair have you tell me you love me that you always wanted a child a girl like me.*

"You're so damned truthful," she said, smoothly altering the gesture and thrusting into her pocket for a handkerchief. She dabbed at her eyes, then sat back bunching the handkerchief in her hand.

"Is that bad?" I asked, my voice thin somehow after the volume of our laughter.

"No, no. It's delightful, not bad at all. Why do you worry so about things being bad? It isn't bad to have the sense of humor you do. It's wonderful. You're the only person I know who can always make me smile, cheer me up. How on earth could something like that be bad?"

I cheered her up? I hadn't known that. Did it mean that there was something I actually gave her, that I didn't just take from her all the time?

"I don't know," I said slowly. "I hate being a clown."

"Then don't be. Just be yourself."

"I don't know who myself is. Would it be all right if I smoke?"

In answer, she slid an ashtray along the top of the coffee table, her voice very soft as she said, "There's quite a wall around you."

I froze.

"Every so often," she went on in that same tone, "I see you peeking out at me and it's encouraging. So many conflicting qualities in you—a bit of a Puritanical streak, and a good deal of the artist. But all of it's behind such a thick, high wall. Do you think you'll ever be able to come out from behind it?"

"Oh . . . I . . ." I choked up, had to stop, wait a moment and then start again. "I don't know."

"What do you want?" she asked softly, leaning a little closer to me.

"I don't know."

"Don't you?" Her eyes burned into mine.

"I'm not sure."

"It's all right," she coaxed. "Tell me."

"I'd like to be . . . you."

"No!" She shook her head emphatically. "Be *you*. Other people's lives only seem enviable when we're young and uncertain. Don't envy what you *think* I am," she said gently. "Don't! My life is the way I've chosen it to be, the way circumstances have shaped it, the way I'm happiest. It wouldn't fit you. You have to have your own life, not someone else's you've borrowed in your mind."

"But I hate my life, *hate* it!"

"You'll grow up and change it."

"But I've already been alive for sixteen years and I can't change anything. I can't even imagine getting to be twenty-one."

"You will," she said confidently. "You'll be here long after the rest of us are gone. And you'll do all sorts of things. I'd like to be around to see."

"You will," I said, ignoring all the signs, the subtle changes. "I'll always want to come here, be with you."

"Do the things you do for yourself, not because you hope to please someone else. When I say that, it doesn't mean I'm not interested. It means *you're* the one who has to choose and decide. You don't need anyone else's approval. Not really."

"I don't know what you mean."

She sighed and I watched her breasts lift under the green dress, then quickly raised my eyes to her face.

"You do," she said patiently. "You grasp things at once, but then, for some reason, you become doubtful. Trust yourself. You have everything you need."

"You scare me when you talk about getting hit by a truck . . . when you say things like that."

"Oh, now," she smiled, resting her head on the back of the sofa, "you wouldn't care to be in an accident and be taken off to the hospital with safety pins holding your underwear together, would you?"

"God, no!" I said, blushing at the idea.

"Well, that's the sort of thing I mean. That's all."

I went away convinced I'd been told something of importance, that I'd been given a message that hadn't any words. It was a long time before all the pieces fell together and I was able to see it.

Often in conversations with others, and often when I least anticipate, my eyes return to the remembered images of that visit. I see her in the garden, her eyes closed and her mouth opening to speak like some exotic flower blossoming in the hot sun. The way she smiled, her eyes and her laughter. Softness and a certain sadness. She was more beautiful to me then than anyone I could imagine.

On a book promotion tour three years ago I met Harry. He was good-looking, charming, and knocked out by the novel I was promoting. In the course of my stay in Detroit, we had dinner—a group of us, including the local publisher's rep. After that, Harry kept popping up at radio stations, and at bookstores where I was to do signing sessions. He engineered it so that he could drive me to the airport at the end of my stay. We talked in the Admiral's Club before my flight was called, and he said he'd telephone. I went home to Connecticut dreaming. A few days later, he wrote and enclosed several clippings. Then came postcards. He telephoned two or three times a day. I was dazed, delighted. Someone I liked actually liked me. We made arrangements for him to fly out and visit.

He arrived and, from the first, danced attention on me, even held my hand when we walked. I wanted it, didn't want it, wondered what the hell was wrong with me. He was generous to a fault: I faulted him. I had to keep on saying, Thank you, but no. I really can't let you buy me that. Or that, or that. But he insisted on buying something and I ended up with an exquisite lace shirt. I was filled with awkward embarrassment. Accustomed to giving, I find it hard to receive graciously. I did try. But I still felt I had to give him something and found some imported cologne, which he accepted with touching delight.

Inevitably, we got into bed together. Once naked, I became a closet critic, my brain actively recording every detail and nuance of the performance. I needed holding, and confirmation of my desirability, so I threw the critic off the bed, opened my arms and closed my eyes.

The next morning, he arose bouncy and elated. I despised both of us. I couldn't rid myself of the sticky depression that settled on me like flypaper. It was the same old thing again: I'd met someone, made love with him and, in the morning, awakened to hatred and despair.

While we were in the kitchen having coffee, there was a sudden, tremendous crash. I got up, walked into the living room, and looked up to see a tree on the skylight. The safety glass was creaking threateningly and the usually bright room was dark. I went outside to assess the damage. Obviously the tree had weakened in the course of an unusually rainy autumn and the rain and wind of the previous night had finally toppled it. The house looked dwarfed beneath the tree.

Harry grabbed his camera and began to take pictures from various angles while I stood gazing at the house and the tree. "Oh boy," he said, emitting a low whistle. "Afraid it got your car, too."

There were dings and dents all the way from the front of the hood to the rear of the trunk. My mood darkened more.

Throughout the rest of the morning and into the afternoon, friends and neighbors kept coming to the door to say, "You know there's a tree on your house?" It was ridiculous and I could see the funny side of it, but I was feeling worse by the minute. Finally I said "Let's get out of here. I'll show you Westport, if you like."

"Fine," he said, and we got in the car and took off.

I had to buy something, needed to spend some money in order to cheer myself up. So I bought a new stereo system and Harry helped me load the various boxes into the car. I was more depressed than before as we drove back to Darien. Not only was there a tree on the house, but I'd spent several hundred dollars for something I didn't really need. I hated having a witness to what I knew was my increasingly bad behavior.

Harry offered to leave. I was so grateful I was able to begin liking him again. I admired him for having the sensitivity not to want to stay when things were obviously not good. He was a nice man, a lovely person; bright, intelligent, funny and generous. He didn't leave. I spent that evening and all the next day still searching for flaws, hoping to find something in him upon which to pin my dislike of us both. But he really was too nice.

The day after he left, flowers arrived. Two arrangements

—one for Jossie and one for me. He continued to telephone two and three times a day until I had to ask him to stop, saying I couldn't take that many calls from anyone. Astonishingly, he took me at my word and wasn't shattered, emasculated or hostile. He began to call once a week.

We got together again a month or so later. Same action, same results.

We met again. The same, the same.

The fault wasn't in Harry, but in me. What do I want? I asked myself. The answer: about ninety percent of what he was offering. Someone who liked and respected me, who lived far enough away not to be able to inflict himself on my rigidly disciplined schedules for writing, who had the money to be able to do whatever he chose. And I *liked* him. So why did I keep waking up the morning after filled with such violently negative feelings?

Through the following months, we talked regularly on the telephone. He sent postcards he'd photographed and printed himself, and letters, funny cards, little notes. He continued to respect my declared need for time alone and I began to trust him. In the interim, came my brief romance with another woman, an experience which clarified many things, but one in particular: I didn't want her, but I did very much want more chances with Harry. So, I arranged to meet him again.

I went into this meeting with my head firmly turned to ON, and told myself I would not ask or expect more of Harry than he was able to give. I would not be awkward or uncomfortable, but would be myself and allow him room to be himself. I would not make unfair or cruel judgments and I would not condemn him because he was a man and wanted me.

We met in Toronto because I was arranging a signing session at the Canadian Booksellers Association Convention and there were final details to be ironed out. He came along to a meeting with the local distributor, and to dinner later with my brother Will and his lady. We had a wonderful weekend. I began to have some sense of what a good relationship we might manage to create.

I returned home to Connecticut happy; I'd spent two nights in the same bed with Harry and not only had I actually been able to sleep, but I hadn't come to in the morning with a crippling hate hangover.

We continued to have long, laughing telephone conversations. He sent more cards and letters and amusing clippings. We got through a year. I was scheduled for another promotion tour, this one a month-long stint in Australia and New Zealand. I spoke to Harry before I left and he spoke of our getting together when I returned. The day before I left, in the mail was a Xeroxed map of Australia with good luck wishes and kisses scrawled all over it, from Harry. I went off thinking about him, and looked forward to seeing him when I got back.

Back home in Connecticut at the beginning of October, I called to tell him about the tour. He sounded tired, atypically down, but said he still planned to come visit in a few weeks' time—as soon as he got over this damned cold he couldn't seem to shake.

November came and went. I was busy writing another book. I wondered why he hadn't called, but it was nearly Christmas and I imagined he must be busy. I was preparing for my annual trip to England to see Norman and Lola, and Walt was taking Jossie off for their usual Christmas vacation in Antigua. Wondering why I hadn't heard from Harry, I flew off. I thought about him often during those two weeks. He'd won my trust and affection and I hoped he hadn't lost interest in me, because what I was feeling was something like love for him.

Christmas was wonderful. The Australian tour had changed me. A month in the company of a twenty-two-year-old woman who was completely intolerant of the views of others prompted me to acknowledge much of my own intolerance, to recognize this truth about myself and allow it to go. I liked people. I was no longer frightened. I was able, for the first time, to accept the people I met in the course of the tour and like them for what they had to offer, not condemn them for failing to live up to my impossible expectations. I had taken a big step forward; I felt calm and unpressured—from without or within—and ready to care about people in a very real way.

When I got home, there was a message that Harry was dead. He'd died while I was with Norman and Lola—of cancer. Three weeks from beginning to end. I was devastated. I'd cared and hadn't had the courage to tell him. I cried at night for weeks, missing him, ashamed of my cowardice, and promised myself never to make the same mistakes again.

But I did care. And he helped me.

Last year, I cared about another man for a time.

Next year, I may do even better. I'm learning how to feel.

Seventeen

WHEN I was a child, the neighborhood kids played a game called "Manhunt." It was simple: someone was picked to be "it," and the rest of the kids ran off to hide. It was played only at night, and the territory available to hide in encompassed an entire block—three streets, an unlit lane that ran behind the stores on Queen Street, and all the cellar entryways, dark recesses between houses, front porches, in fact, any place at all. The game terrified me but I never turned down an opportunity to play. I was invariably scared of the hiding place itself and of coming out and getting caught. But I'd stay hidden until I guessed the game had probably ended, then I'd crawl out from beneath the porch where I'd been squatting, or step out from the deep doorway down the lane, or climb out of the window-well beside some house and walk home.

While counting down the minutes in my hiding place, I'd go off dreaming and the time would pass quite quickly. I was even able to avoid thoughts of the rats and mice that were known to lurk in dark, damp places like this, as well as the bugs and potential ghosts. I dreamed myself out of my life and into other places, projecting scenarios of my future and accomplishments.

I was always a little sorry when the game had to end. Despite the fact that terror was for me the key element in playing it, I was afforded, each time, a rare opportunity to examine slowly the dimensions of the world of possibilities.

When I consider it now, much of the seven years I spent in the house in Connecticut were like a long, long game of "Manhunt." There was no one playing "it," but I did have a splendid hiding place and ample opportunity not only to dream but to put those dreams down on paper and, in the process, create a career. I was, however, afraid to come out: I'd hidden myself well and didn't want to get caught and have to be the next "it." Being "it" meant running up and down dark streets, looking in doorways and under front porches, searching for the other players. It was too exposed a position to play; it was infinitely preferable to be one of the half-dozen kids who got to hide.

There were times when I was overtaken by a terrible, complete and inexplicable sadness; a certain melancholy light tinted everything I said, did, thought, and felt. It was a sadness that made me want to lie down and never get up again. There were never any warnings or hints that it was coming. It simply settled down over me and I'd have to find some way out of it. Going shopping helped. Something new, regardless of whether or not I could afford it, helped lift me past the sadness. Perhaps in defiance of my mother, money had become most useful to me as an antidepressant. I'd go out and buy my safe passage from a depression at the movies, or on classical cassettes, or three new books to read. I'd buy it at the shoe store, or the drugstore, or even at the supermarket.

It took me a very long time to realize that my safe hiding place was becoming a prison, and that the sadness I felt was due to the loss of motion and growth in my life. I'd arrived at a plateau. The house I loved was simply a house, after all, and thirty years from now, some other woman might stand —as I had done, dozens of times—in that wonderful living room, silently intoning, "I love this house, love it. I'll never leave here." This realization was startling, but also freeing. I could go somewhere else, have a different sort of life. I was

starting to feel ready for that and began to consider where
Jossie and I might live, what place would offer what we both
needed. The desire to go back to Canada took root in my brain.
Could I do that? Could I pick up, pack everything, take Jossie
and move? Would I be able to face the memories, and the
changes—both in me and in the city—that I was bound to
find? I had no idea, and was afraid it might end up being a
move backwards. But more and more strongly, I wanted to
go back.

I worked out the summer and set off for my first day at the
new high school both optimistic and depressed. It seemed I
was back to square one, starting all over again in a new place,
without friends. The school wasn't even finished. Carpenters
and workmen wandered around in the halls during classes,
lending an industrial, temporary atmosphere to the place.

I felt old and exhausted from struggling, certainly too old
still to be in school. On my first break, I left the building,
crossed Finch—then a dirt road—and leaned against a tree to
smoke a cigarette, idly aware of traffic on the main road. I
wished I were somewhere else. As always, September filled
me with running-away fever, and I longed to fly off. I missed
my job, and Pamela.

Tracy had told me, "Any time you want a job, you've got
one," and I would rather have been back at the office, in the
cubicle with her. I wanted to be on the bench outside the
library on my lunch hour, listening to Pamela talk about her
one-day plans to return to England, and about her peculiar-
sounding husband; about her childhood in Sussex and the
beauty of the countryside there; about the watercolors she'd
done of the house she grew up in with the river nearby and
the flowers and trees; about her two cats and her house here
with the garden in the rear and how the cats often brought
her gifts of dead birds and mice.

I stood by the tree thinking how easy it would be just to
walk away from the school, hitch a ride home, throw some
things in a bag and leave. My mother would probably be out

shopping. I still had a little money left from my job, as well
as some decent-looking clothes I'd bought, and made. I'd find
a room downtown and fix it up. I could see the room: books
and plants on the windowsill, a bed, a desk and a closet. I'd
have a fully furnished home of my own.

Oh, sure. I'd find a room, fix it up, go to work, and one
night when I came in, my mother and father would be there
waiting to take me home again. I was a minor. And it was
their obvious intention to keep me with them until such time
as I either obtained a husband who would buy my way out,
or attained the age of twenty-one and was legally free to go.
How, I wondered, would I make it through four more years
in that house with Daddy?

A chubby, grinning boy ambled over the road toward me
carrying an impressive armload of books. "Boy!"—he smiled
—"Am I ever glad to find somebody else smokes around here.
Hi. I'm Don."

I told him my name and offered him a cigarette.

We smoked for a while in silence, covertly inspecting each
other. He had a wide, freckled face, black hair and brown
almost black eyes. He was an overweight kid with a nice face
and looked younger and more out of place than I did.

"What grade're you in?" I asked.

"Twelve. You?"

"Same."

I liked him. He didn't make me nervous; I knew he wasn't
someone who'd jump on top of me. I enjoyed his relaxed manner, his differentness, his pure babylike skin and wide, innocent
eyes with their long lashes. It was somehow reassuring to be
with him, perhaps because we both stood out a mile from the
rest of the kids. He was fat, and fat was something to make
fun of. I didn't find it so, and was glad to see Don take the rib-
bing he got with good-natured equanimity. He didn't seem to
mind. We developed a bantering, careless friendship that lasted
through the year and on into the next.

Three days a week, midmorning, we met out by the tree
for a cigarette. We lunched together most days in the school

cafeteria. Don would eat a hotdog in three bites, gulp down half a pint of orange drink, then get out his knitting and spout funny bits of his make-it-up-as-you-go-along personal philosophy. "He who hesitates is lost, but he who dies is dead," was one of his better ones.

The first time he produced the knitting, he explained, "I can't afford to buy a sweater like this. So I figured I'd make one."

He was doing a good job of it, following a complicated pattern. I'd eat my sandwiches and watch him. It was a peaceful interlude and I thought he had a lot of courage to brave the ongoing ridicule of the several hundred students who drifted past our table, most of whom seemed to feel it necessary to make an unkind remark about the fat boy with his knitting. I wondered if any of them ever noticed the sweetness of his smile, or the gentleness of his warm brown eyes, or his remarkable self-esteem. Don was the only tolerable part of my school life.

I was flunking every course except bookkeeping, typing and English. In zoology class, I had to stuff tissues up my nose in order not to get sick from the smell of formaldehyde. At the first sight of a dead frog waiting to be dissected one morning, I excused myself and went down to the office to ask to be withdrawn from the class. The school secretary kept glancing at me with an odd expression until I realized why and turned my back to unplug my nostrils. I was assigned a study hall in lieu of zoology. That was fine. I went out to have a cigarette by the tree.

I stood smoking, thinking about Daddy and wishing he'd finally get himself killed in one of the many collisions he'd been having lately. They were never his fault, yet he had had four head-ons in a year. I knew he drove as he always had—with one foot on the accelerator and the other on the brake, turning to talk to me or whomever happened to be in the car with him, paying no attention to the traffic until the last possible moment, then slamming on the brakes. I had a dreadful, permanent case of motion sickness as a result. And, one evening, my mother arrived home with a blood-soaked handkerchief held to her nose and mouth, saying, "The bastard's trying to kill me." He'd sent her into the windshield. She went off to the bathroom to bathe her face in cold water and I sat down on the telephone bench in the hallway, shaken.

It always scared me when she was ill or not feeling well, because she was all that stood between me and Daddy, and I needed her. Without her to divert his attention, I believed he'd devour me, then keep my bones under his bed.

Night after night I dreamed he was crouched at the foot of my bed, slowly unwinding like a cobra, his enormous mouth opening to swallow me feet first. I'd force myself awake and go sit on the floor by the window to have a cigarette, blowing the smoke out the window so my mother wouldn't find out.

Everywhere I looked people were being injured because of Daddy—accident victims in the hospital or in court for the hearings, my mother in the bathroom bent over the sink applying a cold cloth to her split lip and bloodied nose. Bobby, away now at college, was mute with rage in my father's presence and unable to remain in the same room with him for fear of killing him. Bobby could have done it, too. He had less control and just as volatile an anger as I.

There was such a lot of damage, but Daddy kept walking away from the scenes of the accidents without so much as a bruise, and he managed, with the various insurance settlements, to finance his way up to a nearly new Oldsmobile. He grinned as he cool-talked to his insurance man over the phone, then replaced the receiver saying, "I got the bastards by the balls. They'll pay." He was ecstatic with his collisions. Someone else was paying for a change, instead of him. He was getting back at all the bastards for the shit he had to take on the job. He was making "them" pay. We all found him more and more frightening and hateful. I wondered if he drove the streets at night looking for accidents he could make happen. I believed he did. I was convinced he was out there waiting for someone he could accidentally kill.

I took to going through the Yellow Pages and looked at the

dozens of doctors' names listed, wishing I knew which ones
specialized in what. I wanted to see a psychiatrist, to talk to
someone who could help. I thought, though, that Daddy was
the one who really needed it. He was crazy; I knew it and so
did my mother. When I casually expressed the desire to visit a
psychiatrist, she looked astonished, and exclaimed, "What're
you, nuts? Only crazy people go to psychiatrists."

We both burst out laughing.

"*He* should see one," I said.

"That son-of-a-bitch ought to be locked up somewhere,"
she agreed. "Now don't you let me hear any more talk from
you about psychiatrists. You think I want my sisters, my
friends to know what kind of troubles I've got?"

She couldn't bear the idea that someone might suspect her
life was anything but perfect. If my father started to carry on,
she'd run through the house closing the doors and windows,
crying, "God forbid the neighbors should hear!" before returning red-faced to do battle with him.

The no-talk rule applied in every area: I wasn't to discuss my
family or what went on inside our house with anyone. I'd long
since learned not to voice my observations or opinions of my
parents' behavior to Aunt Brenda because she'd be on the telephone to my mother at the first opportunity. And if I tried to
talk to Uncle Jake, it upset my aunt even more because she
wanted nothing and no one to interfere with the calm serenity
of their household. "Don't go bothering your uncle," she'd
warn, distressed by my audacity. "We can't have you doing
that." I loved her and felt sorry for her, and wondered if she
knew about the things that happened downstairs on the street.
The view from their new high-rise apartment on Avenue Road
was spectacular. The street noises were dulled, distant up there;
muffled by the thick, lined draperies and dense, underpadded
carpeting. I was, I thought, a street noise my aunt allowed in
in spite of herself because she loved me. She simply wished,
aloud, that she understood me. "I wish you did, too," I told
her, then hugged her. I couldn't argue with what she'd arranged for her life; I'd realized some time earlier that the world

was appalling and often terrifying to my aunt. A rude sales-person could shatter her and, once out of earshot and vision, send her into copious tears, while she mourned, "I don't *under-stand*." I'd comfort her and offer my arm as we rode on escalators or descended stairs, climbed into streetcars or just walked along the street. I felt older than she. She seemed to sense this and was relieved, even grateful. Uncle Jake and I were taller, more substantial than she and we ran glad interference between her and life's seamier realities. Frequently, my uncle's and my eyes met over her head and we exchanged a smile of complicity. We knew she was too fragile to make it outside on her own; we were there to protect her.

Don asked me out—to a dance. My first date. I said yes and agreed to drive and to pick him up at his house. Auntie Brenda gave me a full black velvet skirt she'd worn just once or twice, and Lexie gave me a sleeveless white top edged in lace that she'd made only to find it too small. I had high heels, nylons and an evening bag with a cloth rose pinned to it. I got dressed and made up, borrowed Daddy's car and went to Don's house to sit in the living room with his mother, trying not to laugh at this reversal in every known dating procedure, while I waited for Don to finish getting ready.

He looked sweeter than ever in his new suit. We got in the car and took off, heading for the Park Plaza downtown where the dance was to be held. I drove, smoking a cigarette, and felt suddenly so old I couldn't understand what I was doing with this seventeen-year-old boy in the car. Stopped for a light, I had to turn and look at him, gripped by the sad and sudden insight that Don and I would never be more than friends. I'd hoped he might be someone who'd rescue me, but the truth was I was more capable of rescuing *him*, had he required it.

We had a fine evening. We danced and talked and had our photograph taken together. I look so young in that photograph —we both do. Posed in front of some draperies, there I am with short curly hair, freckles and button earrings, wearing an expression that's giving nothing away and a semi-smile meant to hide the two slightly overlapped front teeth; a pretty girl who doesn't bear the slightest resemblance to the woman sitting here looking at her. Don looks more familiar to me than that girl does.

He asked me out again. I said yes, then went home to worry about what I'd do if he wanted to hold my hand or kiss me. Those things happened on second dates, I knew. I sat in a chair in the living room, trying to catch my breath. I'd started having a lot of trouble breathing and could rarely take a breath deep enough to fill my lungs. I gasped and panted, taking rapid, shallow breaths like a drowning swimmer.

I was ready almost two hours too early and flew to answer the doorbell when it rang, anxious to get there before Daddy could shuffle out of the kitchen where he sat in his undershirt, trousers and slippers, reading the paper. His book of crossword puzzles was folded open at the ready, and two packs of cigarettes sat stacked one atop the other, beside the puzzle book. The kitchen was gray with smoke.

I plastered on a smile and was halfway down the front walk before Don had had a chance to say hello. We were double-dating, it appeared. The boy had his father's car and drove with such reckless inattention that I sat half-paralyzed with fear, thoroughly nauseated, my right foot slamming repeatedly on a brake that wasn't there.

Once inside the movie theater, I relaxed beside Don, and we shared a box of popcorn through a run of *Tea and Sympathy*. I cried noiselessly into a fistful of tissues. The woman's beauty and the character's generosity of spirit represented all I wanted to be: soft, giving, caring. By the end of the film, I understood that even if I never did have any of those qualities, I could *pretend* to have them if I was an actress.

This novel thought preoccupied me in the restaurant while we all ate hamburgers, drank lemon or cherry Cokes and dipped our chips into puddles of ketchup. Don had his chips with gravy. I considered being an actress, being someone like Deborah Kerr; or playing those strong Bette Davis parts: women so independent and fierce and determined. Logically, the only way I could possibly have all these qualities was by acting. I certainly wasn't beautiful, but perhaps I could play character roles.

The evening was falling flat. Don and I tried to make conversation disinterestedly, but it wasn't working. What we had on our own alone together simply didn't materialize in the swishy, giddy company of these two other teenagers.

After the restaurant, the other two said they wanted to go to a lovers' lane they'd heard about. I imagined scenes from movies I'd seen: a view of the city framed by overhanging branches. This "lane" turned out to be a pitch-black industrial side road. The boy pulled up, turned the key and switched off the lights, plunging us into an absence of light so complete I felt fear crawling around on the back of my neck; I loathed the darkness.

I squinted out the window and wiped my damp palms on my skirt, wishing I could see, sensing something unpleasant was about to happen. I knew what the something was and didn't want it to happen. I longed to go home but didn't have the nerve to say so.

Don coughed artificially, then whispered, "Why don't you move over a little closer?"

Automatically, as I'd done for ten years upon command, I turned and moved down to put my face in his lap, prepared to perform. Then, suddenly realizing where I was and what I was doing and to whom, I closed my eyes for a moment. Don whispered hoarsely, "Hey! What're you doing?" Sick with shame, I leaped upright, frantically whispering a rambling, incoherent explanation about not being able to see in the dark; I said anything I could think of and went on until it occurred to me to shut up. I was simply making it all worse with my crazed explaining. But God, *God* it was terrible! I felt limp with shame and humiliation.

In the ensuing silence, Don awkwardly put his arm around my shoulders. Both of us were grateful now for the darkness that prevented us from seeing each other's faces. I bore the weight of his arm, wanting badly to cry, to hide somewhere and cry and cry. He kissed me and I was dismayed by his little-boy mouth and sweaty hand gripping mine. It was all pathetic. I was old, so old; ruined, perverted, unable to respond in any way at all except with despair. Daddy had made me old and ugly, turned me into a sexual machine that performed upon receipt of payment.

Don gave up. Relieved, I held his hand while the two of us smoked and kept up an inane conversation; we talked to cover the sounds the two up front made with their noisy necking. I felt a mounting sadness and an enormous sense of loss, knowing now that we couldn't even be friends, as I'd hoped. Unwittingly, I'd revealed myself to him. I didn't think he really understood it, but rather he sensed something wrong and didn't have the experience to define it. There was no way I could go back to school and face this very nice, very normal boy day after day for another six months until the end of grade thirteen.

When the car pulled up in front of my house, I looked at him, click-click, overcome by sadness, thanked him for the evening, said, "Good-bye, Don," and got out. I would miss him. We'd been two mavericks who'd managed to create a place for ourselves in the center of what seemed to us a lot of foolish, juvenile behavior. I never saw him again.

When I was twenty-one and some three-thousand miles safely distant from my parents, I decided, with premeditation and a heart like a stone, to give my virginity to a TV announcer I'd met who seemed most eager to relieve me of my burden. I didn't particularly care for him, but he was good-looking, interested and married. Being married was his strongest attraction. I suspected I wouldn't want to see him again once we'd done what I had in mind.

I needed to rid myself of my fear. And to do that, I'd have to confront what I most feared: penetration. I was positively terrified. We made all the arrangements and he collected me early one Saturday morning in his green Jaguar.

It was a cold, clinical operation performed without feeling on the part of either of us. But I did it. And I told myself that if I'd survived it once, I could get through it again, because

I'd only have to go through that especially painful initiation once. So I did it again with another man. Nothing. I had no feelings, no responses, no awareness of sensation beyond that of grating irritation. What I did have were a lot of old, and some additional new fears. But surely now that I was at least able to perform in relatively normal fashion, the perfect man for whom I'd feel everything was bound to materialize. All I had to do was wait and he'd find me.

I actively assaulted myself through a similarly premeditated use of a number of men. It didn't occur to me then that it wasn't my body that was at fault but my head. I thought it had to be physical, that Daddy had fouled me to the extent where I couldn't function fully. I liked the befores and afters but hated the act itself. It was a matter of accommodating a tremendous, invading weight while my head traveled through stage after stage of recoil and shock and I tried to convince myself that I was a grown woman, doing what grown women do.

I was expecting ecstasy and slowly feeling more and more defective because there was nothing in it for me; once we'd been to bed the men stopped calling. There had to be a *feeling*, I thought, some essence that would make it all quite different.

I managed to get through another year and a half in England before the world finally started to lose its focus for me. The turmoil in my head was a maze through which I had to stagger daily, trying to find a way to some sort of conclusion. And if my various jobs as waitress, secretary, door-to-door bookseller, singer, bit-part actress and occasional model weren't sufficient to accomplish my trip into madness, Daddy's letters arrived with hateful regularity to speed me along.

Huge, closely written declarations of love and lust and pleas for my return; I tore them up as fast as they arrived. I changed jobs and moved every few months. I stood in one rented room after another turning, turning, examining the walls and windows, searching for some exit I might have missed the first time around.

At last, having given up door-to-door bookselling on the

Continent, I offered a Austrian detective who'd befriended me the only two pieces of jewelry I owned as collateral if he'd lend me the money to get back to England. He wouldn't accept the Star of David an uncle had once given me, but he did take my wristwatch. He bought me a hot meal and put me on the train in Vienna. I promised to send the money as soon as I got work in London.

The minute I arrived back in England, I started calling all the variety agents who'd ever booked me and, as a last-ditch effort, I accepted a job as social director of a run-down hotel in Cornwall. I borrowed ten pounds from a Canadian friend, packed my bag and climbed aboard the Cornish Riviera Express from Victoria Station.

A week after starting work at the hotel, I met Norman and Lola. They taught me about love. They gave it, and their giving put chinks in my wall, knocked some of it down.

Six months later, when I knew I couldn't stay, they paid my debts, bought me clothes, put me on the train and sadly waved good-bye. I sat down in my compartment and tried not to let the other passengers see me crying.

Their family and friends said Norman and Lola were mad, that they'd never see that peculiar Canadian girl again. They were wrong. Within three months of returning to Toronto, I'd repaid them, and six months after that, I was on my way back for the first of what would become annual visits. They had believed in me; I couldn't let them down. I took any singing or revue job that was offered in order to have the money to maintain my independence. And when the chance came to make even more money by moving to the States, I took it. I had to get away from Daddy.

But I couldn't escape him. I dragged him with me like a heavy trunk crammed with souvenirs I might one day find a use for. I prayed he would die so I could be free. And every time the telephone rang in my hotel/motel room of the moment, I hoped it would be my mother calling to say it was all over.

In December of '66, as I was making up to go to work at

The Camelot in Minneapolis, the telephone rang. It was my mother. This is it! I thought, and held my breath, waiting to hear her say the words. What she said, in a thick voice, was, "Your Auntie Brenda died last night."

I managed to say, "I can't talk to you now," then hung up and tried to deal with the pain. After a time, I straightened, stood up and went into the bathroom to finish my makeup. I didn't know what else to do.

Two years later, the telephone rang again. My Uncle Jake had died. He hadn't wanted to go on living without my aunt. The loss was complete and unbearable. Who'd put on little fashion shows for me, or let me go through her jewel boxes? Who'd take me on his lap and call me honey? Why did it have to be them, when it should have been *him*? I couldn't bring myself to return to Canada to claim Brenda's mink jacket. It remained in storage for eight years. I think I believed that as long as I ignored the bequest she might somehow still be alive.

I began to think it would never end. I was a hamster running in a wheel, trying impossibly to get to the top. Daddy would live forever and I might be free only by dying first. I became more respectful of razor blades and my various vials of prescribed tablets and capsules: I might need them.

Eighteen

I DUMPED my schoolbooks in the garbage, then telephoned Tracy to ask for my job back. She said, "You can start tomorrow." I went back to work and within a week was enrolled in night courses at two drama schools; in a hurry to get myself trained so I could begin my theatrical career.

I asked Helen, "Do you think it's a crazy thing for me to do?"

And she said, "Well, not if it's what you want. I imagine you'll make a very good actress. I'm just a little surprised."

"Why?" I asked, disappointed. I'd hoped she'd be enthusiastic about my decision.

"I had thought you might write," she said.

I stared at the wall for a moment. "I don't know how to *write*. I can't even write school compositions."

"That's not quite the same thing. In any case, I'm happy you've found something you think you'd like to do."

By the end of the conversation, I was ready to abandon the whole idea of acting because Helen hadn't reacted as I'd wanted her to.

My mother, when I told her, said, "Who says you've got any talent? And you're sure no beauty. Now she wants to be an actress," she told the ceiling. "What next? She wants to take up with all those whores and drug addicts."

"Oh, *Mother!* That's ridiculous."

"Ridiculous, eh? We'll see."

In moments of displeasure, she took to calling me Sarah Bernhardt.

Pamela, however, declared, "You'll be wonderful! You've got such *character*, sweetie, far more than those sickly sweet things I've seen."

She returned me to feeling good about my decision.

Shirley was the teacher at the second drama school—the one I preferred—and I was intrigued by her cool blondness, her highly stylized mannerisms, and her intelligence. I hadn't been prepared to take her seriously because she always seemed to be striking poses. But once the class settled down to work, what she had to say and her evaluation of the students' performances and readings seemed perceptive as well as constructive without being cruel.

After the second or third class, I wrote a note and gave it to her. At the end of the subsequent session, she invited me to join her and Eric, the son of the couple who ran the school, for coffee.

Eric was extremely good-looking, with blond hair and fine bones; he was very quiet but had an appealing sense of humor. While Shirley held forth over a sandwich and coffee, Eric and I listened, every so often our eyes meeting. From the outset, he and I had a friendship that required few words; we understood one another implicitly and explanations were never needed. We accepted each other.

The three of us began to meet often, to engage in what I considered profound, very adult conversation having to do with the theater, with life, and with the problems Shirley and Eric were having trying to maintain their relationship in the face of his parents' intervention. I was sympathetic because Shirley declared they were in love, and the fact that she was older than Eric added, for me, an element of drama. Somehow, although I knew she was serious about Eric, I couldn't see their involvement as real so much as one of my dream scenarios playing itself out in front of me. The weight and anxiety seemed to be entirely on Shirley's side and Eric went where she directed, as if he were exhausted. I almost thought I'd like to have someone do the same for me, and Shirley seemed an obvious candidate.

She displayed tremendous interest in me and offered consistent praise of my "sensitivity." She gave me the "ring twice, hang up, then call back" secret to getting her on the telephone—a momentous step forward in our friendship. I felt privileged; I'd become an ally, someone she could trust. She was going through a messy divorce which necessitated the telephone gimmickry and, again, I was sympathetic. She was mysteriously vague and made only oblique references to the marriage, but spoke openly and bitterly about her mother-in-law who, Shirley contended, was entirely responsible for the breakup of her marriage. It didn't sound quite right, but I kept my doubts to myself because I was becoming obsessed with a growing need to see her as often as possible; she represented the sort of freedom I hoped to have.

At that time, she lived in a wildly untidy bachelor apartment on Jarvis, opposite the C.B.C., an area in the process of being restored to its Victorian elegance, but still home to a good number of drunks and prostitutes. Every time I visited, I had to fight off an impulse to clean up Shirley's apartment. She lived surrounded by stacks of books and papers, by cartons and odd shoes lying here and there.

"I'm very organized," she told me. "I can find whatever I want. I know exactly where everything is." Maybe that was true, I thought; maybe it was the way real artists lived.

She was teaching me all sorts of things, and created in me an awareness of how limited and "provincial" my background was; how limited and "provincial" Canada was altogether. There were foods I'd never eaten, and words I'd never heard, lifestyles and goals it had never occurred to me were within my grasp. She had me hard at work trying to shed my Canadian accent and lower my speaking voice so that I might sound more "mid-Atlantic."

She made me up one evening in her bathroom, then gave me a list of cosmetics and makeup to buy and practice with.

I rode home on the bus admiring my blurred reflection in the window. Upon seeing the results of Shirley's handiwork, my mother turned bright red, and exclaimed, "That woman's turned you into a whore! Look at yourself!" I went to look in the bathroom mirror and silently had to agree with her. What had looked fine in the bus window looked grotesque in the mirror.

"She was just trying to help," I defended Shirley.

"Help? You're only eighteen, for chrissake! No kid of mine's going out on the street looking like that! You wash that crap off!"

She went back to the kitchen and I continued to look at my reflection. She was right: with the heavy eye makeup and the thickly outlined lipstick pencil rimming my mouth, I looked like an outsized mechanical toy: my eyes too large and my mouth too brilliantly red, my cheeks unnaturally rosy.

When I was with her, Shirley asked a lot of questions about my background and my family, and I answered—hedging initially because I felt guilty discussing our family life with an outsider. I also couldn't help but feel that Shirley's questions—like Miss Wentworth's psychiatric tests—were loaded, and I tried to avoid the more conspicuously tricky ones. Yet I was increasingly tempted to tell her about Daddy. I wanted very much to tell someone, but I wasn't sure I could trust Shirley.

One Friday evening, my mother and father and I sat down to a meal of what my mother called "Spanish rice." My father sat staring at his plate, his temples throbbing, then announced "I'm not going to eat this shit!" He picked up the plate and threw it across the table. My mother ducked and the plate smashed against the far cupboard, sending Spanish rice all over the walls, ceiling and floor. There followed a long, weighty silence; then he pushed himself away from the table and stormed off to the bedroom.

My mother and I gazed at each other as we listened to him thumping around in the bedroom.

"He's *crazy*!" I whispered.

She nodded, her face absolutely white.

"What's he doing?" I asked, still in a whisper.

"Who the hell knows?" she said, the color slowly returning to her face.

He tore down to the cellar and came back up with two big cartons which he put on the bed and began to fill with his clothes. I stood in the hallway watching, slowly becoming angry. He'd done all this several times before. My mother would talk to him and eventually, like a child, he'd lose his momentum and allow himself to be stopped. Then he'd sit down at the kitchen table with his crossword puzzle book and she'd put all his things back in the closet and the dresser drawers. Until the next time.

I stepped back into the kitchen. "Let him go this time," I whispered. "We don't need him."

She didn't say anything. I looked at her, the anger getting bigger and bigger inside me, then ran to my room, grabbed my bag and started out the back door.

"Where're you going?" my mother called after me, sounding alarmed.

"Don't worry," I answered hotly without looking around. "I'll be back."

I telephoned Helen from a booth at St. Clair and Bathurst but there was no answer. I thought of calling my aunt and uncle but I was in no condition to play favorite niece. I had to talk to someone, so I rang twice, hung up, then called again and Shirley answered.

"C'mon over," she said.

Trembling now, I went back to the loop and got on a streetcar heading downtown.

Shirley was sitting tailor-fashion in her nightgown in the middle of her unmade bed, eating toast and tea Eric had brought with him from the Lost Atalantis Café down at the corner. Eric always came with food for her; she never seemed to cook. He was in the kitchen now cleaning up, emptying the kitty litter.

"What happened?" she asked, a piece of toast in one hand, a paper cup of tea in the other, the tag from the teabag dangling wetly down the side of the cup.

"Oh, my father threw another of his little tantrums," I said venomously, looking around for somewhere to sit, opting for the floor beside the bed. "He's very good at it. But this time he outdid himself."

"What did he do?" she asked, and reached for another triangle of toast.

"Threw a plate of food at my mother. Jesus! It went all over the place." I could see it: rice and minced meat in a red sauce oozing down the cupboards, the walls, stuck in clumps to the ceiling.

"Why?" she asked calmly.

"Why? Because he's *crazy*!" I was shuddering inside, the way I did when the fathers drove me home late at night after I'd been babysitting.

I could hear Eric running water in the kitchen sink and the clink of dishes as he stacked them. Why was he cleaning up here? Why didn't she clean her own apartment? I looked around, for several moments gazing at the stacks of books and papers on the floor. Fuzz-balls of dust and lint drifted peacefully in the corners. I lit a cigarette and took a hard drag, still watching the fuzz-balls.

She finished the toast and tea and pushed the buttery paper and empty cup into the brown paper bag they'd come in. The noise seemed tremendous. My brain wanted to slide off into the white place; the voices chanted my name very softly. I could feel my eyelids getting heavy. I finished the cigarette and put it out in the overfull ashtray on the floor near the bed. Then, without knowing why, I got up and carried it out to the kitchen to empty it. Eric and I looked at each other. His arms were immersed to the elbows in sudsy water. He looked very thin, despite the width of his shoulders. His chest seemed hollowed. Why are we housecleaning for this woman?

I wondered. *Eric, we should run away together. We're friends. We understand one another. We could run away, be friends forever and never have to explain anything to each other.*

I went back to the living room and sat down again on the floor by the bed. Eric had started on the pots and pans.

Shirley was watching me; I could feel her eyes. She was like a big, lazy cat with her languid gestures, pale perfect skin and green, almond-shaped eyes.

"Why don't you tell me?" she suggested, as if she were asking to hear a pleasant fairy tale.

Don't tell her! the voice inside my head warned. *She's the wrong one. If you tell her, you'll be sorry!*

"It's about your father, eh?" she probed.

I turned to look at her. She looked eager, almost hungry. I was captivated.

"He makes me *do* things," I whispered, wanting her to understand without my having to put it all into words.

"What 'things?' "

"*Things.* Terrible things."

"What kind of 'terrible things?' "

I was going to have to put it into words. Why had I ever started?

Eric had finished in the kitchen and came in now. He sat down on the end of the bed and lit a cigarette. He looked tired, I thought.

"What things?" she asked again.

I hated her. She was going to make me tell it in front of Eric. He'd know all about me and be disgusted.

I put my head down on my arms on the side of the bed and it all came spewing out in a choked, sobbing stream. When I finally ran down, I waited for the sympathy that was bound to come. But raising my head, I saw she was smiling. I couldn't believe it. A different kind of anger started to crowd its way into my chest.

"Oh, listen," she said, smiling and smiling. "All those things you think are so terrible now will be terrific when you meet the right man one day."

It was a movie. She'd dragged The Secret out of me and

now all she had to say about it was meaningless nonsense. I wanted to get up and leave, but I was afraid to. She knew now. If I walked out, she might get mad and tell people and the story would get back to my parents. I had to stay. I sat looking at her, hoping she'd find something sympathetic to say. But after a minute or two of thoughtfully smoking her cigarette, she stubbed it out in the ashtray I'd cleaned, then picked up a pad of writing paper and a pencil and began to make a sketch of Eric.

"Isn't he beautiful?" she said as she worked. "That nose is perfect."

I looked at Eric. He *was* beautiful. And gratifyingly, he looked distressed by what I'd said. *Let's run away and leave her here, Eric! We know each other and we'll always be friends. You'd never hurt me and I'd never make you be a housekeeper.*

"I could handle your father," she said confidently, her hand moving over the page, her eyes shifting back and forth between Eric and the paper.

Was she crazy? I wondered.

"You've got the potential of a multi-talented artist, you know," she said, switching subjects surprisingly. "But you're bogged down by a headful of middle-class values. The way I see it, your real problem's your mother. Filling your head with pedestrian garbage. You want to be an artist *and*, at the same time, a nice little suburban housewife, and that doesn't work. Somewhere along the line, you've got to make compromises, decide what you want and how much you're willing to sacrifice to get it."

I didn't want to hear about that. And I couldn't see how my mother was responsible for what my father had done to me. I wanted Shirley to help me learn how to live—with myself and with the rest of the world. I was too practical to lose myself in the idea of "art." I needed life first. Why wasn't she telling me what I needed to hear? All her talk only confused me and I hated myself for having told her. I'd been weak and stupid and now I felt guiltier and more diseased than before. I wasn't interested in "one day" and the "right man."

I wanted to hear about right now and what to do about Daddy, but she didn't have a thing to say about any of that. I'd made the biggest mistake of my life and told the wrong person The Secret.

My mother hated her.

"But how can you hate someone you've never even met?" I asked.

"Never you mind. What's she interested in you for, eh?"

"She's my teacher, my friend."

"Something fishy about that woman," she said. "I know what I'm talking about."

She was right again, but it was too late for me to agree with her. I felt more trapped than ever; I felt shriveled and dried out inside; lost.

A few nights later my mother opened the door and walked into my room.

"Doesn't anyone ever *knock* around here?" I exploded, embarrassed at being caught emoting into the secondhand tape recorder I'd bought. "Don't I have the right to a little privacy?"

Since the previous Friday, we'd been sniping at each other. It was getting worse daily.

"Don't you talk to me about *rights*!" she snapped. "I'll give you *rights*!"

"This is supposed to be *my* room. I pay enough for it!"

"Shut up and get out here! Your teacher's on the phone."

"Miss MacKay?" My heart stopped. Had she heard my mother and me barking at each other? God!

"That's what she said."

I dashed out into the hall to grab the telephone, pulled it into my room and sat down on the floor with my back to the closed door. My heart started up again—like the repeat key on the typewriter at the office. Helen had never telephoned me. It had to mean something was wrong.

"Helen?"

"Am I catching you at a bad time?"

"No, no. How are you?"

"Fine. I called to ask you a favor."

"Sure. Anything. What?"

"I'm in the hospital for a few days and I wondered if you'd mind coming down and helping me get my Christmas cards addressed."

Oh no God no oh! "What's wrong? Where are you? I'll come right away."

She laughed softly. "It's all right. I'm just in for a few days. You'll be able to come?"

"Sure I will. My God! I was going to call you tonight . . ."

"It's all right," she repeated, more firmly.

"But I feel so awful. If I'd known you were in the hospital . . . I'll come tomorrow afternoon. Okay? Do you need anything? Can I bring you anything?"

"Just bring yourself. I'll see you tomorrow."

I took the telephone back to the stand in the hall, then closed myself in the bedroom, shaking, so scared my teeth were chattering. Something was happening. Please no, no.

The next afternoon, I made my way downtown to the hospital, lost in fearful imaginings. Hospitals meant being more than just a little sick. Being more than a little sick meant you could die. I couldn't think about it.

A nurse gave me directions and I walked down the corridor glancing into open doorways, click-click, geared up to be my better self—sunny and lighthearted, set to cheer her up. I found the room, took a deep breath, and went in. I spent the next two hours trying hard to keep smiling in order to mask the dizzy shock and fear I felt at the transformation she'd undergone in just the few weeks since I'd last seen her. Her face was very pale and puffy, her hair limp-looking and shot with gray; she'd aged at least twenty years. *What happened to you? What did this to you?*

I sat and wrote out the addresses she dictated, everything in me shouting, *TELL HER YOU LOVE HER TELL HER RIGHT NOW THIS MINUTE GO ON TELL HER! I CAN'T! I CAN'T!*

Every time I looked up, I found her eyes on me. My voice dried up and disappeared, words were clotted in my throat. I kept on until all the cards were done and she was sitting against the pillows with the pile of finished envelopes in her lap. She held one up and said, "You have beautiful handwriting. I can't thank you enough for doing this. I'd never have managed without you."

"How long will you be in here?" I asked, looking for the gold bangle on her wrist. It wasn't there. Instead, a plastic name-band encircled her wrist.

"I'll be going home Saturday," she said, and smiled as she set the envelopes and her address book on the table at the far side of the bed.

The hospital gown gapped, exposing her naked spine and I glanced down at the floor wishing I hadn't seen.

"I'm really glad you're not staying here," I said.

"I wanted to see you," she said, as if she hadn't heard me. "I needed a bit of cheering up. It's done me a world of good having you come. Hospitals can be so dreary."

"I'd always come to see you," I said inadequately. *TELL HER YOU LOVE HER!* Was it a hospital, I wondered, a couple of years ago when you were "called away unexpectedly" and were gone those two weeks? Was that where you were? Were you here in this pale-green room with the venetian blinds on the window and that empty bed over there?

"And how," she asked interestedly, "is your theatrical career coming along?"

"Shirley, my teacher, she says I have a literary approach to acting and not an interior, dramatic one. I don't know what she means by that. I thought maybe she was trying to tell me in a nice way that I wasn't going to make a very good actress. She said it after we read out these interpretations she'd asked us to do of Hamlet's soliloquy, you know? I guess we were supposed to write about the emotions or something."

"What did you write about?" she asked.

"Well, there's such a lot in it. I mean, every line seems to have some reference to something else. A lot of Greek mythology, stuff I remembered from Miss White's English class my first year in grade nine. And then, all the metaphors, the different meanings. I wrote what I thought it all meant."

She laughed. "I think your teacher may be right. That is a rather literary approach. But that doesn't mean you won't be a good actress."

"But she also said I was going to have a lot of trouble getting parts because it'll be years before the way I look catches up to my acting and what she calls my emotional insights. A lot of what she says doesn't make much sense to me. I understand, but I don't. You know? It's as if I can *feel* in my brain what she means, but the words won't come into position in my head." Suddenly remembering where we were, my stomach started a jittery dance. I looked at her and she shook her head very slightly as if to say, Don't think about it! Talk to me, keep talking!

"But you're enjoying it all," she prompted.

"Everything always takes so long," I said slowly, distracted by the antiseptic odor of the air and by her ashen face and suddenly gray hair. "What . . . ? I mean . . . why . . . ?"

"A bothersome hip. A lot of nonsense." She waved her hand impatiently, as if brushing away a mosquito.

"Why did you ask me to come and not . . . one of the . . . others . . . someone else?"

Thoughtfully, carefully, she said, "You're one of the most responsible people I know. You are," she said in the face of my visible desire to argue that. "I knew if you said you'd come that you would and that you wouldn't go home and talk about it."

"No one's supposed to know?" I asked. This was alarming. It made everything more serious.

"I'd prefer not. I just wanted to get in and get out again without any fuss."

I looked around the room, nodding. "I guess I'm really glad that you'd ask me, that you think that way about me. I'd never say anything."

"Of course I think that way about you," she said, appearing surprised. "You're reliable and responsible and you can be very discreet."

"Discreet?"

"How is your job?" she asked, changing subjects almost too quickly for me to keep up with her.

"Oh, fine. They're really nice to me. You're going home on Saturday for sure?"

"Yes. You'll want to run along now, won't you?"

"Oh! Yes." I was, I realized, being dismissed. I reached for my bag and coat and stood up, wetting my lips while I groped for something appropriate to say.

"It's such a relief to have those cards done," she said, smiling again.

"I was glad to do it." I wanted to close the distance between us, to take hold of her hand and press my cheek against hers and tell her how much I loved her. But I felt too graceless, too clumsy with shock at being here and seeing the changes in her to make any move. So I said good-bye and moved to go.

I stopped to look back from the doorway. She'd sagged back against the pillows and her forearm rested across her forehead, her eyes on the ceiling. An expression of sadness and a look of extreme fatigue made her seem terribly old. I had to lean against the wall in the corridor with my eyes closed for several minutes before I could get my legs to move and take me out of there.

Going home Saturday. You'll go home and I'll visit on a Sunday soon and it'll be the same the same nothing will change you've got to be there I need you. Where will I go if you're not there please be there!

For the next few weeks, I threw myself into my escape plans. I wanted to get to England. But how? My mother would never give me permission to travel with Shirley and Eric who were planning to go in a matter of months. But Pamela was another case altogether. A librarian, someone with education, intelligence, age, and a thoroughly respectable job. When I spoke of her to my mother, I carefully omitted mention of her obsession with the mystical sciences, or her passion for strange foods. Pamela was married and therefore even more respectable. Married was what Shirley and Helen were not, which made them both suspect in my mother's eyes. What

kind of woman didn't want to get married? An unmarried
female was anathema, akin to drug addicts and whores; unnatural. My mother's highly placed premium on women with
husbands set Shirley and Helen well on the minus side: hopeless lost causes who'd failed socially because no man had staked
a claim on them. The fact that Shirley had been married and
was now getting divorced made her even more of a failure
because she'd been unable to sustain a marriage. Women who
gave up and got divorced were quitters, failures. And a woman
who'd never even been asked—like Helen—had to have something horribly wrong with her.

My only chance to get to England would be if I could
somehow work it out to go over with Pamela. But her plans
were very indefinite, contingent on problems with her husband and his yet-to-be-formed plans.

I latched onto Pamela like a life preserver, knowing she
was my only possible chaperone to freedom. I visited often
and sat with her in her kitchen, drinking the cups of tea she
offered. Lapsang Su Chong with brown sugar and milk. It
tasted, I thought, like boiled tires. We discussed the prospects
of England and firmed up the arrangement that we'd travel
together when we went.

"You're the only one," I admitted truthfully, "my mother
would let me go with. So when you do decide you're ready,
I really want to go with you."

She said, "Fine, sweetie."

It was settled.

Nineteen

IN APRIL, Helen telephoned a second time.

"I called to ask," she said, "if you'd like to come out and have lunch with me this Saturday."

"I'd love to!"

"There is one minor problem, though."

"What's that?"

"It's a nuisance, but I'm afraid I can't drive. I was wondering if you'd mind ferrying us about in my car."

Can't drive why can't you drive? "I can get my father's car. I'll be glad to drive."

"Perfect! I'll see you Saturday then."

Saturday.

My hair was long again, carefully coiled on top of my head, securely anchored with numerous pins; eyeshadow, mascara, lipstick, a new bright green-printed Empire dress and four-inch stiletto heels. I picked up my bag, the car keys, and drove downtown.

Mrs. MacKay offered me a smile and her hand, then showed me into the living room where Helen sat waiting, a cane propped against the arm of her chair. Her expression upon seeing me underwent quite a change, and made me wonder if my own face changed quite as drastically at the same moment. Both of us were so different. She looked even older than she had at the hospital; horribly thin, yet swollen somehow, with orthopedic old-lady shoes. Where were the beautiful Owen's & Elm's spike heels? And her hair. *Oh God! Your hair your face the way you look where are you what happened to you where have you gone?* Her hair had turned gray, with streaks of white.

She got up, leaning heavily on the cane as she traveled slowly across the room, saying, "How grown-up you look! And so tall! It seems just a few months ago you were the smallest child in the school and my curiosity got the better of me so I had to ask Leslie Redfield who you were and what you were doing in with the grade nines."

"You *did*?"

Smiling, she admitted, "I did."

"I didn't know that," I said stupidly.

"Will I be needing a coat?"

"Oh, no. It's really very warm."

Her mother hovered anxiously in the hall as I opened the front door. I turned to look at her. Her face was deeply creased with what might have been sadness or fear; her eyes told me to go slowly, go very carefully. I was in charge of someone she loved. I felt both frightened of and equal to her expectations.

Making myself strong, steady, I took hold of Helen's arm to help her slowly, one step at a time, down the stairs, and into the car. My lungs seemed to constrict as I walked around to the driver's side. I wanted to deny what my eyes and intelligence were telling me; everything inside me was sinking down, down in despair. I slid behind the wheel, turned to smile at her as I pushed the key into the ignition, then put the car in gear and pulled away from the curb.

"You drive very well," she said after a few minutes. "You really are the most amazingly competent girl. Good at everything."

"Oh, I'm not. I'm really not."

"What are your plans now?"

"I want to go to England eventually."

"Why England? Surely there's work to be found here."

"Oh, it won't be for a while yet. My mother . . . they wouldn't let me go now. I'm too young, they think. It's a miracle they're letting me go into summer stock next month."

"And how is your family?"

"Oh fine, fine." I gave the standard, dismissing lie.

"Are you sure," she asked, "acting's what you really want?"

"I think so. Why?" I glanced over at her, shocked each time by the face of this familiar stranger. She was an old woman inside a younger woman's loose-fitting clothes.

"I keep thinking you may change your mind and decide to write."

"But I *can't* write. I'm *terrible* at it. I told you about those compositions. I couldn't ever think of one single interesting thing to say. 'How I Spent My Summer Vacation.' " I laughed.

"That isn't writing," she said a little impatiently. "Your letters were more what I had in mind."

"But that isn't really writing, either. And I'm always writing letters. They're nothing."

"Those letters were wonderful," she said quietly. "They showed talent and imagination."

"I could never," I argued, "sit down and write a whole book. I wouldn't even know what to say or how to say it."

"I know you don't want to hear it, but I have a feeling you'll end up writing. Now I won't say another word about it."

"I thought . . ." I stopped and wet my lips. "I thought you'd think I was crazy. Because of those letters." I looked over again. Again the shock. "I didn't even know why I was writing them."

"I did." It was an enigmatic response I didn't dare risk investigating. I was afraid to hear her say anything that might have to do with feelings. I'd break down and disintegrate.

"I write letters to everybody," I said, thinking about it somewhat abstractedly. "Every time there's someone I think I'd like to know, I write a letter."

"One of these days, you'll stop feeling you have to do that."

"I guess."

Neither of us ate very much of the lunch. She ordered a drink and I watched her sip at it, riveted. Drinking was something it hadn't ever occurred to me she might do.

"Does my having this bother you?" she asked. Her gold bangle hit against the side of the glass, making a pretty sound.

"No. Just that I've never seen . . . I mean . . . I didn't know you did, that's all."

"Have a cigarette," she suggested. "That should put us on even ground. One bad habit for another."

Returning her smile, I got out my cigarettes, lit one, took a hard drag and exhaled to one side, taking a look around the room. I felt old and all the way grown up; I also felt young and utterly out of my depths.

"You're not eating," she noticed.

"Neither are you."

"I haven't much of an appetite these days."

"Me, neither."

She laughed softly. "Seems somewhat of a wasted effort."

"Oh, no. I'm glad we came out, that you invited me. I like being with you." Flushing, I looked intently at the ashtray, at the burnt-out match I'd dropped there.

"*I* like being with you," she said, her hand around the sweating glass. "I always enjoy you."

"I thought I was being such a nuisance, the way I came around all the time, imposing. Calling you on the phone, intruding."

"Had that been the case, don't you think I'd have let you know?"

"I never thought of that. I suppose that's right."

"You really have grown tall," she changed subjects. "Or is it just the heels?"

"I think it's the heels. I've always thought of *you* as being tall." My throat lumped up again and I quickly took another drag on the cigarette.

She laughed, looking and sounding highly amused. For those moments, she was once more completely recognizable to me. Our eyes met and held. *The way you look is murdering me*

*is it murdering you too? I don't want to think about this don't
want it to be happening. We're not saying what we're saying
what we're saying is good-bye and I can't bear it I can't.*

She took another swallow of her drink before signaling to
the waiter for the check. It was like an old film being replayed.
I remembered the luncheon at the Royal York with Miss Fielder
and how she'd gestured to the waiter. And now here it was,
at the Seaway, happening again. Would people think she
was my mother? I looked around hopefully, defiantly, wanting
them to think precisely that. *This is my mother someone who
loves and respects me I think she's dying will somebody please
come and stop this from happening?*

"We might as well go back," she said, "and sit where it's a
bit more comfortable."

I parked and hurried to help her out of the car, and up the
front steps. My hand on her arm. *I've never before touched
you now I've touched you half a dozen times all in one afternoon.* My hand on her arm, her hand wrapped around my
wrist for support, we went into the house and through to the
living room, to sit once more in the chairs by the side windows. I lit another cigarette. Both of us looked out at the
blossoming trees. I felt her eyes on me for long moments before she said, "You've grown so pretty."

I shook my head, no.

"Someday you'll believe that when someone tells you. Because you'll feel it. And then you *will* be."

"I used to think I wanted to be a teacher." I smiled suddenly. "Like you. But I knew I couldn't. For one thing, I
hated school. I like the *idea* of things, but when it comes actually to doing them or being there, it's never the same as I'd
thought it would be."

"Things rarely are. I'm terribly tired," she said. "I hope you
won't be offended if I send you on your way now. I'm going
to go upstairs and rest."

"I'm not offended."

Rising, I watched her struggle out of the chair and reach
for the cane. I knew it would be wrong now to offer to help

as I'd done before. Her movements, the set of her head, made it clear she wanted to stand and walk alone. We moved toward the front door.

"Thank you for coming today," she said. "I did want to see you. You always brighten things up. Don't ever lose your sense of humor. It's one of the best things about you."

We stood looking at each other. The voice in my head commanded me, *DO IT, TELL HER! RIGHT NOW TELL HER!* I opened my arms then closed them around her, aware, as I did, of her surprise. Holding her, my eyes closed, I breathed her in: the scent, the feeling, the softness that still remained. Pressing my lips to her cheek, I found more softness, and felt the return of her embrace, her arms, and her lips on my cheek. I didn't want it to end, didn't want to go. But it had to end, and I had to go. I stepped away, opened my mouth, and forced out words.

"Thank you for the lunch." *God don't let me cry please not in front of her.* "I'll call . . . call you during the week."

A smile plastered over top of the threatening tears, I flew away down the front steps on those treacherous stiletto heels. I held off until I'd driven down the hill, turned the corner, was well away. Then a cry erupted from the bottom of my chest, loud inside the car.

The following Saturday morning, early, my mother threw open my bedroom door and dropped a folded newspaper across my chest.

"What?" I asked, groping my way up from sleep. She looked strange: confused, embarrassed.

"Your teacher died," she said, then stared at me for a moment before turning to go out, quietly closing the door after her.

Propped up on my elbows I looked at the newspaper, hearing her rattling dishes in the kitchen, hearing Daddy's complaining murmur; unable to move. If I didn't touch the paper or look at it, none of it could be real. I sat up and the newspaper slid down to my lap. With unsteady hands, I lit a cigarette. At last, I slowly opened the paper and began to read.

I lay back against the pillow with my eyes closed, and finished the cigarette, my stomach convulsing.

The cigarette done, I put it out, got up, and got dressed, then sat down with a pair of scissors and cut the notice out of the newspaper. I carefully refolded the paper and put it down on the kitchen table, then went downstairs to the cellar to pump up the bike tires.

As I was maneuvering the bike out the back door, my mother asked, "Where are you going?"

"For a ride. Just a ride."

The day was cold, the weather so changeable. I swung myself up and started down the road, going nowhere, just away. Unable to see, I rode the bike into a drainage ditch and sat there with my head on my knees, arms folded over my head, crying. A trickle of blood made its way down my leg from the gash on my knee.

That night, after putting myself into the white space with the late, late show, I got into bed and fell at once into a heavy sleep. I had The Dream for the first time.

I was twelve years old again, riding the bike to the house on Indian Valley. The bike left secured to the fence with Will's old combination lock, I climbed the front steps and knocked at the door.

Mrs. MacKay opened the door. "Helen's upstairs, dear." She held her hand warmly over the top of my head, searching my eyes for a long moment before leaving me to make my way up the stairs and along the hall to Helen's room.

There was a fire in the grate and Helen, in a pale pink robe of some silky fabric, was on the chaise, jabbing at the logs with a poker.

"You *told* her The Secret!" I accused, quivering with anger and confusion at this devastating betrayal. "How *could* you when you promised you'd never tell *anyone*?"

"Come in here and close the door!" she said evenly, her eyes commanding.

"*Why* did you tell her?" I demanded, standing with my back against the closed door, my hand on the knob.

"I had to," she said simply. "It was necessary to explain my involvement with you. It isn't as if there are great numbers of girls who come here at odd hours of the day and night. Mother won't tell anyone. You know that."

The voice in my head told me, That makes sense. That's true. I moved away from the door to sit beside her on the chaise studying her face, her eyes and mouth, her hands clasped loosely over her crossed knees, her legs where they emerged from the opening of the robe. I realized she wasn't wearing anything under the robe. Her nipples were plainly defined by the shiny fabric.

"What is it?" she asked.

"Nothing. I don't know."

"Do you have sexual feelings about me?"

"Oh, no!" I shook my head vigorously. "I know the difference. I know what that is. It isn't that," I said, yet was unable to look away from her breasts.

It was so real, and a thought transcended the dream: This *is* Real! It's too clear to be a dream. She's here, really here. We're together. This is *happening!*

"I think I understand," she said slowly. "You'd like to go all the way back and be an infant again, have all the things they've deprived you of. You'd like to be *my* baby. I can't," she said, her voice going softer. "I've never been a mother. I can only guess at what you need." Looking perplexed, she stood up and walked across the room, to stop by the desk and stand with her hand on the curtain, gazing out.

"It's snowing," she said, and let the curtain drop. "You'll have to stay here tonight."

"Yes, all right."

"Telephone your mother and tell her where you are."

"Yes, all right."

"Tell her you'll be staying and you'll be home in the morning."

"Yes, all right."

Magically, the call got made without my awareness of using the telephone. Then she handed me a nightgown, and said,

"There's a bathroom through there." Her hand on my shoulder guided me in the right direction.

Upon returning with my hands and face properly washed, clad in the nightgown, I saw she'd turned down the lights and set a screen in front of the fireplace and made up a bed on the chaise. She stood beside her bed with her hand held out to me saying, "Come here."

I went to her, my eyes again on her breasts.

"Why do you keep staring at me?" she asked, raising my chin with her hand. "Why here?" she asked, her hand over her breasts.

I shook my head mutely.

"You don't know about love at all, do you?" Her voice and manner seemed deeply sad. Mysteriously, she said, "This is my final obligation, what I must do. This, and then I am free. I need to be free now." She looked deeply into my eyes "You have to let me go. You must." She took a deep breath, then went on. "You think love is sex, love is being mistreated, lied to, abused. I know what you want." Her eyes widened. "You want to touch me. Isn't that it? Isn't that what you've always wanted: to touch me?"

I nodded, swaying slightly, overcome by her closeness, her perfume, her misted features, the altogether ethereal look of her.

"Final tests," she sighed. "The understanding will come to you in time. Ends to be tied before it's all finally over." The gold in her eyes was dominant, glowing. "This is love." Her voice almost inaudible, she moved closer. Her eyes fused to mine, her hands moved up to loosen the top of the robe, opening it. "Love," she repeated hypnotically, taking hold of my hand. "Love," she whispered, placing my hands over her bared breasts. "God help us both. *Love!*"

I stood with my hands curved over her breasts, my eyes half-closed, overwhelmed by a tremendous influx of emotion, caring, understanding; messages; exquisite pain.

"Please, no more," she whispered, with tears on her face. "Believe!" Her eyes fluttered closed. I could feel her trembling. "I wish you could have been mine, so I could properly tend to you. But I can't breastfeed you. It isn't there." She let her arms drop to her sides and stood motionless with my hands still on her. "This is as close to me as I'm able to bring you. You will *never* be closer. There is nothing more I can do for you."

I could feel the meanings penetrate and spread; could feel the incredible texture of her skin, cool and silken beneath my hands. She was so still, I could feel the erratic heartbeat beneath her breast. Abundant, filling my hands; yet contained. *My hands on your flesh, the woman in my hands. Real, so real.* Slowly, I withdrew and carefully closed the robe, whispering, "I love you love you love you. Don't leave me I'll be good I will I promise please don't leave me. I'll make you so proud of me I will and I'll be good so good I love you love you. You're the only one the only one who's listened who's allowed me to breathe I *love* you."

"You must go to sleep now," she said, and drifted away from me to go into the bathroom. The door closed.

I lay down on the chaise and stared through the screen into the dying fire. Then, suddenly, it was dawn and I was fully dressed, standing beside the bed where she lay on her side. The sheets were tangled and bunched. I gazed at the somehow too vulnerable figure in the pale gown, with a pulsing ache in my throat. I reached out to straighten the bedclothes, then stopped, my hands unmoving in the air; I was entranced by the profound serenity of the face on the pillow. Utter stillness, silence. There was a certain waxy perfection to her skin. Her throat long and white, her arms slender, her breasts full and white, blue-veined with delicate tracings.

Don't LEAVE me! I want to go WITH you! COME BACK AND TAKE ME WITH YOU! I'll be very quiet I'll lie still there'll be room for both of us I'm not very big. DON'T LEAVE ME!

The curtains billowed suddenly, causing me to turn and look. It was a warning: *Go on, you've got to go!* I touched my fingertips to the gold bangle on the bedside table, then looked at the plastic name-tape on her narrow wrist. The bracelet was cold under my fingers. I took a last look at her, at the room. Then I opened the window, climbed up onto the sill and stepped outside onto the ledge. Raising my arms, I soared up above the trees and deserted streets; flying home.

The Dream. I've had it dozens of times in the last twenty years; without variation.

In 1970, very shortly after I married Walt, I received a telephone call at the office one afternoon from my brother Will. I knew what he was going to say, and waited.

We talked for several minutes and I promised to fly up that same afternoon. Then I hung up and, feeling giddy and weightless, walked into the inner office to tell Walt I had to leave for Toronto.

"He finally died," I said.

Walt understood.

Twenty

THE TUESDAY evening after Helen's death, I went into the living room where Daddy sat reading the newspaper. Filled with a new sense of myself as a person, as someone with definite rights and powers, I waited until he put aside the paper. Then, kneeling on the floor in front of him, with one hand gripping the arm of the sofa, I said, "It's over. You're never going to touch me again. *Not ever!* It's all over. I want you to understand what I'm saying, because I mean it. It's *over!* Do you understand? Do you hear what I'm telling you?"

"Oh, I hear all right," he said bitterly, then smiled suddenly, knowingly. "But you'll be back. I know you. Next time you want five or ten bucks, you'll be back."

I shook my head and got to my feet, trying to suppress the rage and loathing I felt at his treatment of me.

"No, not ever. And if you so much as put your hand on my arm, I'll kill you." My voice was very steady, very quiet. "I'll kill you. I'm going to stay here, in this house, because I have to. I'll stay until legally I'm free to go. And then I'm going and never coming back."

I moved several steps away and waited to hear if he'd say anything further. He didn't. Casting a murderous and ludicrously petulant look at me, he pulled himself heavily up off the sofa, threw down the newspaper and shuffled off to the bathroom.

I went to the telephone and called Shirley. "Are you busy?" I asked.

"Eric's here. Can you give us an hour?"

"It'll take me that long to get there. I'm leaving now."

"Okay, fine."

I pulled on my coat, checked to see I had my keys, then walked out. There was a curious, expanding sensation inside my chest, and not a sound in my head. Just silence. I began to run and ran all the way down the road to the bus stop on Bathurst where I paced back and forth, brimming with a strange energy, until the bus came. I'd done it! My God, I'd actually done it!

I studied my reflection in the bus window all the way downtown to the loop. It was the last time I ever saw The One, actually saw her. She got lost in a bus window. The Other had moved to take control of me with all her optimism, conviction and determination.

It took two and a half years before I was able to get away from Daddy. It was that long before Pamela assembled all her scattered plans. It was a time in which Daddy became daily more sullen and morose. He was ominously silent except for his usual grumbling complaints and sudden and maniacal tirades against his employers, my mother and me. He never looked straight at me but rather gazed slit-eyed with his head slightly turned away. He tried everything he could think of to move me into the bedroom with him, but was met always with my hating glare and the impenetrable wall of my resolve.

And finally, just after my twentieth birthday, with Pamela standing at the rail beside me, we waved good-bye to Aunt Brenda and Uncle Jake and my mother down on the pier. My aunt and uncle waved gaily, but my mother wouldn't look up at me. I couldn't understand why. I wanted her to approve my departure and send me off into my life with gladness.

In the lounge later, over tea, Pamela said, "She couldn't bear to see you go, sweetie."

"What does that mean?" I asked.

"As long as she didn't actually look up and see you, she didn't have to accept that you really were going."

"I don't know," I sighed. "That seems somehow too complicated for my mother."

"Oh, no," Pamela disagreed. "It isn't complicated in the least. It's very simple, very uncomplicated. And now there's no one left, is there?"

I could feel my eyes grow wider. It hadn't occurred to me that I was abandoning my mother to Daddy. She'd be all alone with no one to stand between her and his rage.

"She'll be all right," I said at last. "She'll be fine."

Upon arriving in England, I changed my name, changed the color of my hair and took to wearing makeup full time as a kind of daily applied disguise. I wanted to get rid of that other girl; I believed I had to relegate her to the past so that I might, a step at a time, teach myself to deal with the pain of living with a head filled with flashback horrors that distance didn't seem to diminish. I believed I had to become someone entirely new to escape completely.

I did not land starring roles the moment I set foot in England. I sent out dozens of photographs and résumés and got several bit-part jobs, but nothing with more than five or six lines of dialogue and a few modeling assignments. When I was hired, it was to play foreigners—Russians or Germans or Italians. I had a talent for accents and that was what the producers wanted, not someone who looked about fifteen and hoped to play heavy dramatic roles.

I took an office job and continued to send out résumés. In the meantime, I practiced the guitar. Most evenings I sat in my fifth-floor walk-up room in South Kensington looking out the window at the treetops and roofs of nearby houses, singing while I played my fingertips raw.

On lunch hours at the office, I wrote stories on the typewriter, and sent them off to magazines hoping someone would buy something I'd written so I could stop trying to be an actress; I knew I would never make it. Deciding on the theater had been another mistake. I didn't actually think I'd be a writer, but I hoped I might earn a little extra money. The fifty pounds I'd brought with me had gone very quickly, and the ten or twelve pounds a week I earned at the office didn't go very far.

Shirley accused me of "copping out" in taking the office job and I lost my temper.

"I don't see anything 'artistic' about sitting around all day waiting for the telephone to ring," I said angrily. "I also happen to like eating."

We argued while Eric listened, looking grieved. And then we parted to go in different directions for a year.

I began to get singing jobs here and there, but was reluctant to give up my job. The job was security. And I'd long ago learned from my mother that it was important to have something to fall back on.

So, I moved from one rented room to another, always imagining the perfect place where I'd one day live, and Daddy's letters followed me. My skin erupted with fierce, angry infections that refused to heal. I plastered on more makeup and accepted a job selling magazines door to door.

It was when I was about to topple off the edge that I met Norman and Lola and fell in love with them. They gave me a family and a home. But we all knew I couldn't hide out indefinitely. Whether I was ready or not, I was—in the eyes of the world—an adult. I had to go forward. I returned to Canada briefly, then went to the States. I spent the next seven years constantly moving. Like someone shadowboxing, I bobbed and weaved; moving, moving.

When I fell in love with Rob and gave up my singing career for another office job, I felt a complete failure. I was twenty-nine years old and no man wanted me for his wife.

Walt came along and was kind. He listened to my stories about Daddy and wasn't sickened, but rather, was sympathetic.

We each had needs we believed the other could satisfy, so we got married. This was it: the fantasy made real. I was a married woman with a wedding band, married to a good-looking, considerate man who was the president of his company: everything my mother had ever told me to look and hope for in a man. I worked frantically at being happy, but it wouldn't come Not even Jossie's birth added any more glue to the marriage.

Walt and I talked and talked, and then we agreed to live apart. I began to take very small, uncertain steps forward. I found I could actually face that woman in the mirror and smile at her. So what if she was ugly? *I* was beginning to like her. Daddy was dead and receding into the distance.

Around 1965, my parents had separated for close to four years and Daddy had gone to live with Will and his wife and children. During that time, Daddy staged a repeat performance on his granddaughter. Will didn't discover this until his daughter had a breakdown years later and, in the course of her therapy, the truth surfaced. Will called me to say, in a thick, strangled voice, "If he were alive, I'd kill him."

It brought everything back; I felt as if it were all happening again. I wanted to help but there was nothing I could do. I was driven to examine my past as I had never done before to see why I was living the way I was, why I felt the way I did, why I was the person I was. I finally faced Daddy.

Three years ago, returning from a promotion trip in St. Louis where I had sat at a table piled high with copies of my books in a long row of authors behind tables piled high with their books, I came down the ramp—relieved as ever to be off another terrifying plane and on my way home to Connecticut and Jossie—and headed toward the baggage claim area. I heard a small child's voice crying out. It was an eerie sound. As I walked on, I saw that people were cutting a wide path around two women by the windows. One of the women was so like Helen in size and style of dress that I had to pause for a mo-

ment, to watch. The child's voice was emerging from the
second woman who was perhaps twenty-five. She cried out,
sobbing, her head turning in anguish as the older woman held
and tried to comfort her.

The scene was deeply distressing. As I passed them, the
younger woman shrilled in that penetratingly high child's
voice, "I want my mummy! It's *no good* telling me all that!
I want her! *I want her!*"

"It's real," I thought, stricken. "My God, this is real!" The
woman was lost, trapped inside the little girl she'd once been.
This insight was so painful that I all but ran toward the baggage area.

I found my bag, telephoned the Connecticut Limousine and
gave my name; I was told I'd be picked up in ten minutes.

I sat on a bench to wait, with my bag at my feet and lit a
cigarette, thinking, It could have been me. That child-woman
could have been *me*. I'd come so close. But I'd managed to
find my way out.

I unclenched my fists and leaned back against the railing,
concentrating on relaxing, and wondered how long, if ever, it
was going to take me to find my way out completely.

Maybe never. It's impossible to forget what happened. I
can't use Liquid Paper on ten years of my life and put a nice,
thick white coat over it the way I do typing errors. But I have
finally accepted it and put it into some perspective.

Nine years ago, when I began to write this book, I became
angry when a literary agent suggested I put it away for a
while because I really wasn't ready yet to write it.

I understand now what he meant.

Toronto, August 1979

Afterword

THE INCIDENTS related in this book all took place. Certain of them have been shifted in time, and some occur with people other than those who were actually involved.

The majority of the names have been changed, but the places have not.

There are many dear and valued friends and family members who don't appear here, but who have their place in my deepest affections.

ABOUT THE AUTHOR

CHARLOTTE VALE ALLEN has been a professional writer for five years. In that time she has published sixteen books, many of which have also been published in Germany, Holland, Britain, Spain, Mexico, Australia and France. While her previous works have all been fiction, *Daddy's Girl* is autobiographical.

Born in 1941, the author was raised in Toronto. She left school in her late teens to become an actress, and in ensuing years lived in England and then in the United States. In 1971, while pregnant with her daughter, she began to write fiction about contemporary women and their problems. She is now a full-time author—with a broad range of interests including photography, drawing and needlepoint.

Charlotte Vale Allen was recently married to the actor and writer, Barrie Baldaro. She and her family divide their time between homes in Toronto and Connecticut.